SALISBURY
From Old Photographs

SALISBURY
From Old Photographs

PETER DANIELS

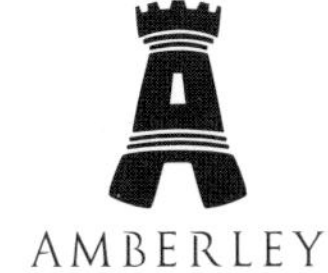

AMBERLEY

First published 2015

Amberley Publishing
The Hill, Stroud
Gloucestershire, GL5 4EP

www.amberley-books.com

British Library Cataloguing in Publication Data.

A catalogue record for this book is available from the British Library.

ISBN 978 1 4456 1597 4 (print)
ISBN 978 1 4456 1606 3 (ebook)

Typesetting and Origination by Amberley Publishing.
Printed in the UK.

Contents

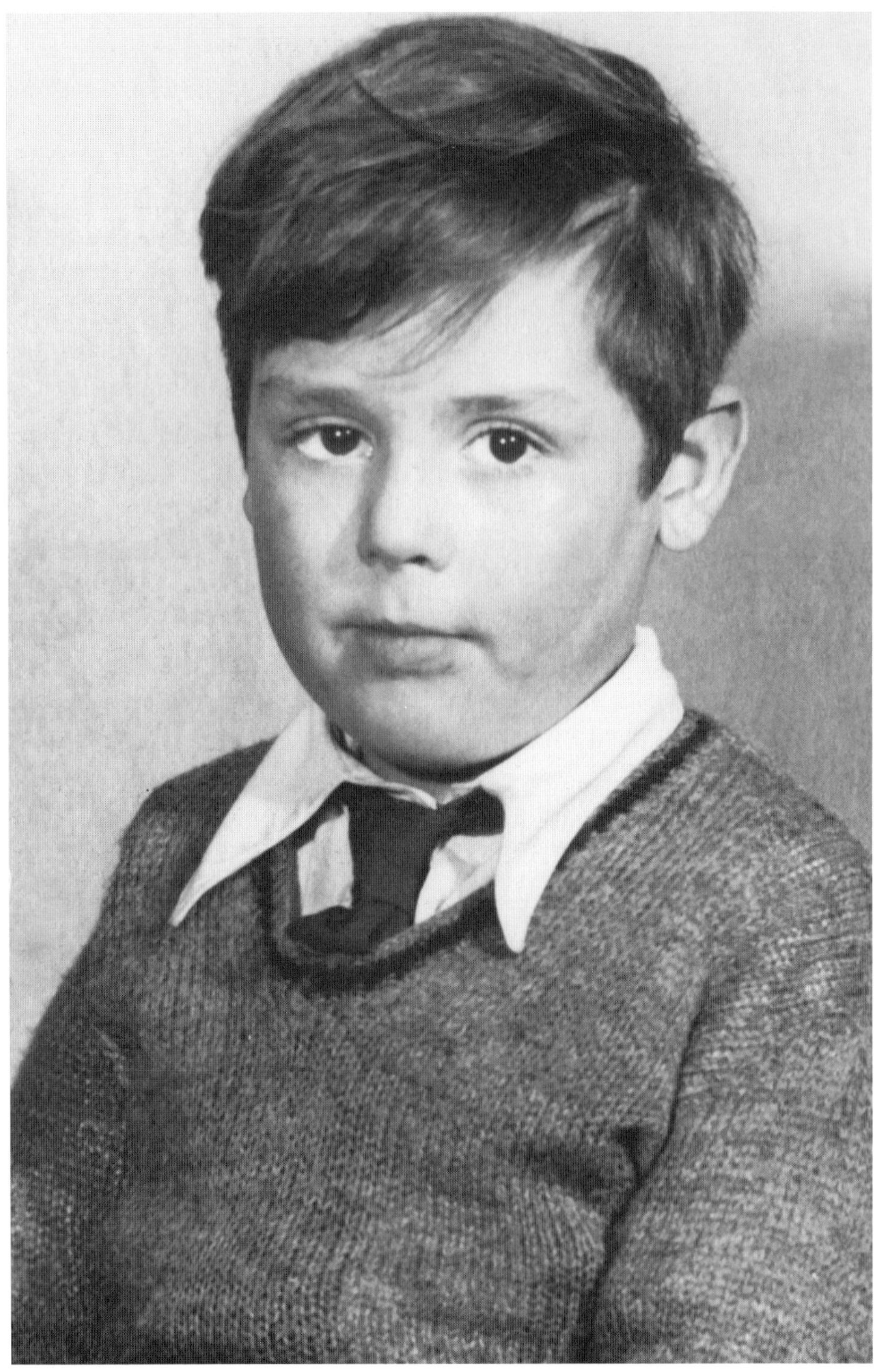

Peter Daniels at the Age of Six
Dating from 1954, the photograph was taken at St Martin's Primary School in St Martin's Church Street. Peter was brought up at 102 Love Lane, just a few minutes' walk from the school.

Introduction

The Victorians were enthralled by photography, it was a craze that led to the way we capture images today and reflects our own present-day fascination for digitally recording the world we see around us. Here in Wiltshire, we have the distinction of being the home county of William Henry Fox Talbot, the inventor of the first ever photographic negative that depicted a small window at his home, Lacock Abbey. Talbot published his first article in 1835, documenting his photographic discovery – that of the paper negative from which multiple positive prints could be made.

Fortunately for us a number of pioneering commercial photographers believed that Salisbury would be the ideal location to establish a photographic business, and several portrait studios opened in the city in the late 1850s. Although no precise details have been found, it is thought that the first 'photographic artists' in Salisbury were Henry Brooks of No. 60 High Street; William Thomas Pitcher of St Ann's Street, and James Wesley Miell of No. 21 Catherine Street, all of whom are listed in the 1859 edition of Kelly's *Post Office Directory* of Wiltshire. Over the next few years, quite a number of professional photographers followed their example and set up shop in Salisbury. A few disappeared almost as quickly as they came but others were more successful and continued to provide a useful service well into the twentieth century. The quality of their work, its content and quantity varied immensely, but nonetheless they all contributed something to the visual record of the life and times of the city of Salisbury, its people and their environment. Only a relatively low percentage of their total print output has survived to the present day but many aged photographs have yet to be discovered hidden away in old family photo albums, scrapbooks and in attics. A representative selection from those that have already come to light is reproduced in this book.

My interest in local history and photography emerged in the mid-1970s following a day out with a friend's 35-mm camera. I recall spending an enjoyable day at the Great Dorset Steam Fair, which was then held at Stoupaine Bushes, near Blandford. Returning home later in the day with four rolls of exposed black and white film, there is no doubt that full advantage was taken of all the photo opportunities that presented themselves on that particular occasion. It was fascinating to see how people lived, worked and played in the days of long ago. The images I had taken of some steam road locomotives were quite impressive but I was even more delighted with the photographs of a few old cars, buses, lorries and vans.

With the desire to learn more about England's industrial heritage I read a few books on the history of road transport and began searching for contemporary material. Among the items I sought were original photographs, postcards, commercial stationery, books and sales brochures. The hunt was very rewarding and I gathered together a great deal of information. A year or two after starting my collection I obtained a small booklet from a dear old friend, the late Jim Smith, proprietor of The Little Junk Shop at No. 73 Greencroft Street, Salisbury. It was a purchase that was to have a profound and lasting effect on my new hobby. Written by Jeremy P. Farrant, the pamphlet was titled *Scout Motors of Salisbury, 1902–1921*. I was fascinated with the book and after reading it several times there were a number of questions that needed to be answered but I could find no one to answer them. Keen to know more about this local motor manufacturer, I carried out a lot of new research, learning a great deal about the company and the vehicles they made. I compiled a list of names of the earliest Scout car and commercial vehicle owners, who appear to have been mostly professional people such as doctors, solicitors, farmers and even a few shopkeepers.

It was at this point in time that I realised my research had only just begun as there was so much more that could be done with the catalogue of names, with dozens of leads to be followed up. For example, what about Revd William Page Roberts, who purchased a blue and yellow Scout limousine with Wiltshire registration No. AM-1342 in February 1909? What did he look like, what was his background, and where did he live? Fortunately those particular enquiries were quite rewarding as I found several photographs of the distinguished gentleman and also a lot of detailed information about him. Residing at The Deanery, in The Close, he was the Dean of Salisbury from 1907 to 1919. A fine photograph of him can be seen on page 10 of this book. My research is not always successful, however, and sometimes facts about a certain person, organisation or event just refuse to be found, even if the search is a particularly thorough and extensive one. There remains much work to be done.

On 21 August 1980, my first ever illustrated 'local history' article appeared in *The Journal* – the first of many, each one featuring at least one old photograph. There were regular appearances of series called *Flashback* and *Then and Now*. In the year 1987 came an opportunity that could not be missed – I was offered a regular slot in the *Salisbury Times*. Under the heading *Puzzle Picture*, the series featured a different mystery photograph each week, and readers were invited to get in touch if they could provide answers to questions such as who, what, where, when and why? The articles proved to be very popular indeed, running continuously for 810 weeks, transferring eventually to *The Journal*, where the last puzzle picture appeared in December 2003. It was during this time that readers of the *Salisbury Times* and *The Journal* started to call me 'The Old Picture Detective'.

Old photographs certainly seem to appeal to a wide audience, some of whom enjoy the feeling of nostalgia while others are more interested in the historical aspects. It has been a great pleasure and a privilege to have met so many interesting people during the time I worked on the puzzle picture articles. Through the years I have been sent a great many photographs, postcards, books and numerous other items of printed ephemera from all parts of the world. There is enough material to keep me busy for many years to come. As a means of sharing the images and information obtained through the puzzle picture articles, a new nostalgia feature was introduced in *The Journal* on 1 January 2004. The 'Journal Scrapbook', as it is known, has appeared on the Heritage page of *The Journal* every week since then and is now in its twelfth year with 614 appearances thus far, as of 1 October 2015.

This moves us neatly on to my latest project, *Salisbury From Old Photographs*, an album of remarkable photographic images depicting the people of Salisbury and their environment over a period of more than a hundred years, from the 1850s to the 1960s. Many of the images are being published for the first time and there should be a few surprises for even the most avid local history enthusiast.

For the first time I have included a section of photographs taken from above. Some of the pictures are shot from aeroplanes and helicopters and others from very tall buildings such as Salisbury cathedral. One or two images were even snapped from the top of high-level rescue appliances from Wiltshire Fire Brigade – a probably never-to-be-repeated experience for an enthusiast like me due to modern-day concerns about health and safety. These aerial photographs are among the most revealing of all scenic images as there are very few obstacles in the way to obscure the view. There is so much more to be seen from above – concealed gardens, buildings and other features that are just simply hidden and out of sight at ground level.

The year 2015 marks the centenary of the Wilts & Dorset bus company that began operations in Salisbury in 1915. To acknowledge this milestone in the company's history, I have included a section of photographs featuring fifty years of local buses, covering the period 1915–1965. There are also a few images of the company's early employees.

A major section in the book appears under the heading 'Memorable Occasions', a visual record of sixty-seven notable events that have taken place in Salisbury between the years 1887 (Queen Victoria's Golden Jubilee) and 1953 (Coronation of Queen Elizabeth II). There are also selections of photographs featuring the people and places of Salisbury.

Peter Daniels
Alderbury
5 October 2015

Chapter 1
People

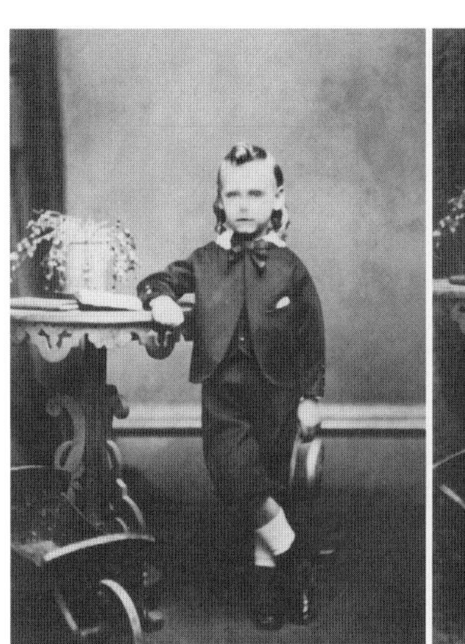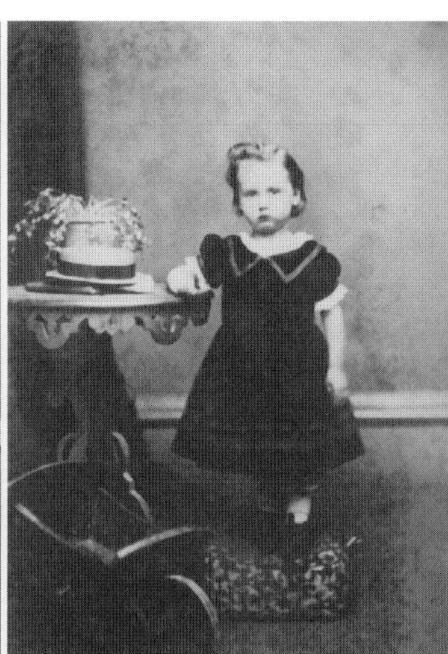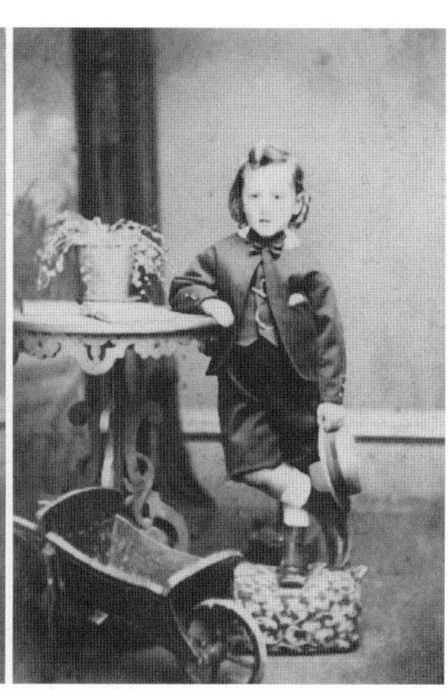

The Sewell Children, 1873

The father of these three charming children was William Sewell, proprietor of Sewell's Stores at 21–23 Milford Street, trading as pawnbrokers and general dealers. Pictured to the left is William (aged five years and nine months) and in the middle is Eliza (two years and eight months). Their older brother, Edward Granville, sadly lived a very short life. Born on 26 June 1869, he passed away on 8 June 1874. These carte-de-visit photographs were taken at Edward's photographic studio in St Ann Street in October 1873.

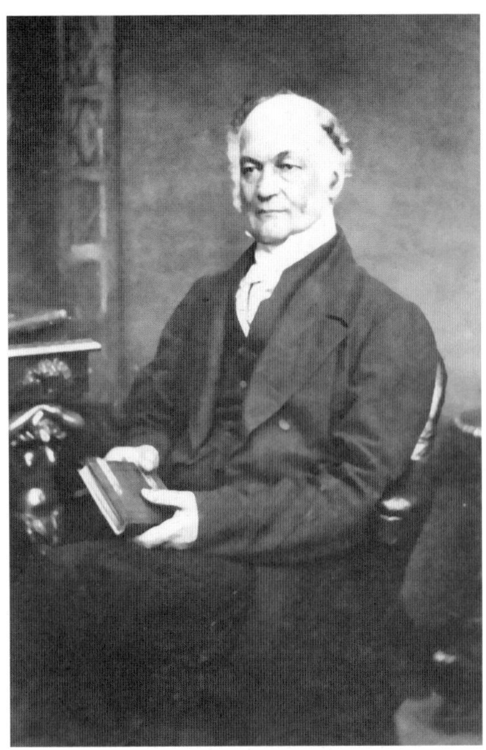

Bishop Moberly, 1875
One of Salisbury's more memorable bishops, George Moberly was born on Monday 10 October 1803 in St Petersburg, the seventh son of Edward Moberly, a Russian merchant. At the age of ten, and living in England, George was left in the care of his eldest brother, who arrange for him to attend Mr Richards's school in Hyde Street, Winchester. Then, in 1816, Lady Pembroke nominated him for a scholarship at Winchester College. Following a distinguished academic career he became headmaster of Winchester College in 1835, a post he held until 1866. In August 1869, Prime Minister Gladstone called Dr Moberly to become bishop of Salisbury. He was consecrated on Thursday 28 October. He passed away on 6 July 1885. Moberly Road in Salisbury is named after him, and his tomb and memorial can be found in Salisbury Cathedral.

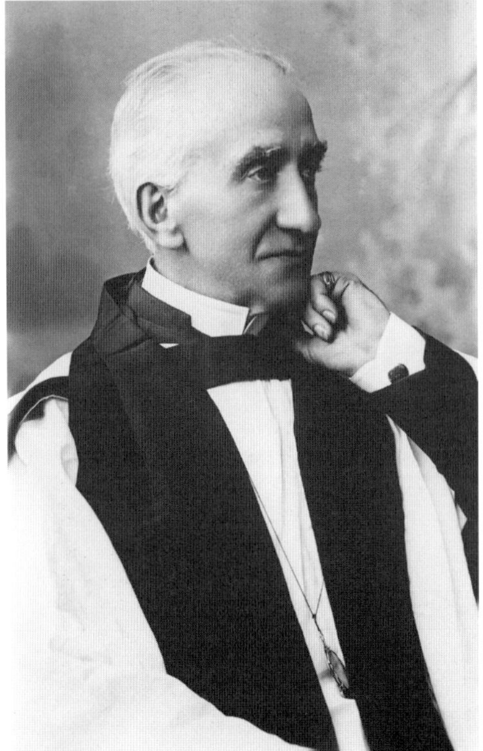

Dr William Page Roberts, 1907
William Page Roberts was born in Liverpool on 2 January 1836. A much respected and eminent clergyman in the Church of England, he was a Canon Residentiary at Canterbury Cathedral from 1895 to 1907, and Dean of Salisbury from 1907 to 1919. Residing latterly at Shanklin, Isle of Wight, he died on 17 August 1928, at the age of ninety-two.

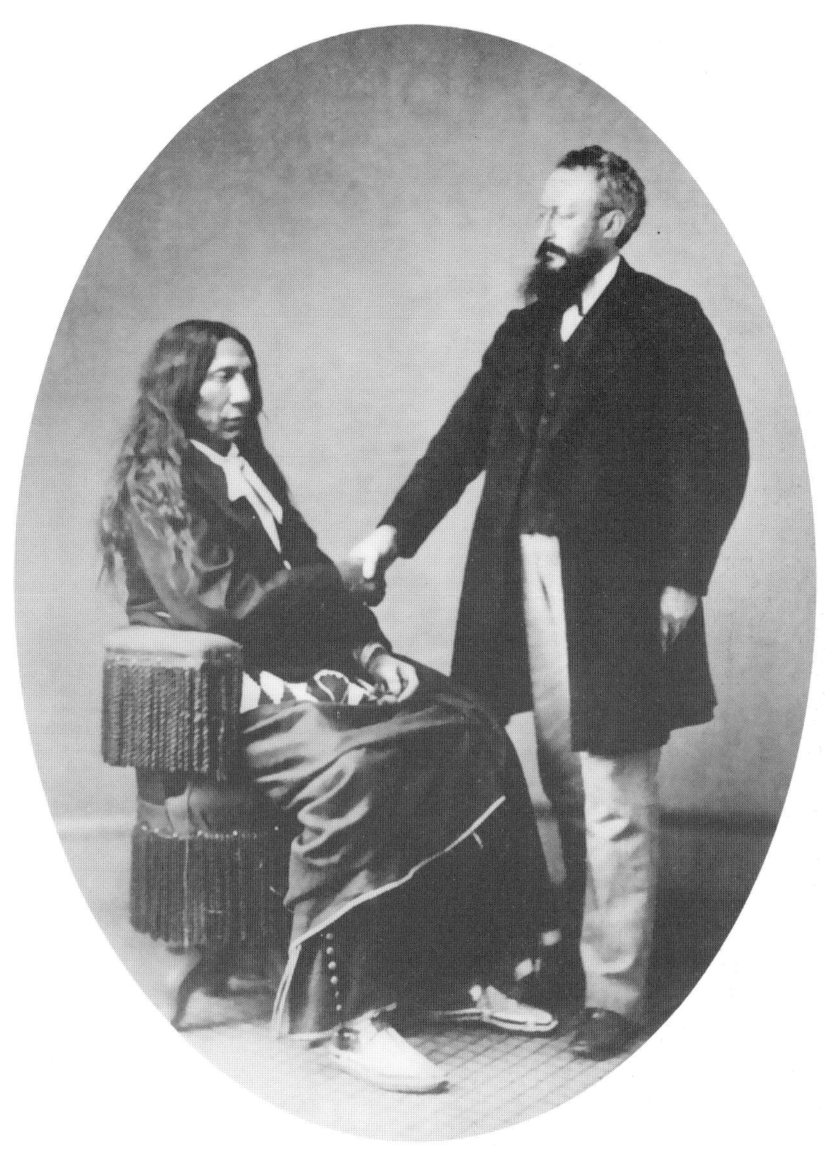

William Henry Blackmore Meets Red Cloud, 1872

William Henry Blackmore was born in Salisbury on 2 August 1827. During a business trip to America in 1863, he met some investors in New York who encouraged him to invest in a freehold land and emigration company. Having made a fortune, he became a philanthropist, primarily centred on his interest in Native Americans. Then, having acquired a collection of archaeological artefacts excavated from the mounds in the Mississippi valley, he returned to Salisbury and founded The Blackmore Museum in St Ann Street, which opened on 4 September 1867 (amalgamated with the Salisbury and South Wiltshire Museum in 1902). William was fascinated by photography and he commissioned a large number of photographs of Native Americans, prints of which were displayed at The Blackmore Museum. Red Cloud (Makhpiya-luta) was an Oglala Sioux chief who helped establish the great Sioux Reservation in 1868. He passed away at the age of eighty-seven in the year 1909. William Blackmore died in rather tragic circumstances on 12 April 1878.

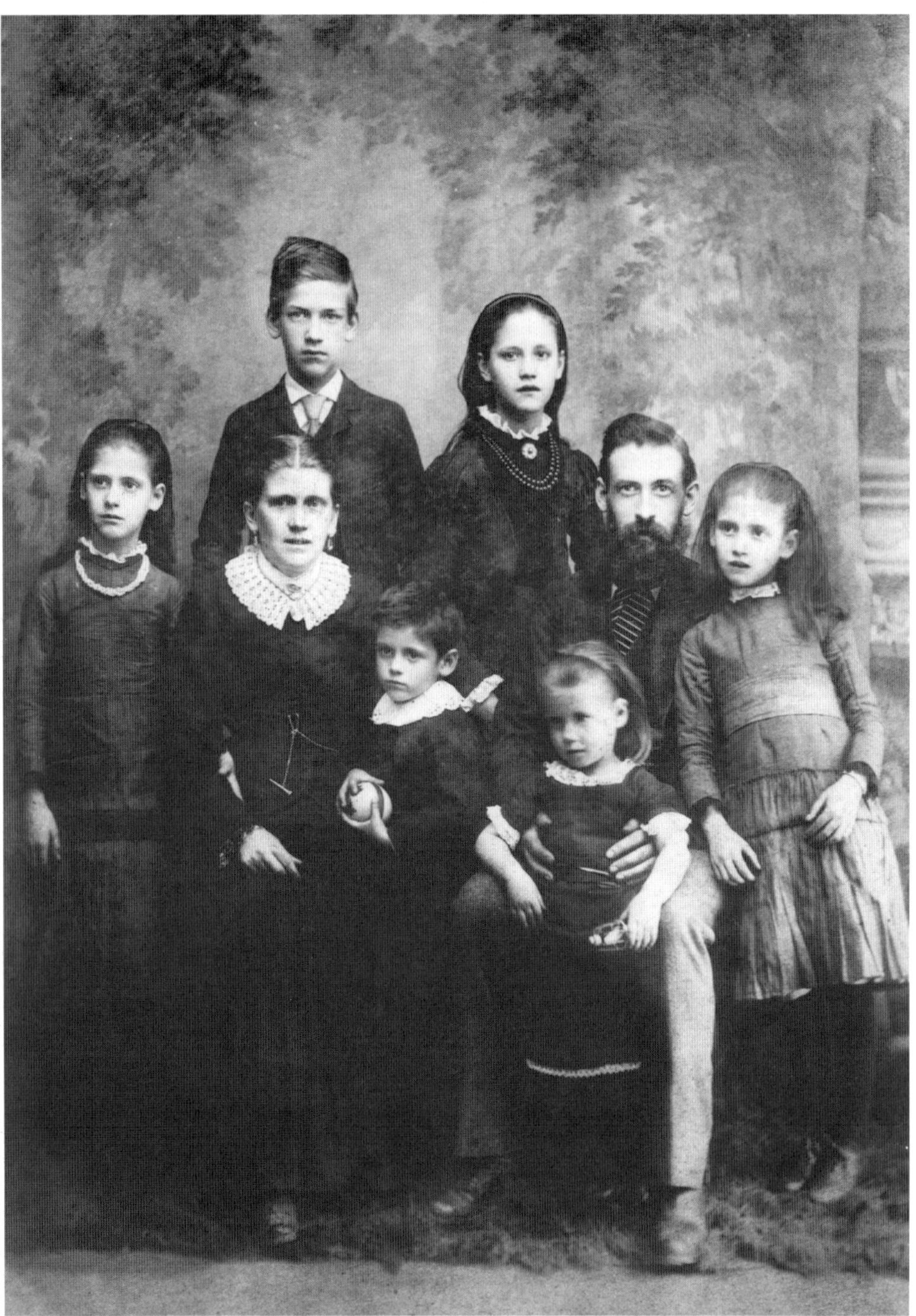

A Medway Family Portrait, July 1885

This delightful photograph was taken by Charles John Witcomb at his 'daylight studio' at 10 Catherine Street, Salisbury. Mr and Mrs Harry Bywater Medway are pictured here with their six children: Henry (aged fourteen), Edith (twelve), Alice (nine), Maude (six), Horace (four) and Amy (two). The couple celebrated their golden wedding anniversary in 1914. Mr Medway was a Justice of the Peace – he ran a thriving tailors shop at 34/36 Winchester Street, and he was the elected Mayor of Salisbury in the year 1922. The family home was at 64 Hamilton Road.

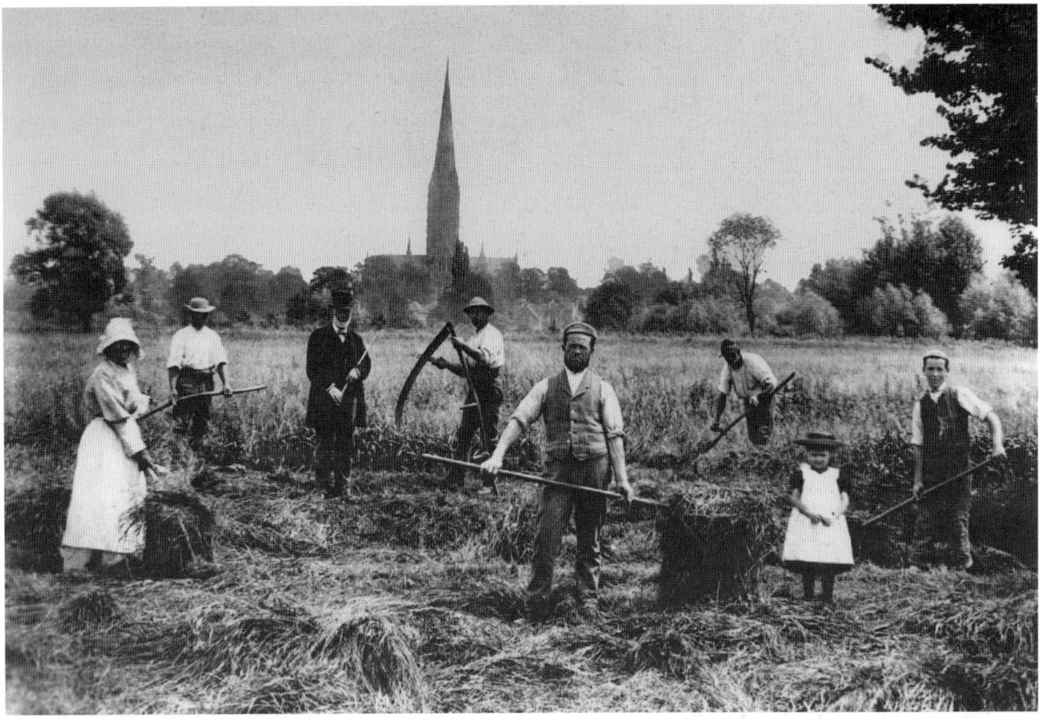

Harnham Water Meadows – Reaping the Harvest, 1890
Haymaking involved all members of the family in Victorian times, including children, as can be seen here. It is thought that the gentleman in the dark jacket and top hat is Edmund Main, who was farming around here at that time. The man pictured at the back appears to be sharpening the blade of his scythe with a whetstone, which was known as peening. A good reaper could cover thirty yards before the scythe required resharpening.

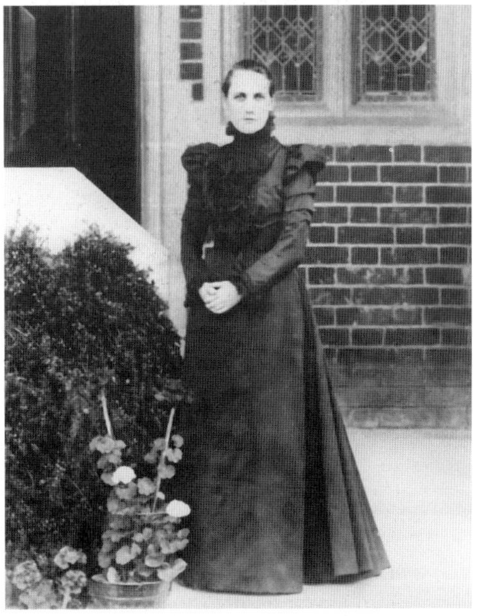

Godolphin School Headmistress, 1899
Mary Alice Douglas was born at Salwarpe, Worcestershire, on 29 November 1860, the fifth daughter of William and Frances Jane Douglas who had fifteen other children. In January 1890, Miss Douglas became headmistress of the Godolphin School, a position she held until the year 1919. She passed away on 7 November 1941, having never been married. This cabinet-style photograph was taken by James Owen, a portrait painter and photographer who had a studio at 29 Catherine Street.

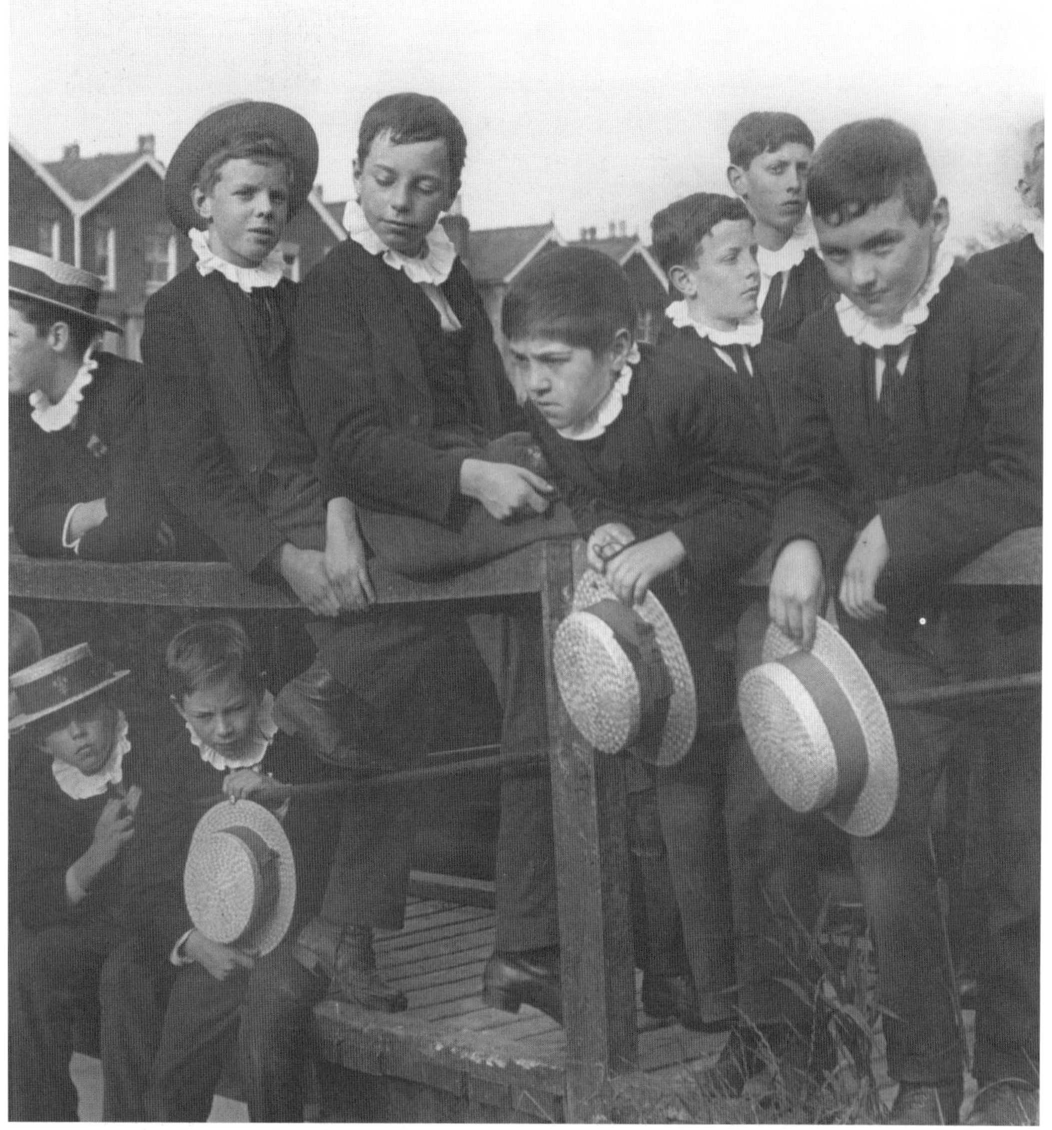

Salisbury Cathedral Choristers Relaxing on Long Bridge, 1909

This delightful photograph is reproduced from a magic lantern slide, one of many taken in the early 1900s by Rev. Arthur Gordon Robertson, headmaster of the Choristers' School. He was appointed headmaster on his thirty-second birthday, 18 June 1900. He started a camera club at the school, and also set up a darkroom for photography. There are some wonderful Edwardian images surviving of the choristers boating and playing cricket. Looking very smart here, the boys are wearing the obligatory white ruff collar, black tie and straw boater hat.

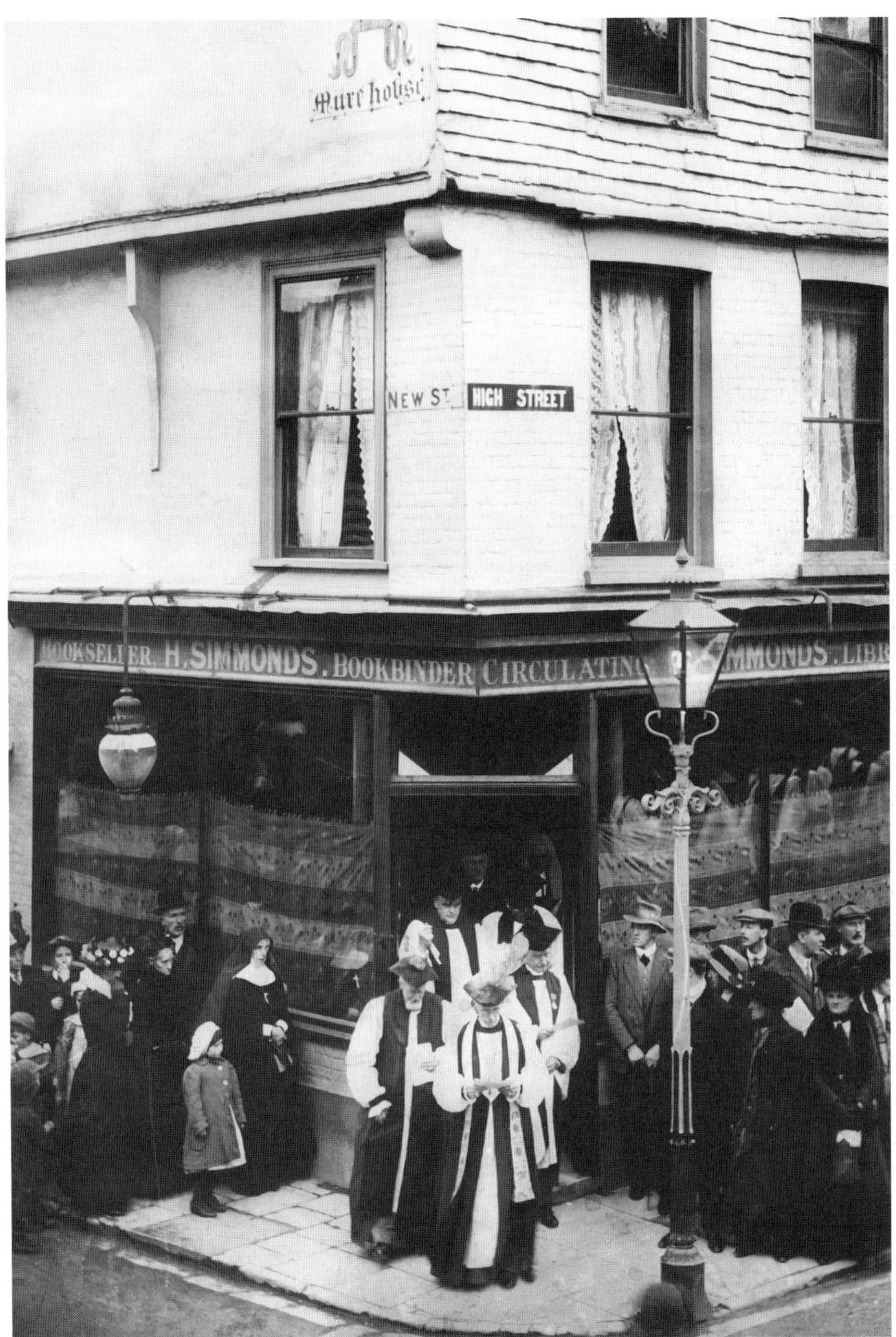

Bishop Ridgeway Enrobed at Mitre House, 1911
It has been a tradition since the fifteenth century that newly appointed Bishops of Salisbury would be enrobed at Mitre House, on the corner of High Street and New Street, before processing to the cathedral for their enthronement. Bishop Poore built a house on this site as a temporary residence while the cathedral was being built.

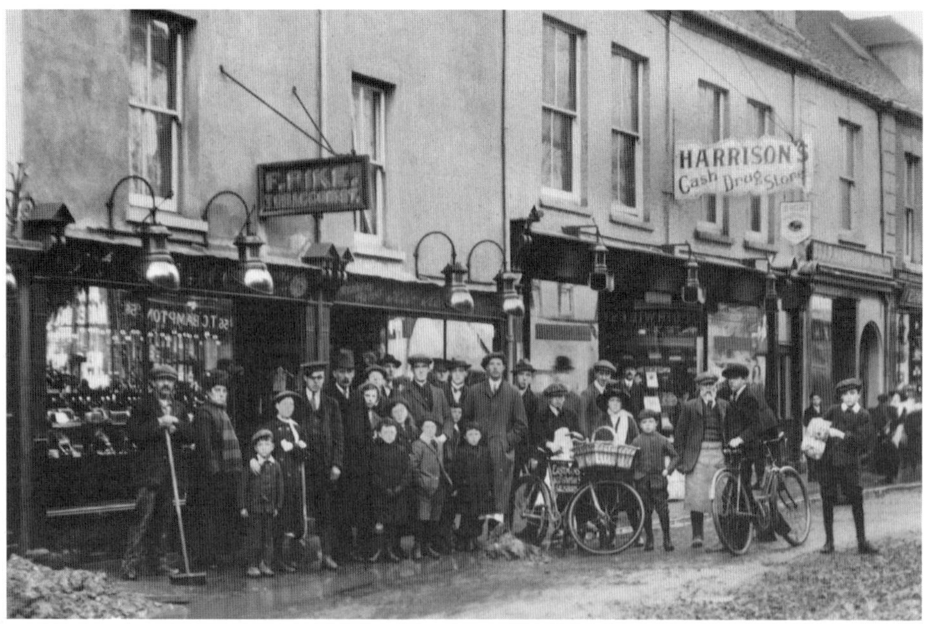

Cleaning up in Fisherton Street after the Flood, 1915
These individuals seem to have spontaneously formed a group while Mr Futcher, a commercial photographer, was taking an informal picture of some men removing debris and cleaning up the area following the disastrous flood of January 1915. Mr Futcher's shop and photographic studio are just out of view to the left.

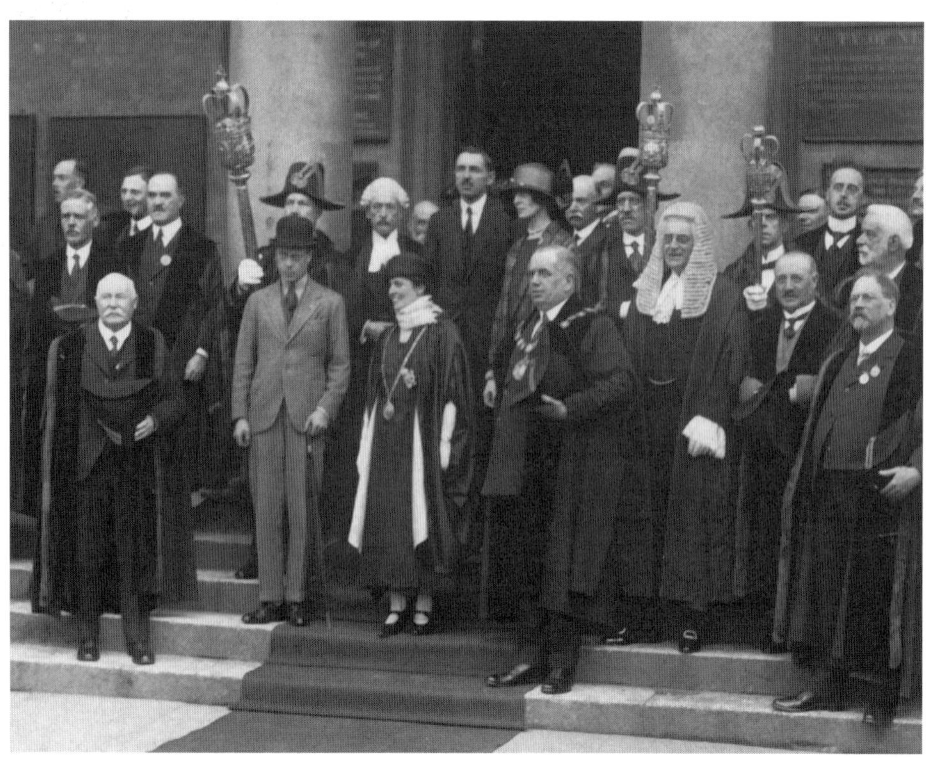

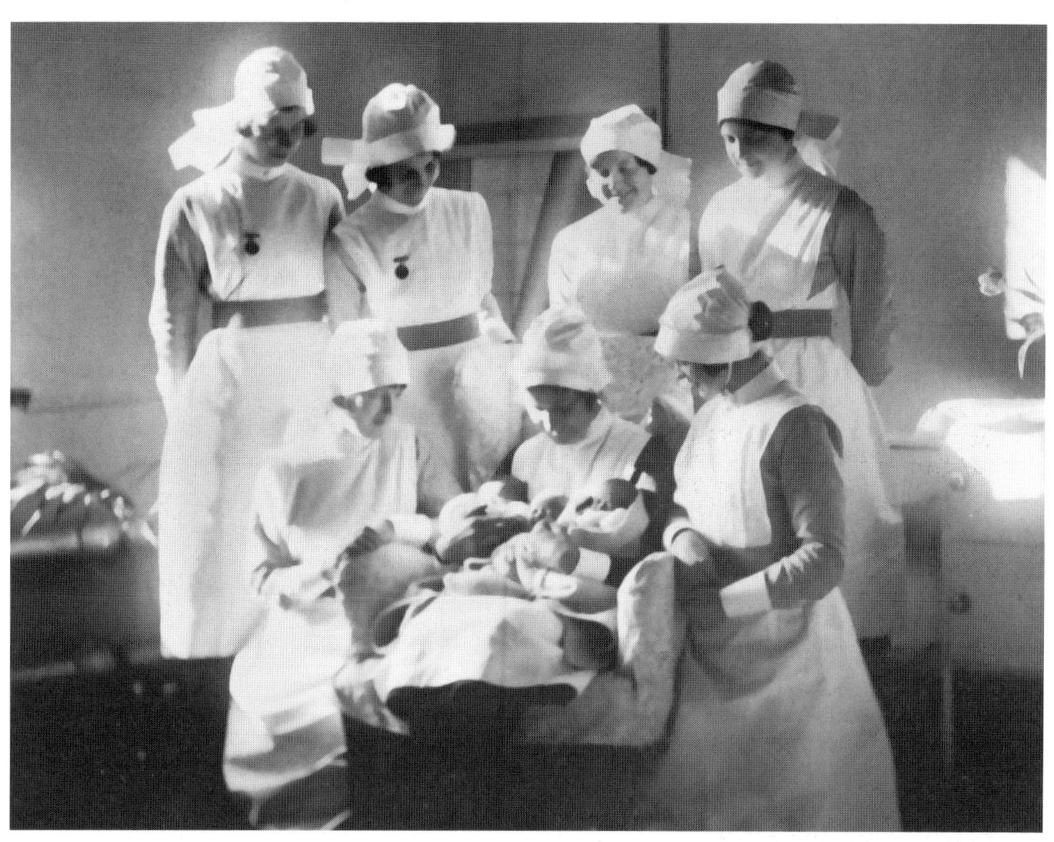

The Gates Triplets at Salisbury General Infirmary, 1931
Pamela, Patricia and Peggy Gates arrived in Beatrice Ward on the morning of Wednesday 11 February 1931. They weighed in at 3 lb 5 oz, 4 lb 9 oz and 4 lb 13 oz, respectively. They were the first triplets to have been born at Salisbury General Infirmary in its 165-year history. Nurse Wainwright was the Ward Sister at the time, so perhaps this is her pictured with the trio? There were already six girls in the Gates family before the arrival of the triplets, making Mr and Mrs Walter Gates, of 6 Rampart Road, the proud parents of nine lovely daughters. There were no boys in the family at that time but Ronald came along later – he was their only son.

Edward, Prince of Wales at the Council Chamber, 1923
Opposite bottom: The prince visited Salisbury on 24 May to open the Wiltshire Agricultural Association's annual show at the Butts Fair Field (later the site of Five Rivers Leisure Centre). Having had some formal photographs taken with invited VIPs on the steps of the Council House (Guildhall), he inspected a contingent of wolf cubs from the third Salisbury pack.

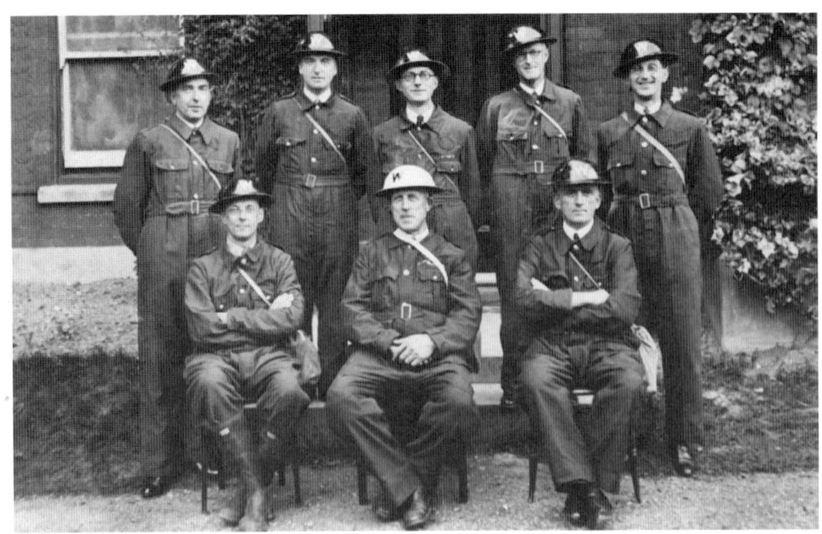

Salisbury Air Raid Wardens, 1940

Standing left to right: William 'Bill' Bowden, Archie Sanger, Frederick 'Freddy' Hayward, Mr Paine and Edward 'Ted' Holloway. Seated are Mr Withers, Mr Ross (Section Chief) and Charlie Sparrow. In a booklet, *Notes and Advice on Air Raids – Before, During and After*, published by Salisbury City Council in June 1941, citizens were advised to 'Get to know your Warden – he is specially trained to help you'.

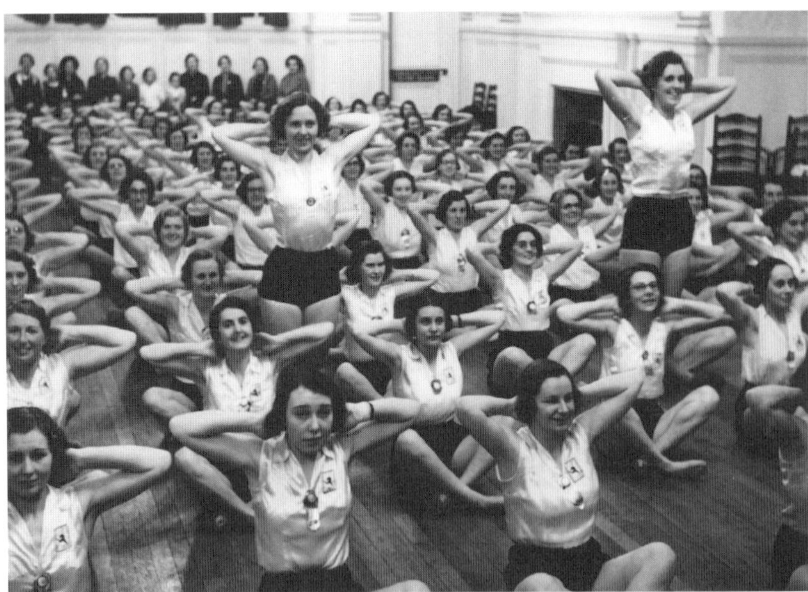

Women's League of Health and Beauty, 1938

Here we can see the Salisbury members of one of the first exercise systems to have been conceived in the UK. The movement was founded in 1930 by Mary Bagot Stack, a First World War widow, who suffered from rheumatic fever. The teacher was Miss Madge Brown, who ran the sessions in The Canal at the Assembly Rooms (later a Waterstone's bookshop). Among the Salisbury members at the time were (names before marriage): Bridle, Couldrey, Davies, Ducket, Jenkins, Packer, Potter and Robins.

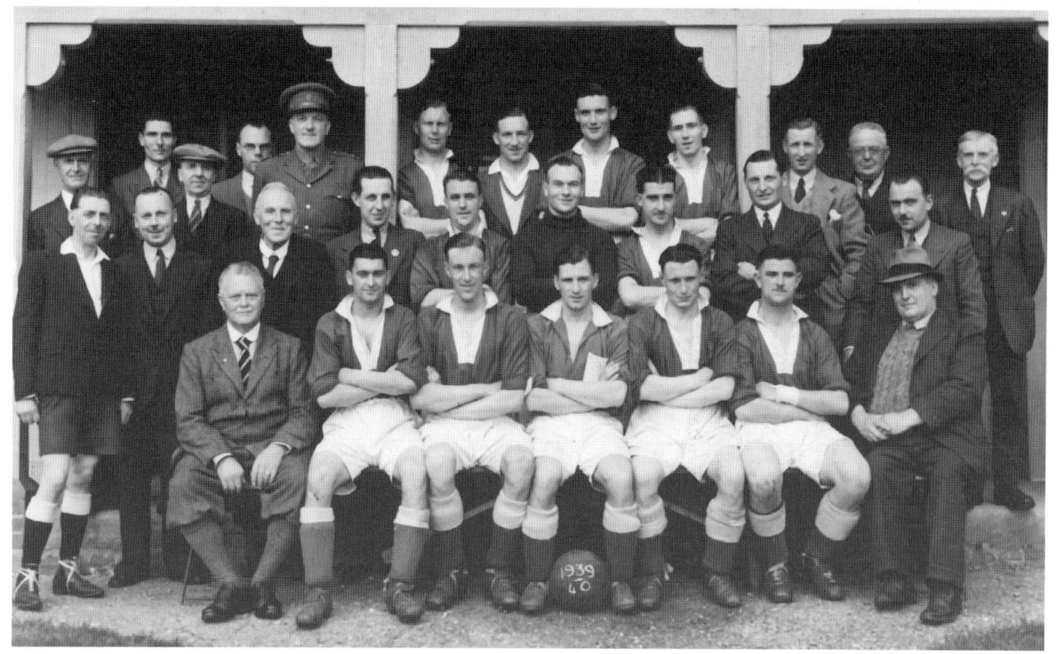

The Salisbury Corrinthians Football Team, 1939/40
Pictured here at The Pavilion in Victoria Park is a team of professional footballers nicknamed 'The Corries'. The club secretary, Jack Marchant, is seated to the right, wearing a trilby hat, and the linesman on the left is Fred Bevis. Arthur Ingleby can be seen second from the left in the third row. The club folded in 1947.

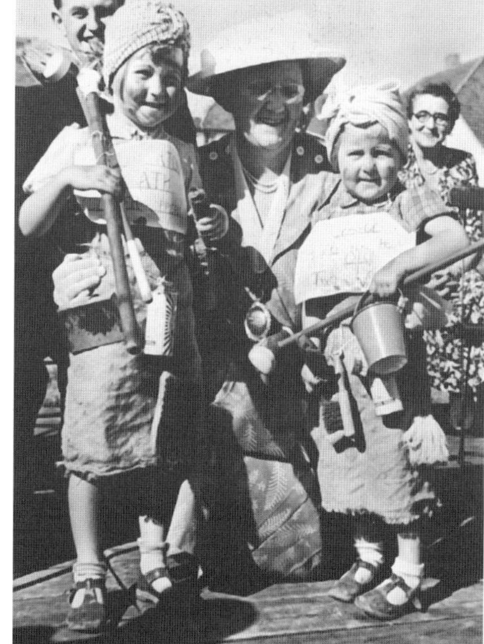

The Bemerton Heath Cleaner-Uppers, 1951
The Mayoress of Salisbury, Mrs Chalke, is clearly enchanted by these two little Misses Mop, Pauline and Penny, who took part in the children's fancy dress competition at the first 'Festival Day' organised by the Bemerton Heath Tenants Association on 28 July 1951. Dolly Roles can be seen at the back on the right. She was awarded an MBE for her work at the Eventide Centre.

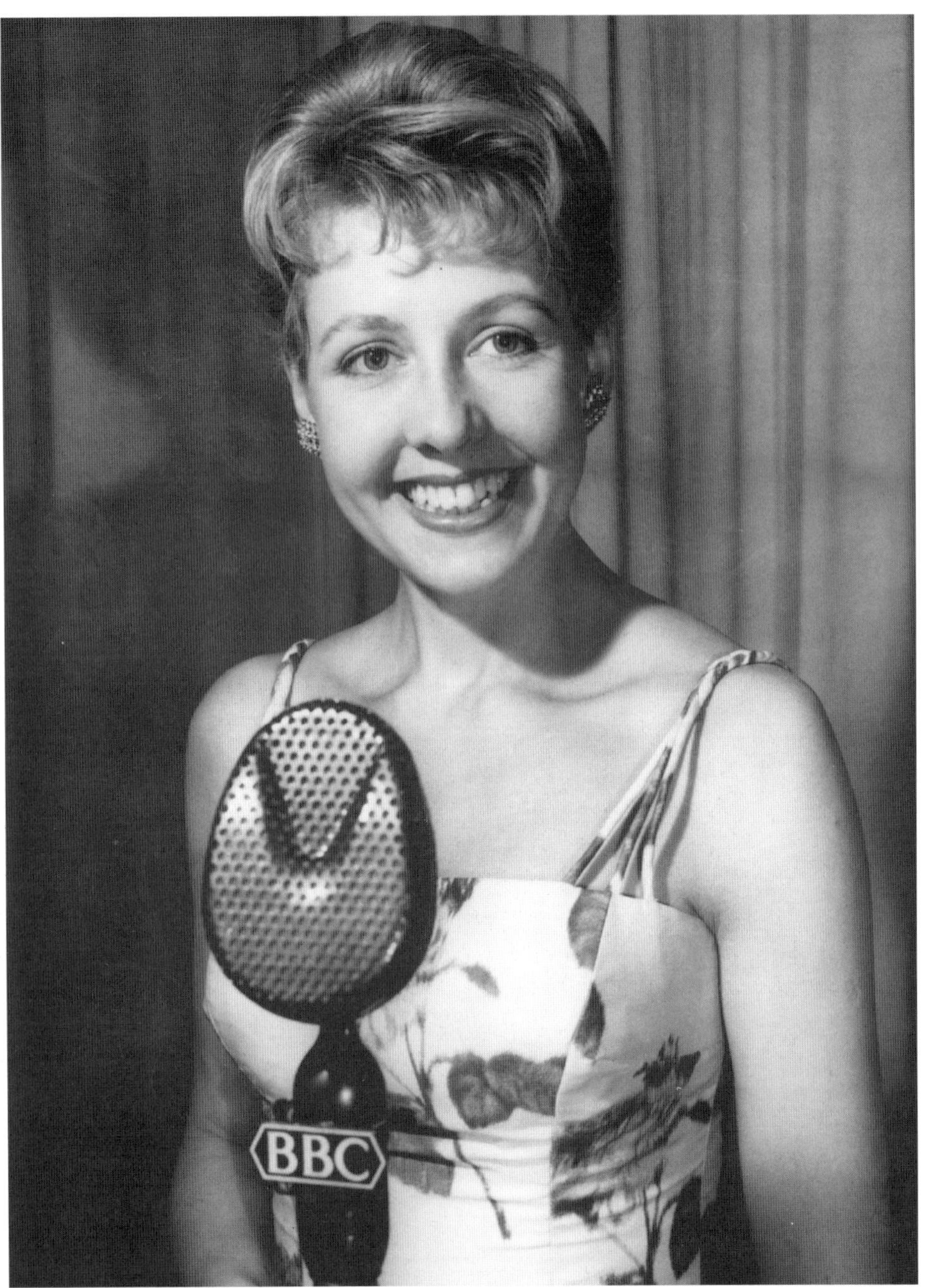

Rosemary Squires, Salisbury's Queen of Song, 1958
Having moved to Salisbury at the age of ten, Rosemary attended St Edmund's Girls' School where she was presented with a Certificate of Merit for Speech and Drama. Her teacher, Ada Gething, encouraged Rosemary to join a concert party, and having done so she has never looked back. One of Rosemary's claim to fame is that she recorded the longest running jingle, *Hands that do dishes* for Fairy Liquid, which was broadcast for more than thirty-three years. The year 1998 was her 'Fifty-Fifty' year, celebrating the anniversary of fifty years as a professional singer and fifty years of broadcasting.

Chapter 2
City Scenes

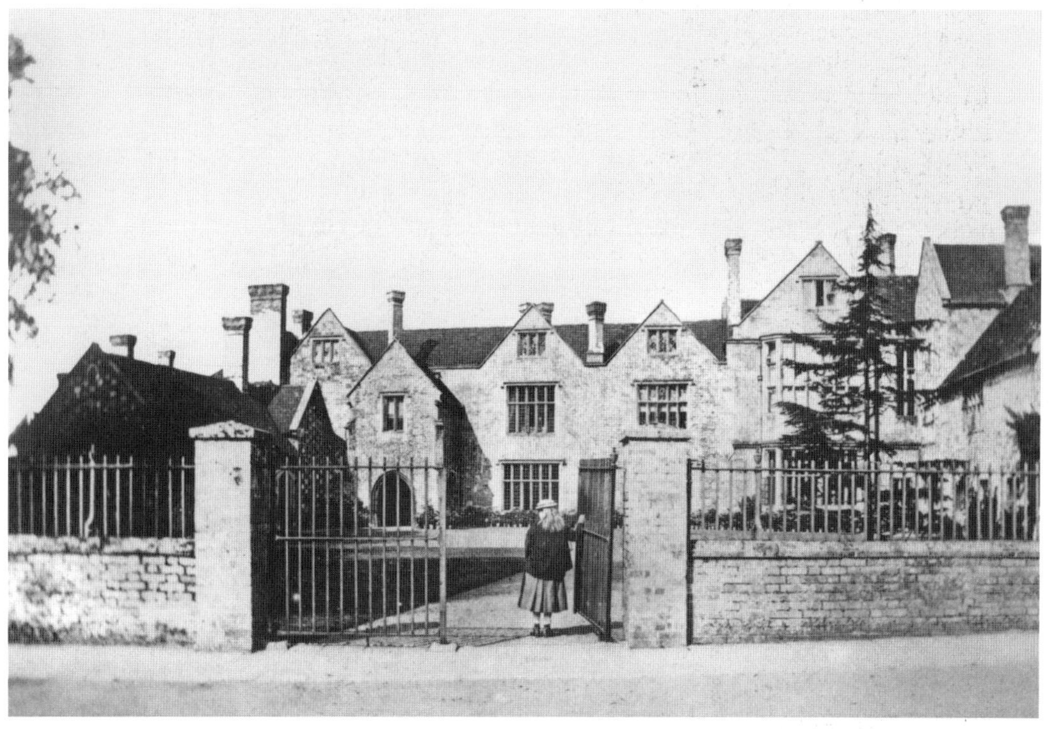

Salisbury Diocesan Training College, King's House, *c.* 1875
The teacher training college opened in Salisbury Cathedral Close in January 1841, having been founded by the National Society for the Church of England. Later to become the College of Sarum St Michael, it settled at King's House in the early 1860s, where it remained until its closure in 1978. Three years later, in 1981, this Grade-I-listed building became the home of Salisbury Museum.

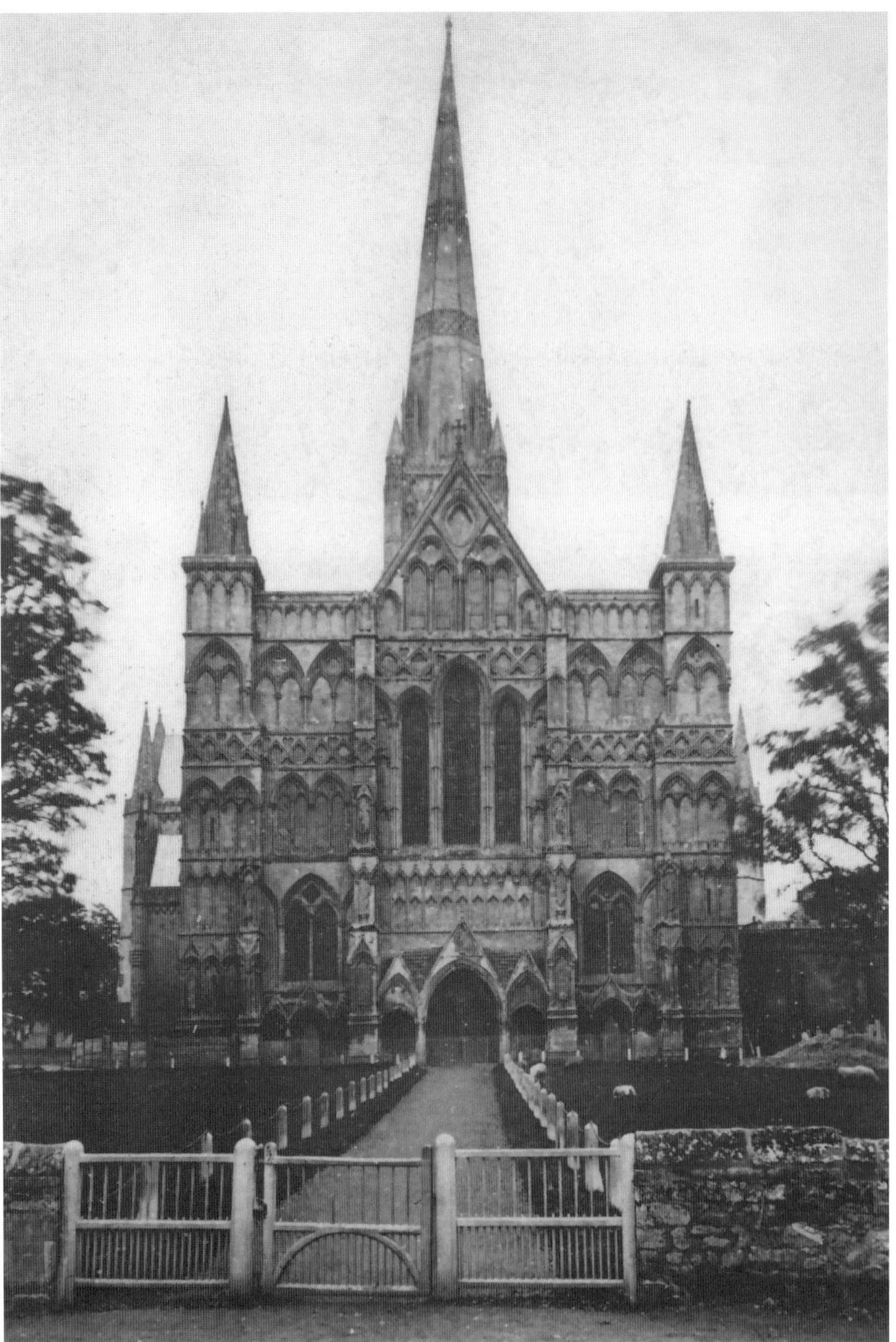

The West Façade of Salisbury Cathedral in the 1850s
This remarkably early photograph records a number of changes that have long since passed from human memory. Wooden posts and linked chain fencing lead to the West Door, in front of which can be seen some metal railings and gates. There appear to be only six statues displayed in the niches on the West Front at this time. Sheep are grazing on the west lawns.

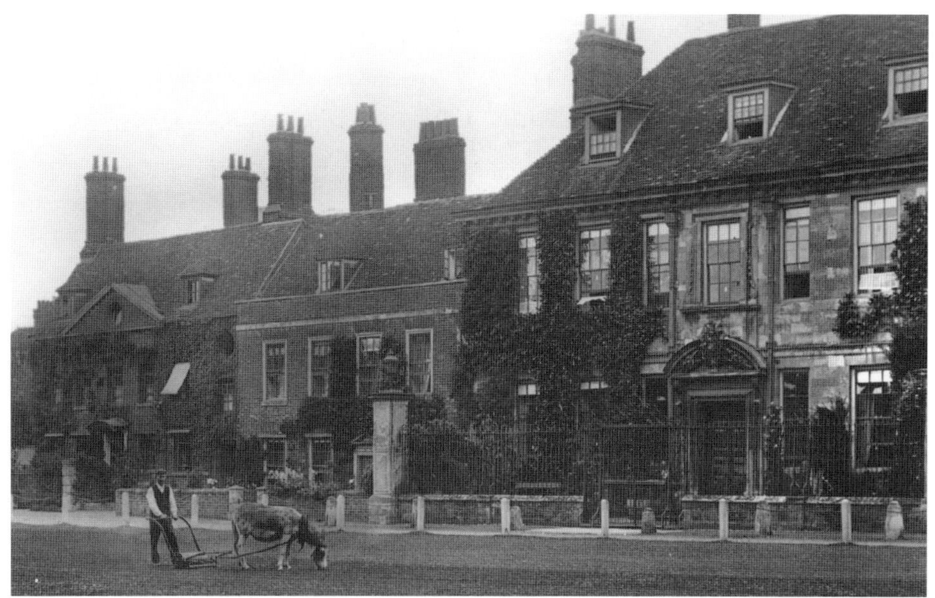

Grass Cutting in the Close, 1906

The groundsman pictured here on Choristers Green in front of Mompesson House would have got the job done a lot more quickly if only he had encouraged the donkey to actually pull the lawn mower along rather than let it munch the grass short. Life really does seem to have been lived at a slower pace all those years ago. In a Salisbury street directory of the period, the occupants of Mompesson House (53 The Close) are shown as William M. Hammick and The Misses Townsend.

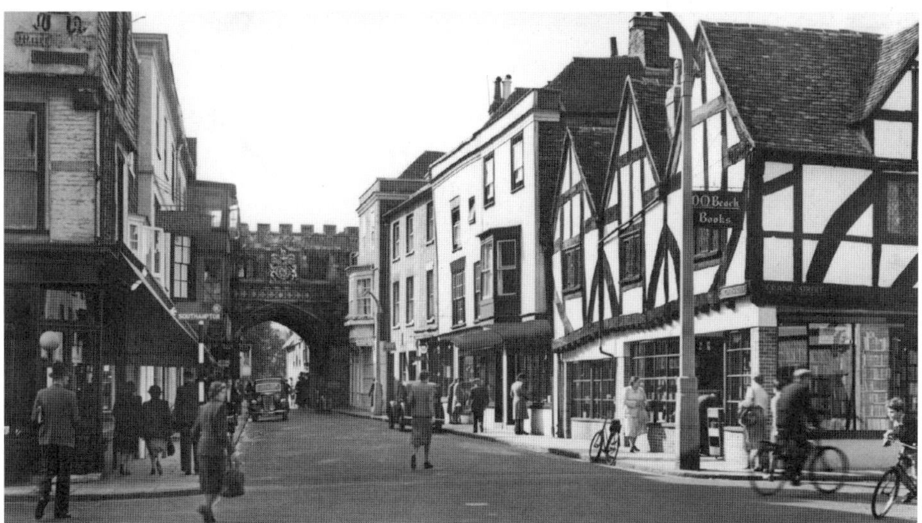

High Street and High Street Gate, 1953

Coming into view on the left is Mitre House, at the junction of New Street, where you would find Herberts ladies hairdressers and perfumers. On the opposite corner, at the Crane Street junction, we can see D. M. Beach Books, a very well-known and respected bookshop of the era. Having successfully run the shop until his retirement in 1998, Tony Beach passed away in 2014 at the age of eighty-four.

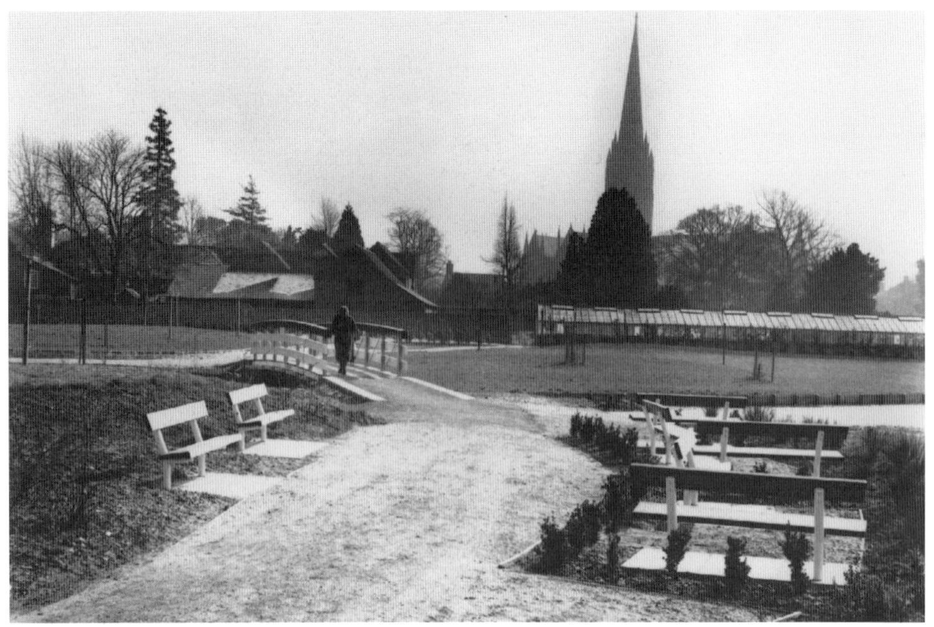

The Development of Queen Elizabeth Gardens, 1957
The land was developed by Salisbury District Council as public walks and pleasure grounds to commemorate the Coronation of Queen Elizabeth II. The area was formerly occupied by Keynes, Williams and Co., nurserymen, whose slogan was 'We Supply Everything required in a Garden', specialising in 'fruit trees, roses, dahlias and seeds'. The company had not entirely vacated the site when this photograph was taken – one of their greenhouses can still be seen in the background.

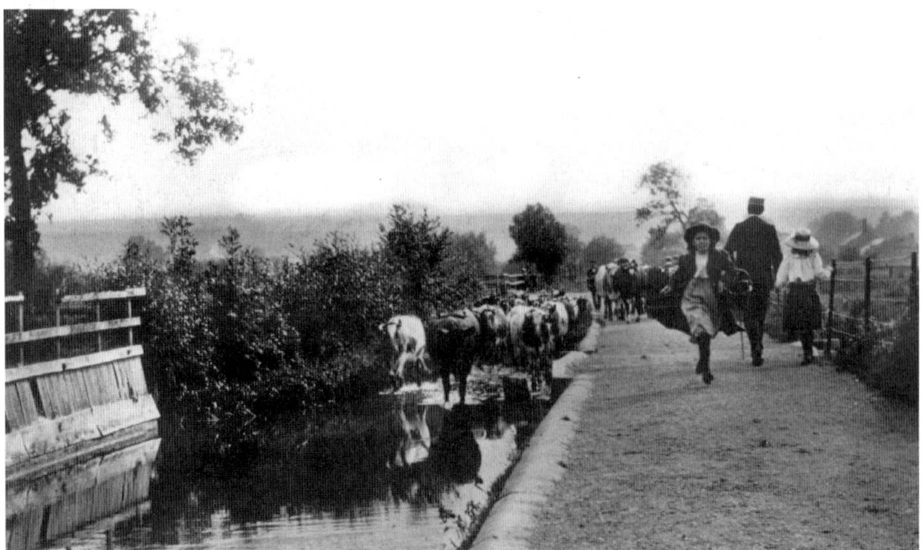

Town Path, 1909
The thoroughfare linking the old settlement of Fisherton with the scattered suburb and village of Harnham is believed to have been constructed by Salisbury City Council, maybe with the help of Harnham Parish Council, in the mid-nineteenth century. Although it has been some years since cattle last used the path, sheep can still be seen crazing in the surrounding water meadows.

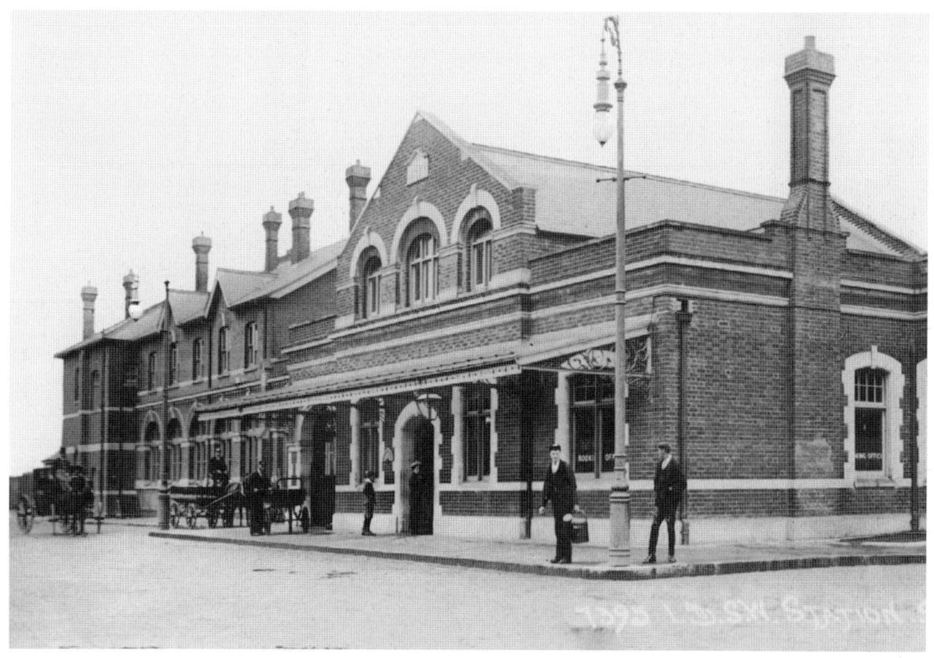

London and South Western Railway Station, 1907

The original station, which stands out of view to the right of the picture, came into use on 2 May 1859. Work on extending the station commenced in 1899, and by 1902 the building shown here was competed. George Lawrence was Station Master when this photograph was taken.

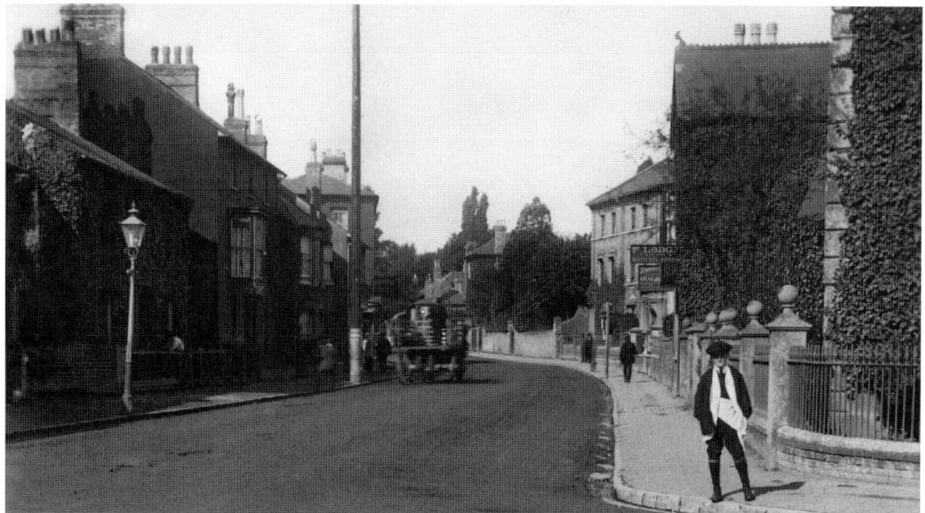

Wilton Road, 1914

The ivy-coverd building on the right edge of the photograph is Portland House, formerly the residence of Theodore Brown, who in the late 1800s and early 1900s was a prolific inventor of stereoscopic cameras and other items of optical entertainment. Coming into view on the left is another ivy-covered house, 19 Wilton Road, which was the home of George Prince, a commercial traveller. The Muslim Association of Salisbury acquired the building in the early twenty-first century.

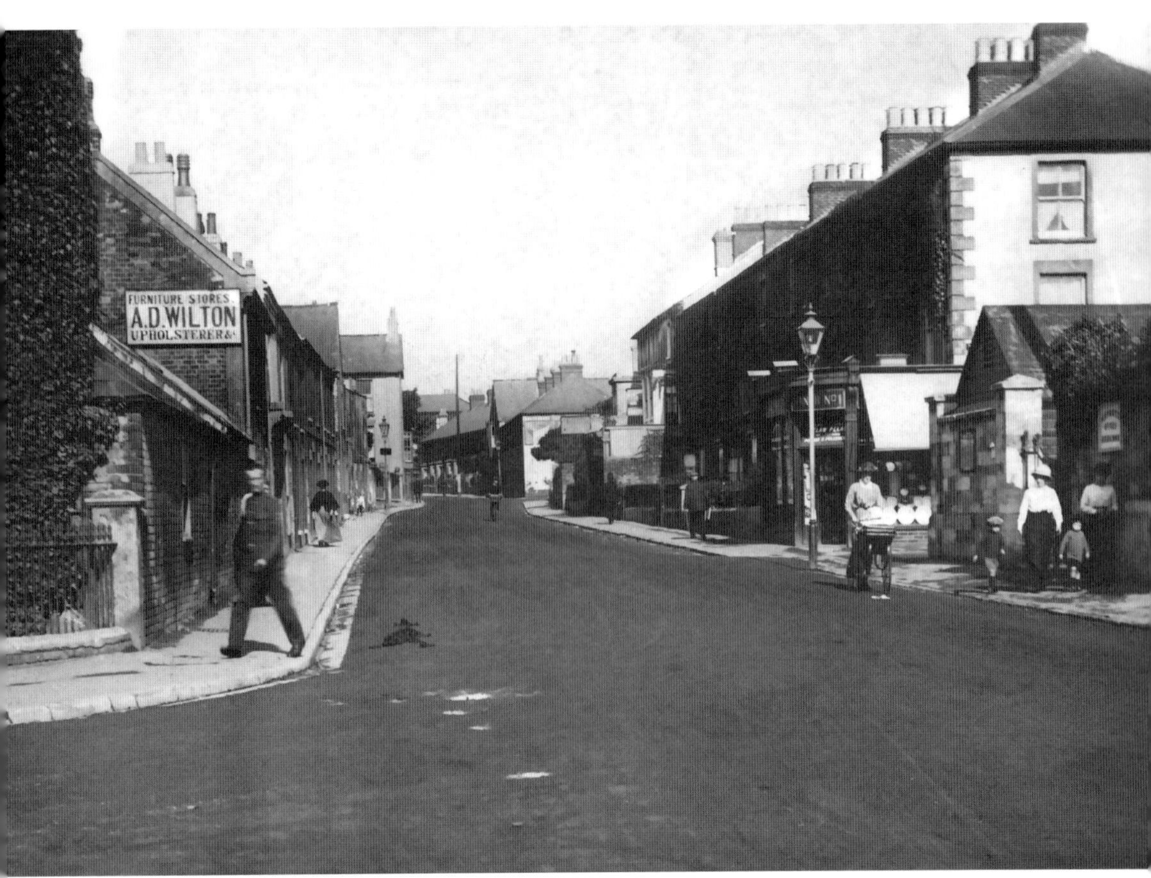

Devizes Road, 1914

Portland House can be seen to the left, and York Road is to the right. When the central parts of Salisbury were bypassed in the early 1970s, and Churchill Way was constructed, many features of the city were lost forever. The lower end of Devizes Road was completely remodelled to make way for the St Paul's roundabout, and this photograph is now a vivid reminder of how it used to be. The women and children pictured to the right had just passed Branch No. 1 of the Salisbury Co-operative Society at the junction of York Road, and they are approaching the perimeter wall of the old goal ground. It was about this time when workmen unearthed some human remains near this spot, which is not surprising because the bodies of executed murderers were sometimes buried in the grounds of Fisherton Goal. There may well be human skeletons lying under the foundations of Churchill Way.

Fisherton Street, from the Tower of St Paul's Church, 1930

Opposite bottom: On left of the photograph can be seen a Pratt's motor lorry delivering petroleum products to Bown & Sons, motor engineers, of 159–161 Fisherton Street. Next door, at No. 163, could be found Harry Dawkins' fruit and vegetable shop; then the London and Central Meat Co., butchers (165); Frank H. Tribbeck, jewellers (166); Thomas Brockway, game dealer (167), and finally Fisherton School, at which point Wilton Road starts.

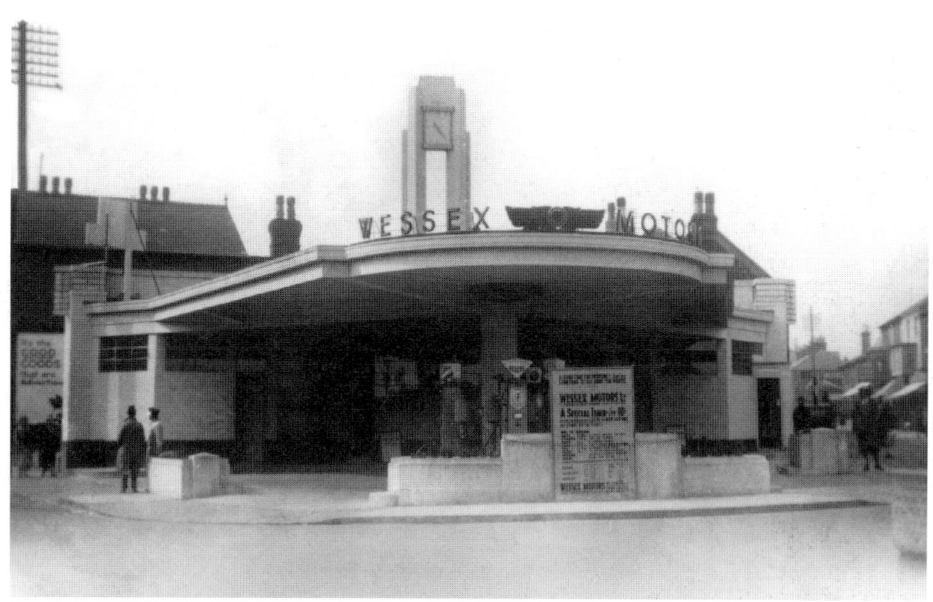

Wessex Motors Ltd – Petrol Filling Station, 1947
This splendid art deco petrol station with its imposing clock tower was ideally situated at the Devizes Road and Wilton Road Y-junction (the actual address was 2 Wilton Road). The garage opened in 1933 or thereabouts on the former site of Portland House. Wessex Motors were agents for Morris and Wolseley cars, and more significantly the Bentley marque. A large polished-steel Bentley badge can be seen displayed between the Wessex Motors lettering above the canopy. Cleveland Discol petrol pumps are in use at this time.

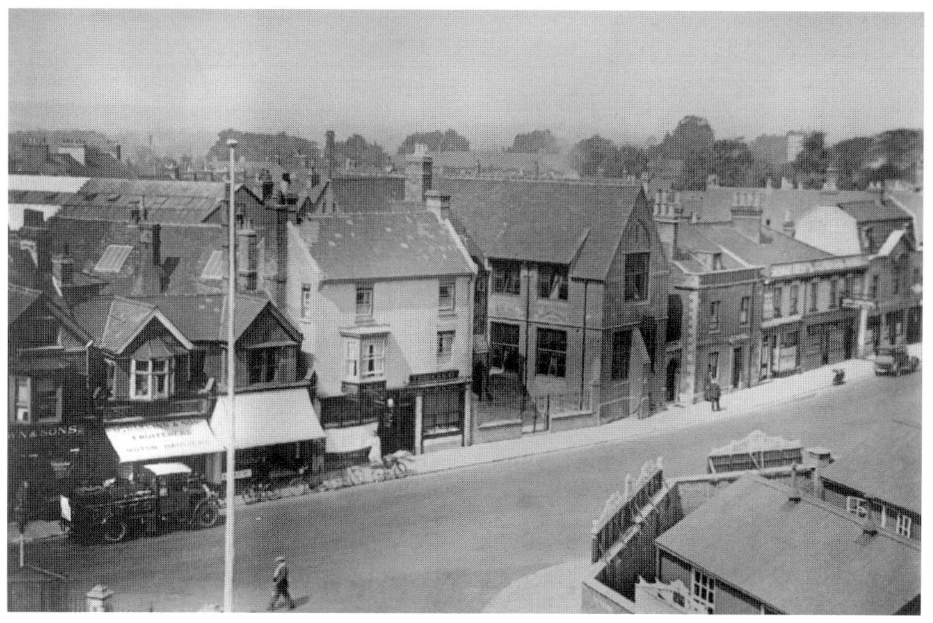

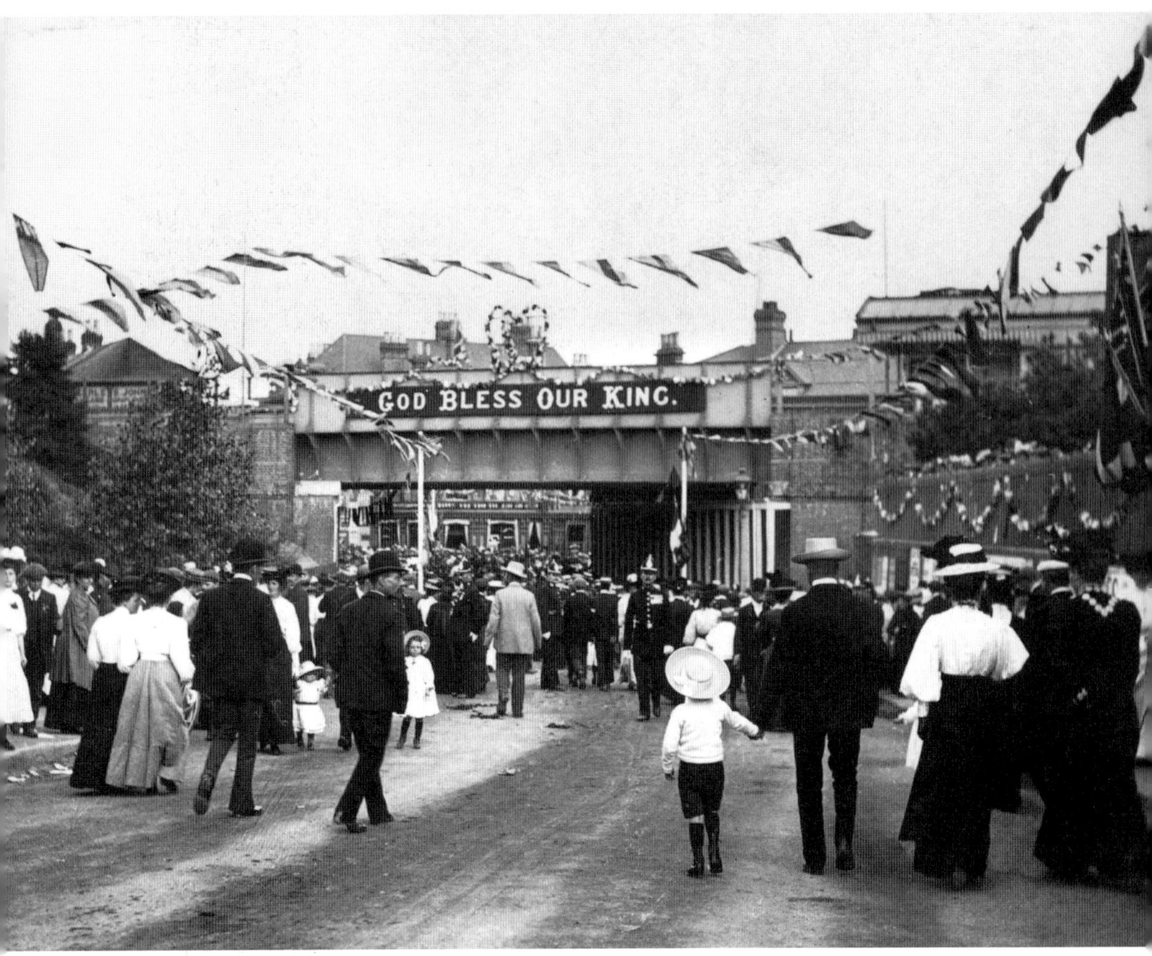

Dressed to Impress in Fisherton Street, 1908
This was the scene near Fisherton Street railway bridge on 27 June 1908, when thousands of people put on their Sunday best clothes and headed in the direction of Salisbury railway station, where King Edward VII and Queen Alexandra were due to be greeted by the Earl and Countess of Pembroke. The king and queen had been invited to spend a few days at Wilton House. By the time the royal train had arrived from Waterloo, all available spaces in Fisherton Street and much of Wilton Road had been taken up by smartly dressed onlookers such as these who hoped to catch a glimpse of the royal visitors as they drive to Wilton in open horse-drawn carriages.

The Summerlock Bridge Area of Fisherton Street, 1915
Opposite bottom: On the left of the photograph, Case & Son's horse-drawn delivery van can be seen parked outside William Sutton's bakery, near the entrance to Water Lane. And on the opposite side of the street an open cart appears to be delivering animal carcasses. The vehicle has pulled up near the shop of Henry Rattue, a pork butcher at 110 Fisherton Street. The local offices of Pickfords, the very well-known household removals and warehousing company, were to be found a few doors away at No. 100 Fisherton Street.

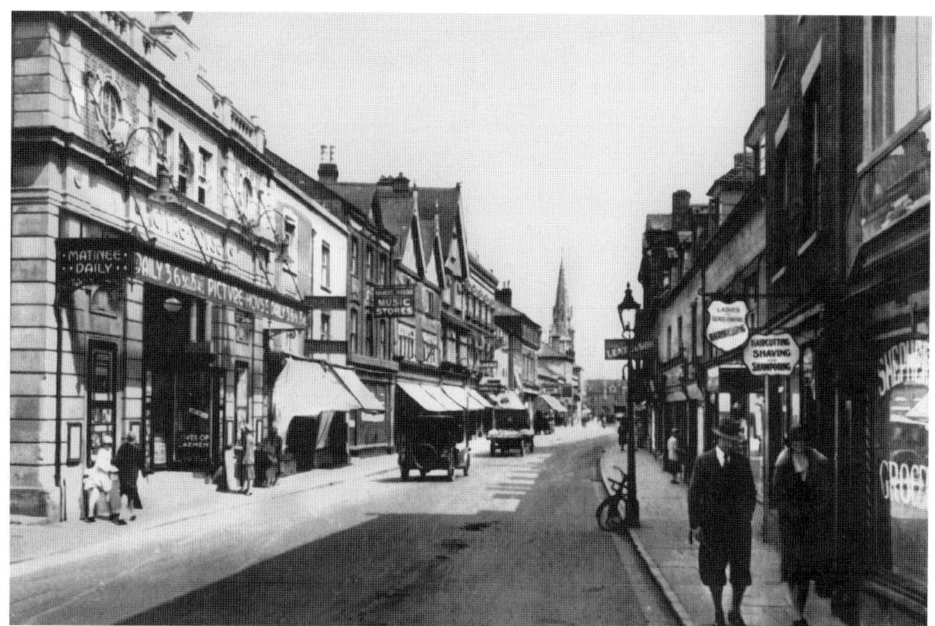

Fisherton Street in the Late Twenties
Albany Ward's cinema, The Picture House, can be seen to the left, where there were three screenings daily, at 3.00 p.m., 6.50 p.m. and 8.45 p.m. On this particular day the film *Loves of Carmen* was being shown – a 1927 American silent romantic drama starring Dolores del Río and Don Alvarado. Also coming into view on that side of the street is Handel's Music Stores and the Angel Hotel; and on the opposite side, Leate & Sons, leather merchants, and Bridle & Sons hairdressers are now part of history.

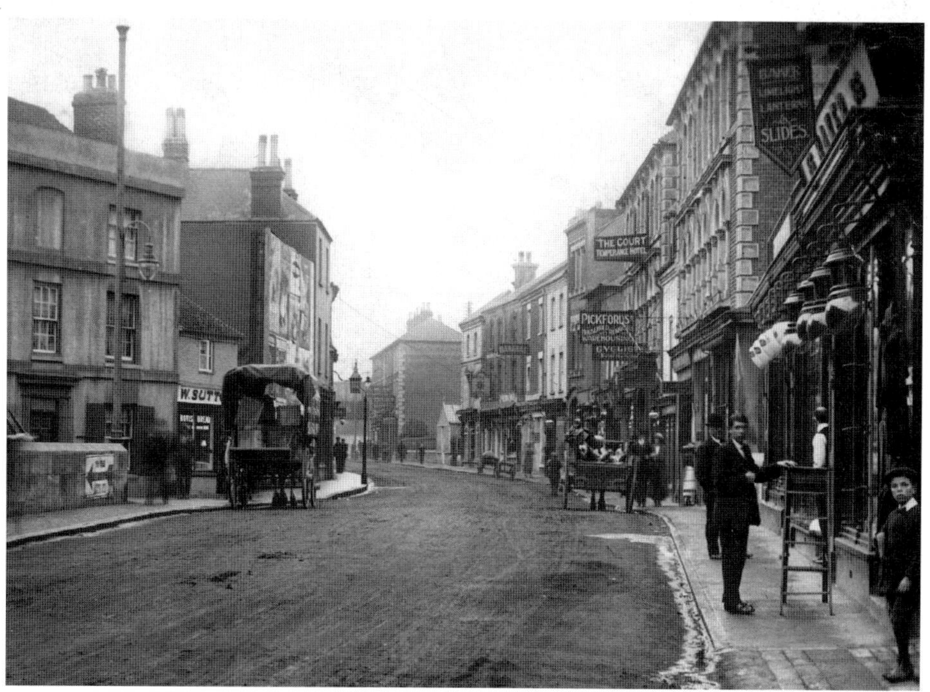

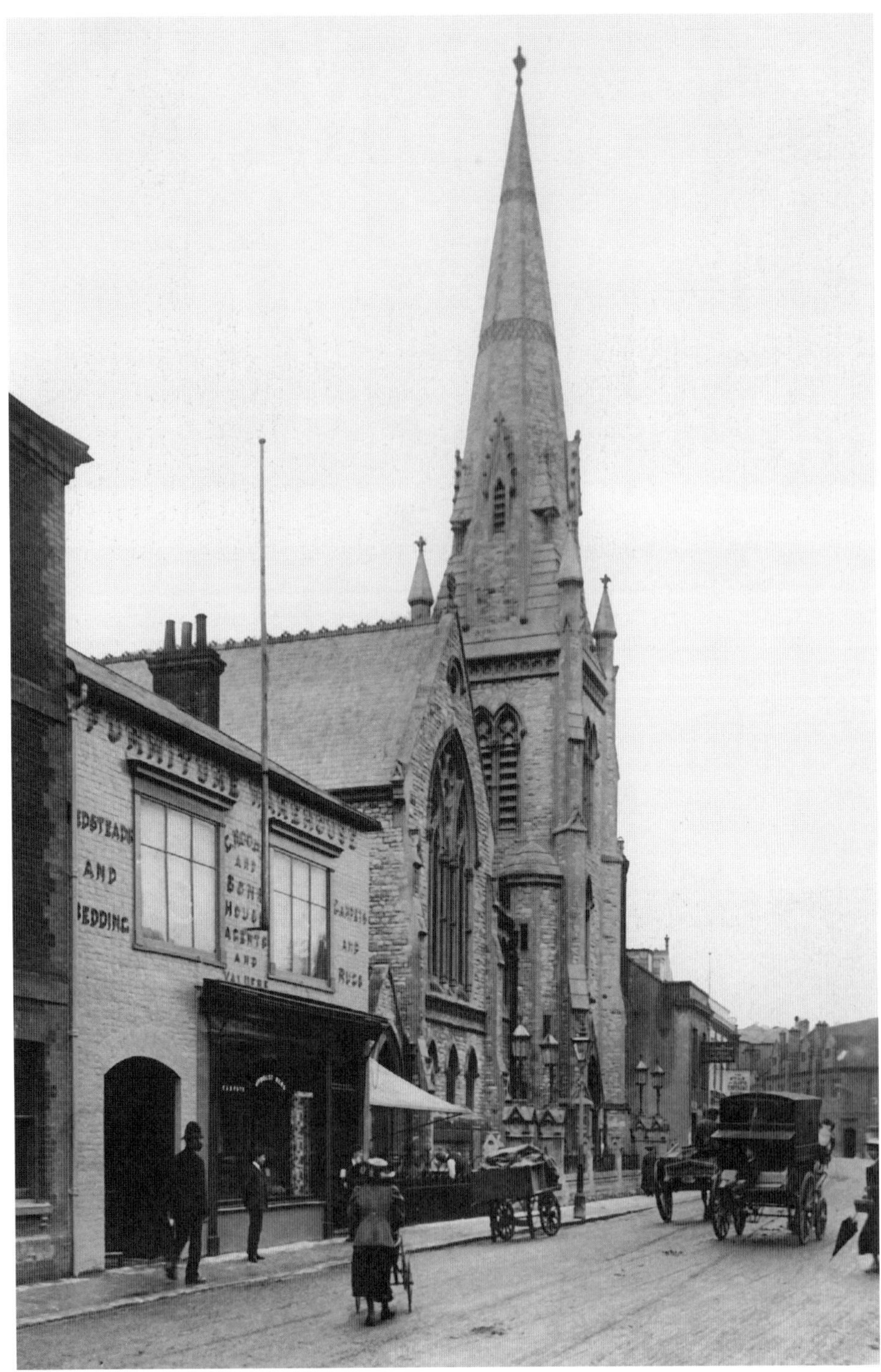

The Congregational Church in Fisherton Street, 1907
The pastor at this time was Revd Percival Neale Harrison who lived at Honiton Lodge, Milford Hill. Built of stone in the early decorated Gothic style, the church was completed in 1879.

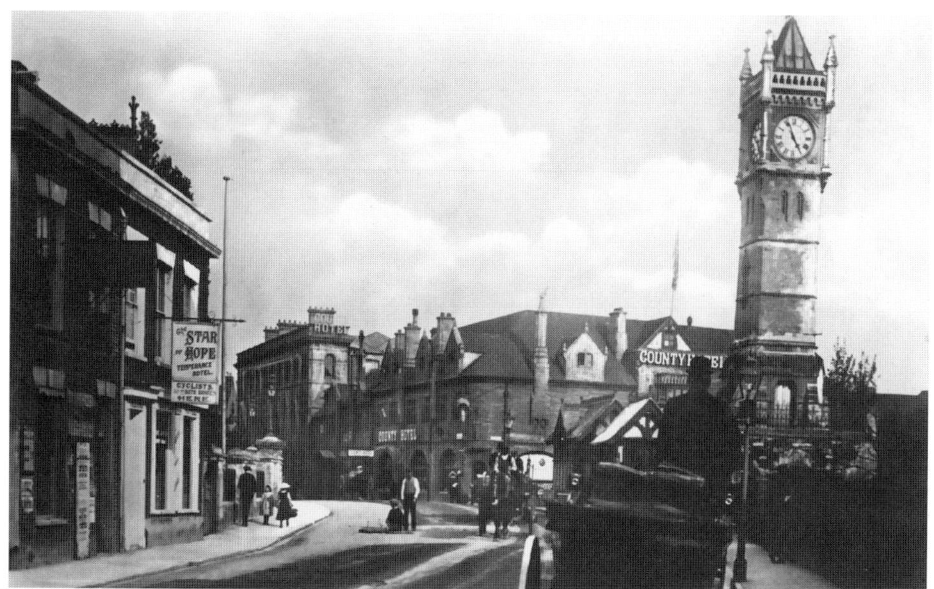

Fisherton Clock Tower and County Hotel, 1918

The clock tower was presented to the city of Salisbury by Dr John Roberts in 1893 as a memorial of his beloved wife, Arabella. The County Hotel seems to have originated from the King's Head, which is the only hotel recorded in Bridge Street in 1891. The next reference to a hotel in that thoroughfare is in the year 1897 when advertisements appear for the New County Hotel.

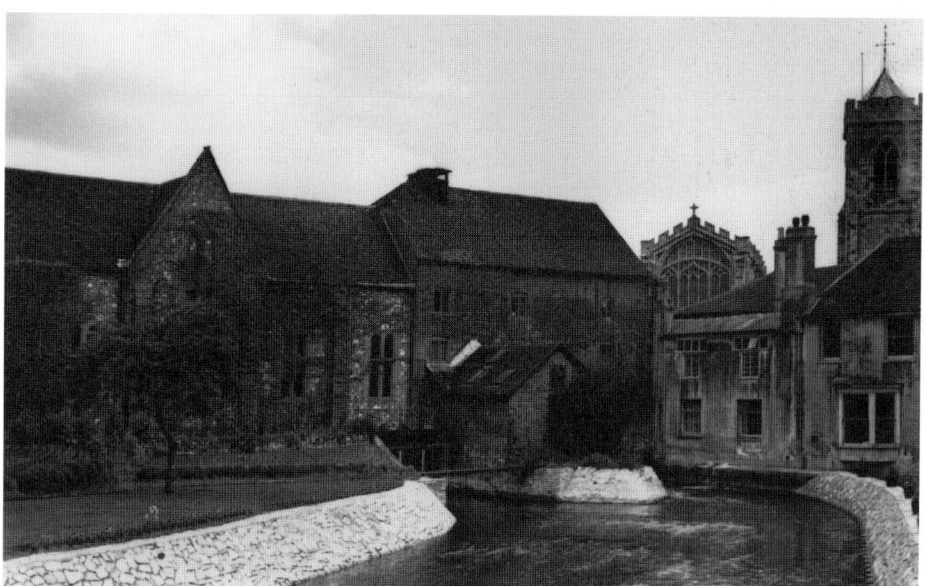

Town Mill, September 1962

When the late Austin Underwood took this photograph of a former electricity generating station, it was managed by the Central Electricity Generating Board. An eighteenth-century riverside building, originally owned by the bishop of Sarum, it appears in the Doomsday Book. To provide access to The Maltings shopping centre from Fisherton Street, a pedestrian footbridge was later built across the river at this point.

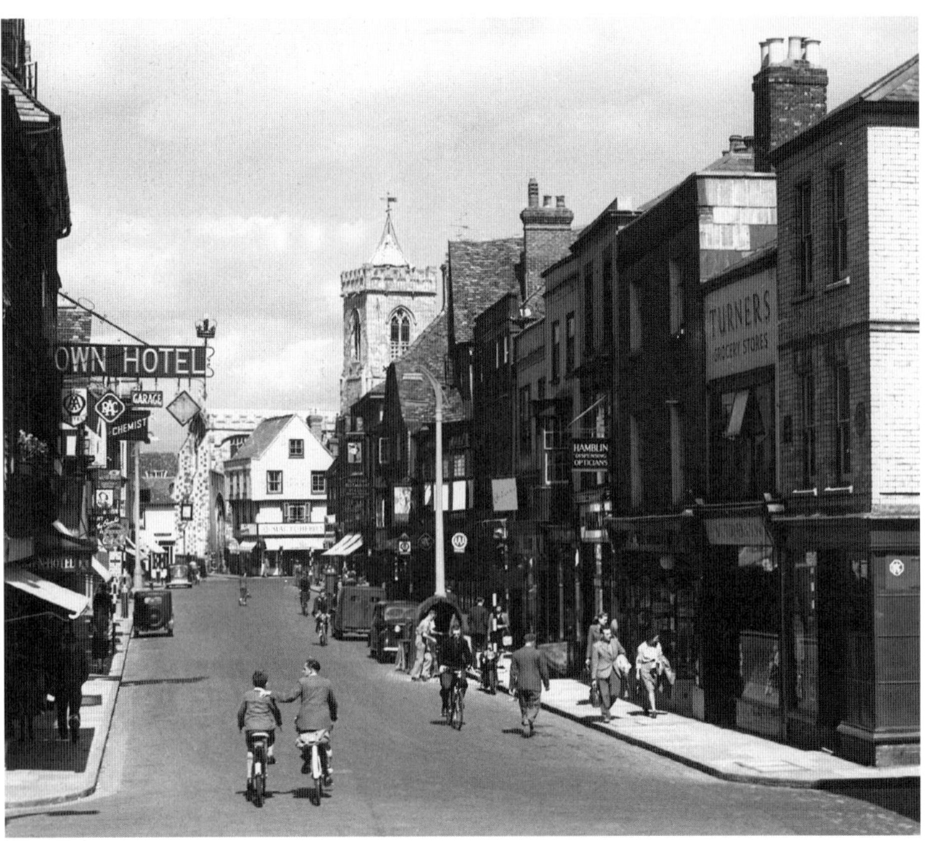

Two Way Traffic in High Street, 1949

How times have changed! No yellow lines or traffic wardens to be concerned about (the first double yellow lines and 'No Waiting' signs appeared in London in 1958, a few years ahead of Salisbury) and a two-way traffic system operation in High Street. Cyclists were a common sight after the Second World War, people were inclined to get around on bicycles out of necessity rather than for pleasure. Of the four motor vehicles pictured in this scene, all were made in England– a Morris van, and Austin, Morris and Vauxhall cars. Taking a look at some of the High Street shops: Nearest to the camera on the right can be seen the large fascia sign of Turners Grocery Store (No. 33), next to which is H. Simmonds' second-hand book shop (29–31). Then follows Hamblin Opticians (27), Crown Wallpapers (25), Percy Bates' antiques (23), B. E. W. Roberts commercial photographers (23a), H. B. Nicholas chiropodist (21a), and South Western Dry Cleaners (21).

Silver Street and High Street, 1868

Opposite bottom: The road surface at this time was basically earth with stones rolled in. The only hard surfaces were the pedestrian crossings that were to be found at many of the principal road junctions. The crossings were laid out with bricks, stone slabs, sets or tiles such as the one shown here at the bottom of the photograph. The high street shops that come into view in the distance were at that time occupied by Tovey, a retail and wholesale boot and shoe manufacturer; and Thomas Barber, a chemist and druggist. In 1872 the old shops were demolished and a new large building was erected on the corner of Bridge Street and High Street. There appears to have only ever been two occupiers of the new building. Richardson Bros, wine and spirit merchants (founded in 1672) from 1872 to around 1929; and then Barclays Bank.

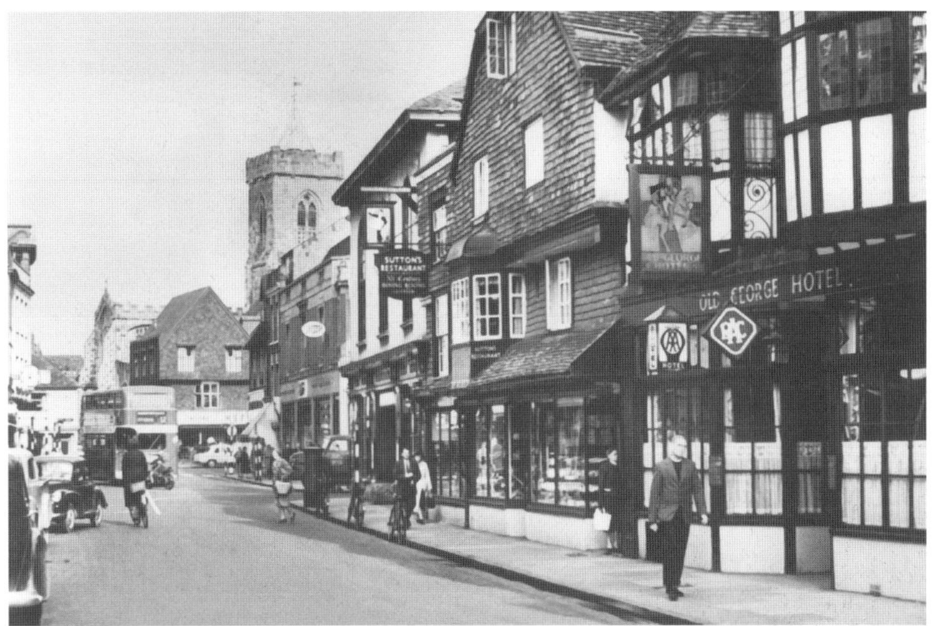

High Street, Looking North, 1960

On the right can be seen the Old George Hotel, an ancient coaching inn built around 1320. In its courtyard, the strolling players of the sixteenth and seventeenth centuries gave some dramatic performances; it was here, according to an old book, that Shakespeare acted when he visited the city. Any list of famous guests believed to have stayed at the hotel should include Oliver Cromwell (1645), Samuel Pepys (1688) and Buddy Holly (1958). The ground floor of the hotel was removed in 1966/67 when the high street entrance of the Old George Mall shopping centre was created.

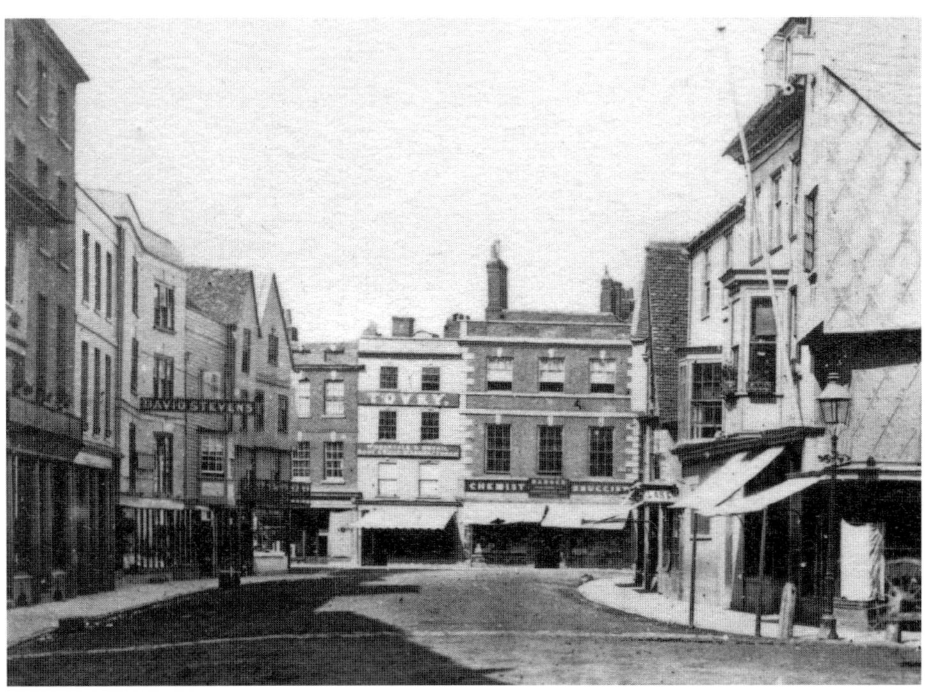

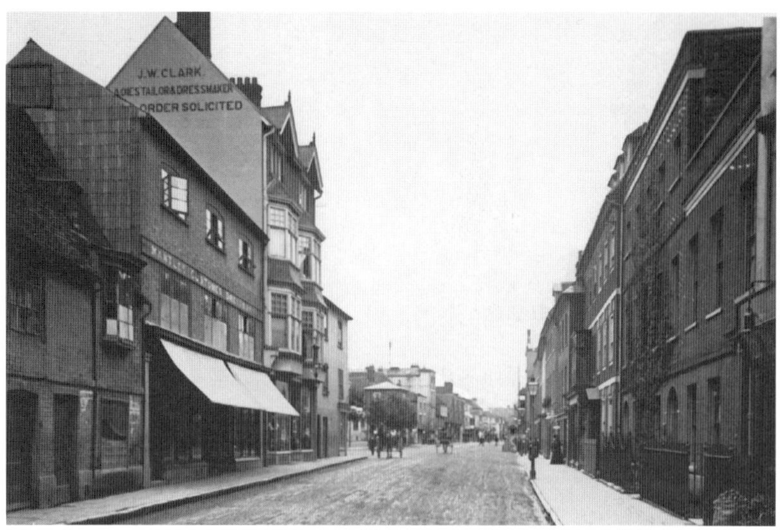

The Canal, 1911

The name of this thoroughfare has changed through time. It has been called Canal, The Canal and New Canal, which is its modern name. Its appearance has altered dramatically too, particularly at street level where brick façades have been replaced by shop windows. J. W. Clark's four-storey building, with the bay windows, and the lower building beyond it have been completely rebuilt.

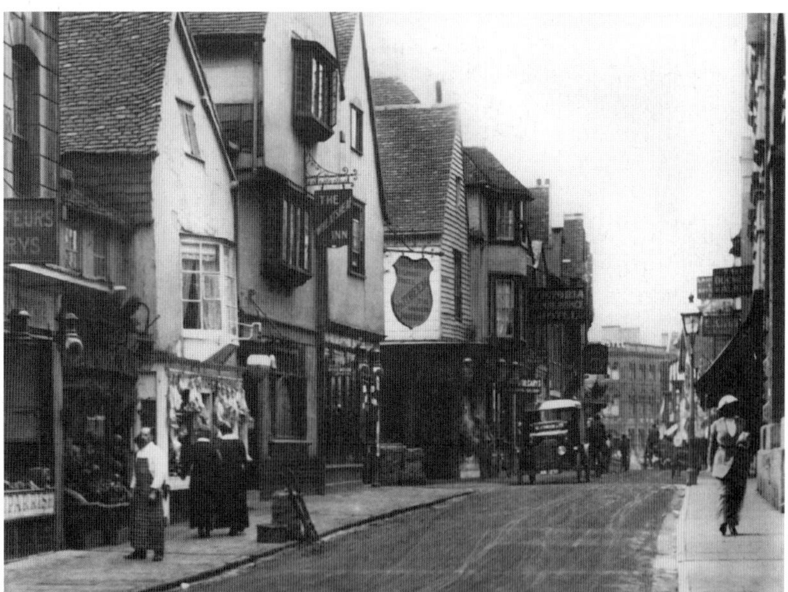

Fish Row and Butcher Row, Looking West, 1916

On the left edge of the picture we can see the butchers shop run by Harry Parrish (2 Fish Row), next door to which is A. G. Bedford, a florist and fruiterer. Then comes Alan Pritchett, butchers, where sawdust was scattered on the shop floor, and unprotected cuts of meat and poultry are hung on hooks outside the shop. The Wheatsheaf Inn comes next (F. G. Gurd, licensee) and then A. Nutbeam's tobacconists shop. The first building on the Butcher Row side of 'no name street' was then occupied by William J. Snook, butchers (9 Butcher Row). The shop's Ford model T delivery van (AM 5230) can be seen parked outside.

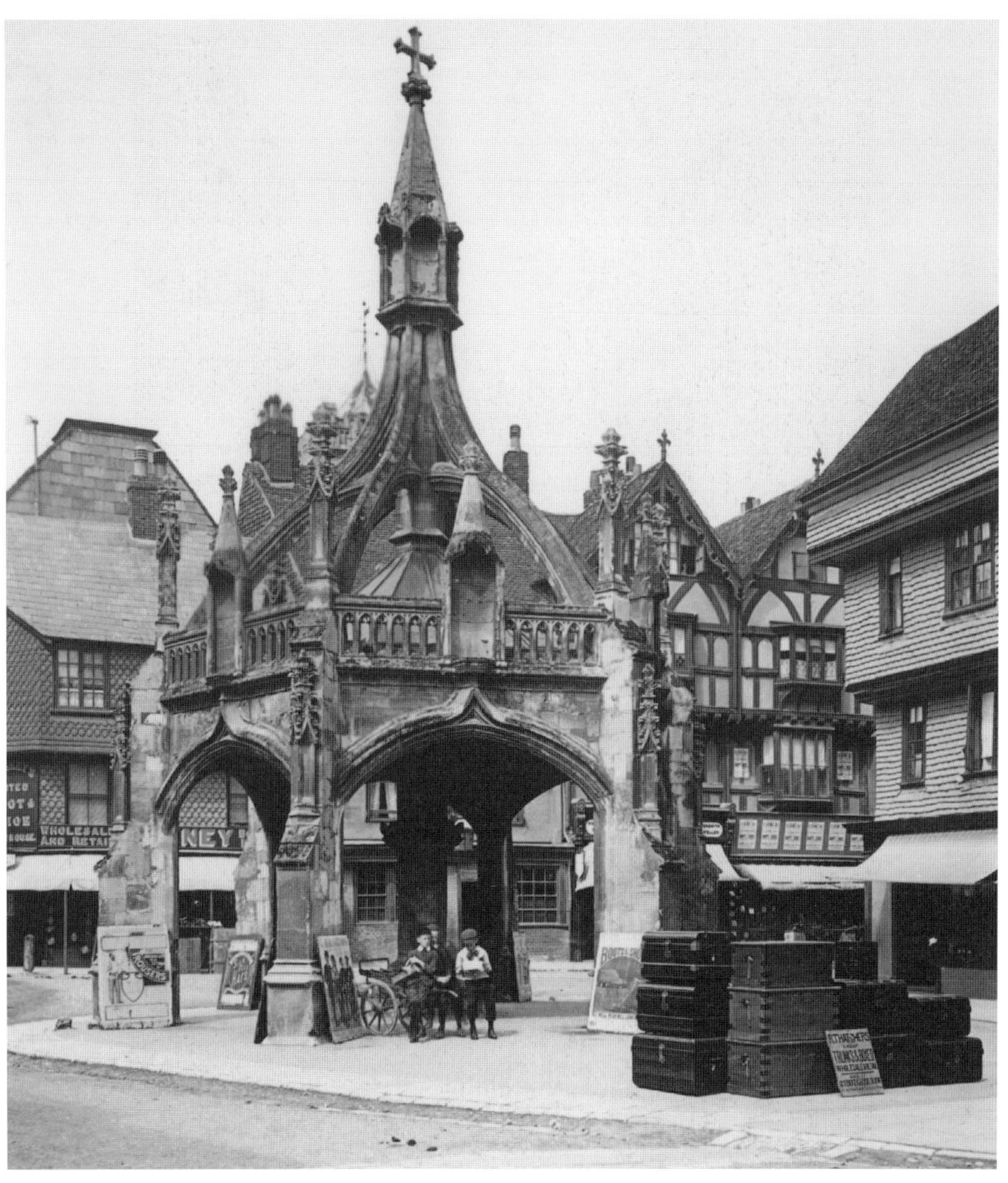

The Poultry Cross, 1890

Dating from around 1450, the Poultry Cross was one of four market crosses to be found in the city in medieval times. A dairy cross was situated in the present-day Cheese Market area; a wool or yarn cross was positioned in Market Place close to where the war memorial now stands (originally marked by a large elm tree, before the stone cross was built); and the Barnwell (or Barnard's) Cross, at the junction of Culver Street and Barnard Street, where livestock was traded in the middle ages. When this photograph was taken, several local companies were blatantly using the Poultry Cross as an advertising platform: Richard Thatcher, whose shop was at 27 Butcher Row, frequently exhibited a selection of his 'Cheap Trunks and Boxes' on the pavement; and Charles Haskins displayed a number of large art posters around the pillars of the monument. The placards feature advertisements for 'boots and shoes, silk and straw hats, and trousers'.

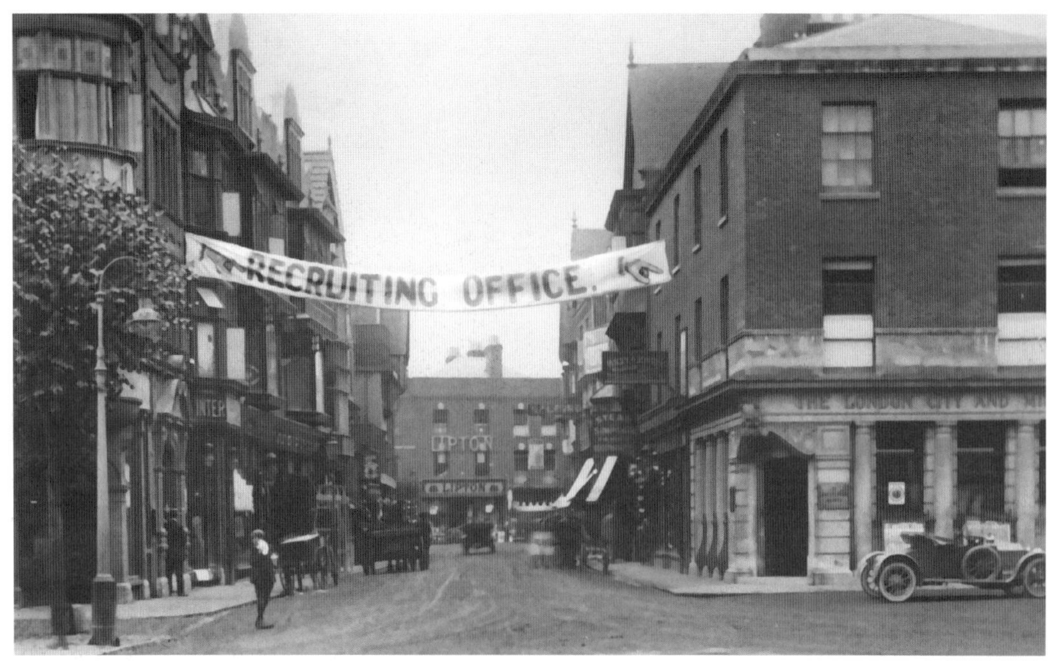

War Department Recruitment Office in Minster Street, 1915
Recruiting offices were hurriedly opened in cities, towns and villages across the UK. Here in Salisbury, an office was set up at Minster Chambers, on the first floor above what was then the London City and Midland Bank (later HSBC) on the Corner of Minster Street and Market Place. The large sign-written fabric banner would certainly have attracted the attention of passers-by.

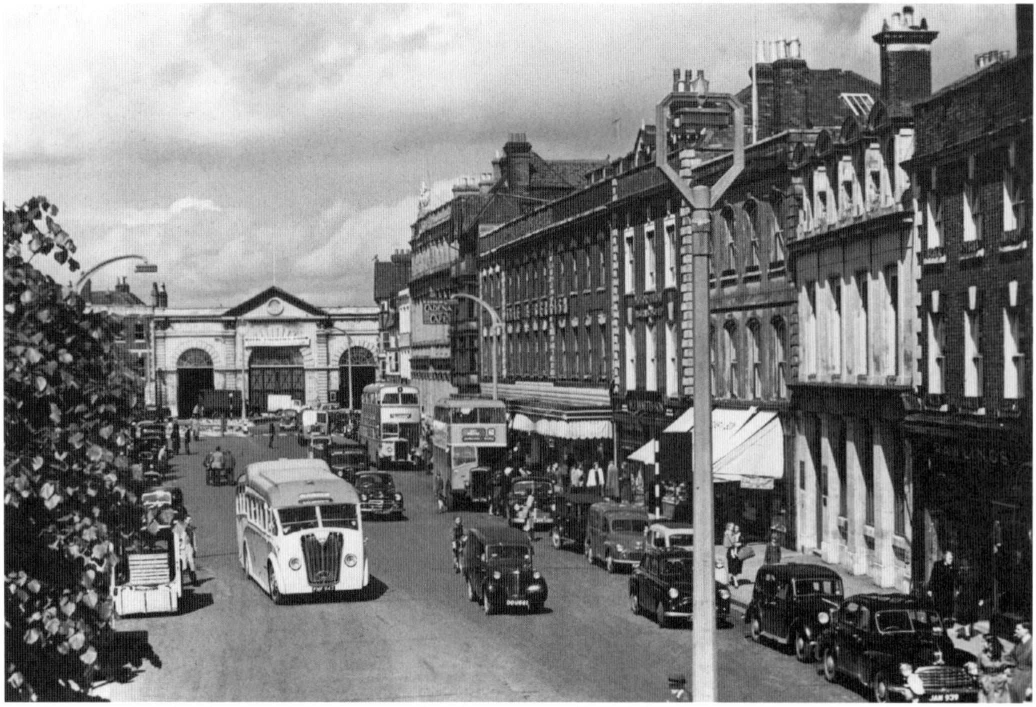

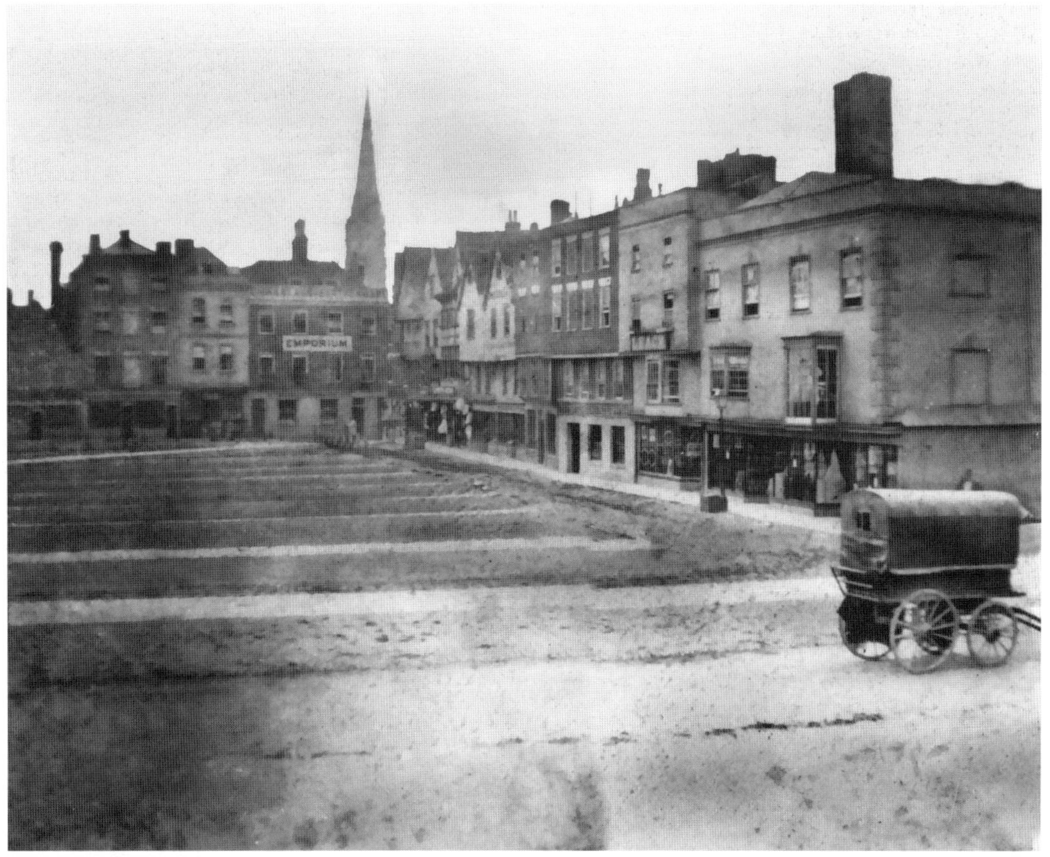

Market Place in the Early 1870s
The square was evidentially laid out specifically to function as a market at this time. The surface is fundamentally earth, on which the market traders could set up their stalls or animal pens in the spaces between the rows of paved walkways that had been provided for the shopping public. There seems to be little distinction between the market square and the thoroughfare known as Blue Boar Row. To the right can be seen Oatmeal Row, where you would find, among others, Thomas Leach (grocer and provisions merchant), Henry Neesham & Co. (cutlers) and the Hampshire Banking Co., where Francis William Ponting was the manager. Alfred Marcus Melville's China Glass & Earthenware Emporium comes into view in the background (to the right of Ox Row), the entrance to which was by Poultry Cross.

Blue Boar Row on a Busy Day, 1956
Opposite bottom: Pulled up at bus stops in front of the Style & Gerrish department store are two double-deckers: Wilts & Dorset service 62 to St Mark's church, and Silver Star service to Winterbourne. The streamlined coach appears to have Downton showing on its destination blind. The names of a few once-popular businesses can be seen here: Cadena Café, Higgins & Sons (chemists) and H. J. Annetts & Sons (china and glass).

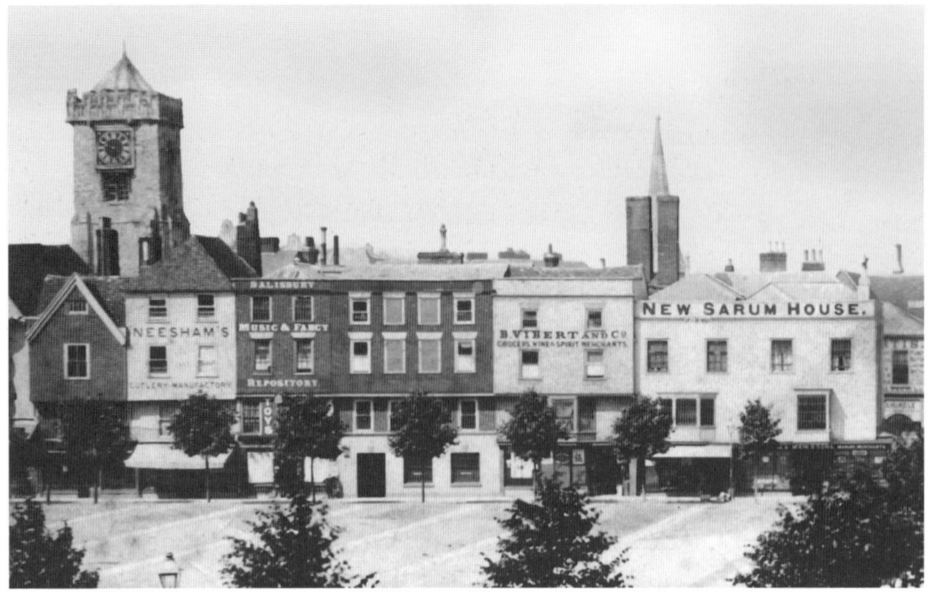

Oatmeal Row, From Market Place, 1895
The light-coloured shop to the left is Neesham's, cutlery manufactures, beside which is Salisbury Music & Fancy Repository, where toys were also sold. To the right of centre is B. Vibert & Co., wine and sprit merchants, and grocers. This building was seriously damaged by fire in 1901 and had to be demolished. New Sarum House, to the right, was removed a few years later to be replaced by a new building that was erected for William Main & Sons, seed dealers, and manure merchants.

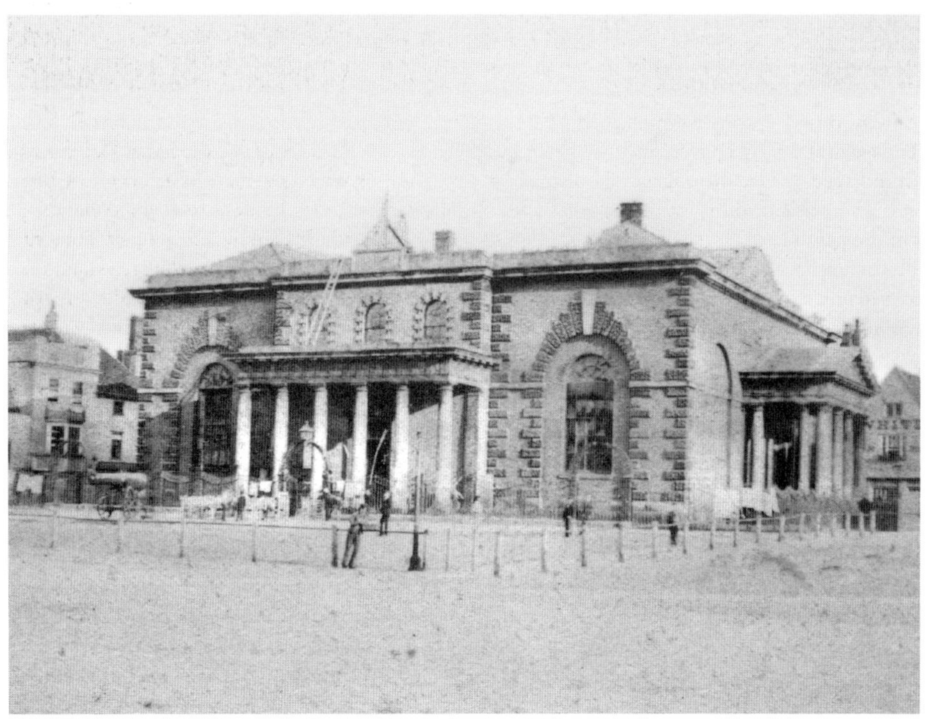

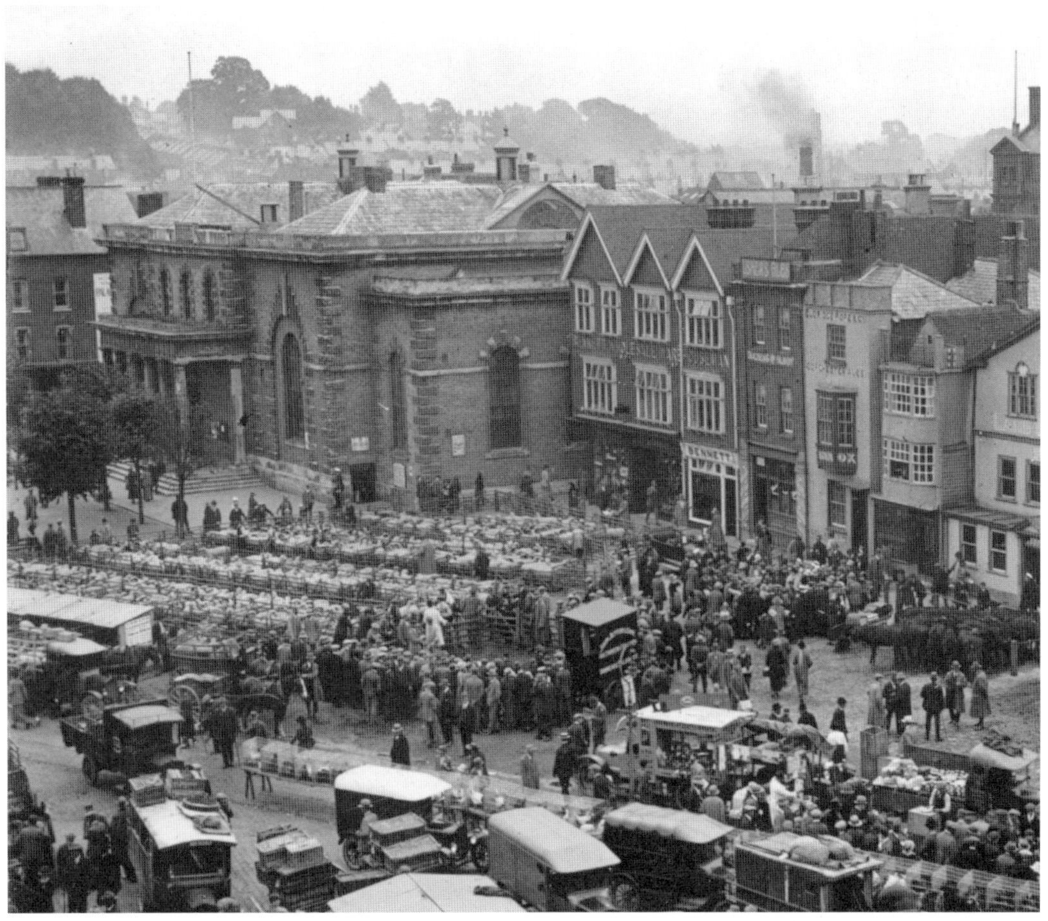

A Very Busy Tuesday Market Scene, 1928
The event certainly appears to have been well attended – a quick count of the assembled farm animals
would suggest that they outnumber the people by more than two to one. Sheep pens had been set up
in the south-east corner of the square, where John Jeffery & Son, auctioneers, were conducting a sale.
On the south side, facing Ox Row, fifty or sixty head of cattle had been tethered, awaiting their fate.
The central area is occupied by poultry, where perhaps as many as a hundred cages stand on trestles
in a diagonal line across the square. The remaining space is taken up by market traders offering dairy
and farm produce and items such as agricultural tools and equipment. Horse-drawn and motor vehicles
are in use at this time.

The Council Chamber, 1858
Opposite bottom: This remarkably early photograph is a rare survivor, revealing numerous changes
that have taken place over many years. The western portico was carefully taken down in 1889 and the
columns kept for repairing the northern portico. The ornate wrought iron railings and arches that were
erected on the north and west boundaries of the council chamber can just be seen in the photograph.
They were taken away sometime before 1885. To the left of the chamber stands a Sebastopol Cannon
that was captured from the Russian Army at the battle of Sevastopol during the Crimean War (1854–56).

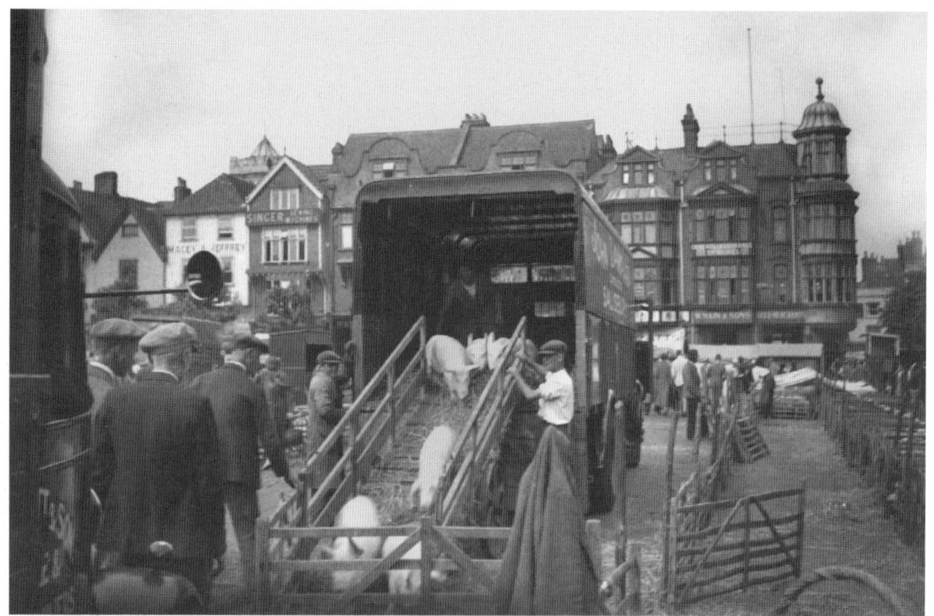

Pigs Arriving at Tuesday Market, 1947
Here we can see some young pigs being offloaded from the back of one of John Lampard's lorries. Coming into view in the background, on the right, is the building erected for William Main & Sons (seed dealers and manure merchants) a few decades earlier.

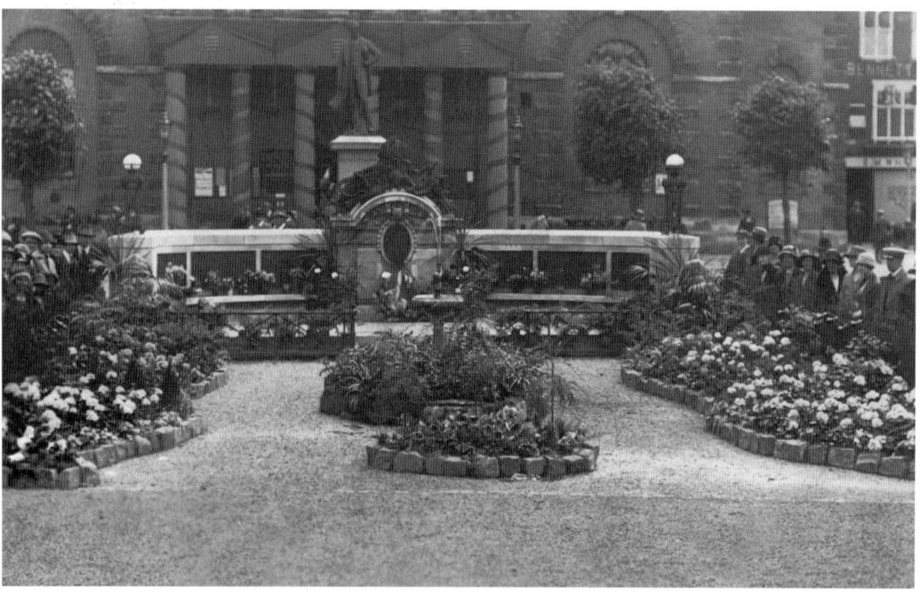

Salisbury War Memorial, 1927
Having been dedicated on Sunday 12 February 1922, the monument can be seen here surrounded by floral displays on the occasion of the 700th anniversary of Salisbury in June 1927. The following words have been set into the oval dedicatory plaque: 'In Honour and Remembrance of the Citizens of Salisbury Who Served, Who Fought, Who Died for Freedom, Home and Humanity 1914–1919'.

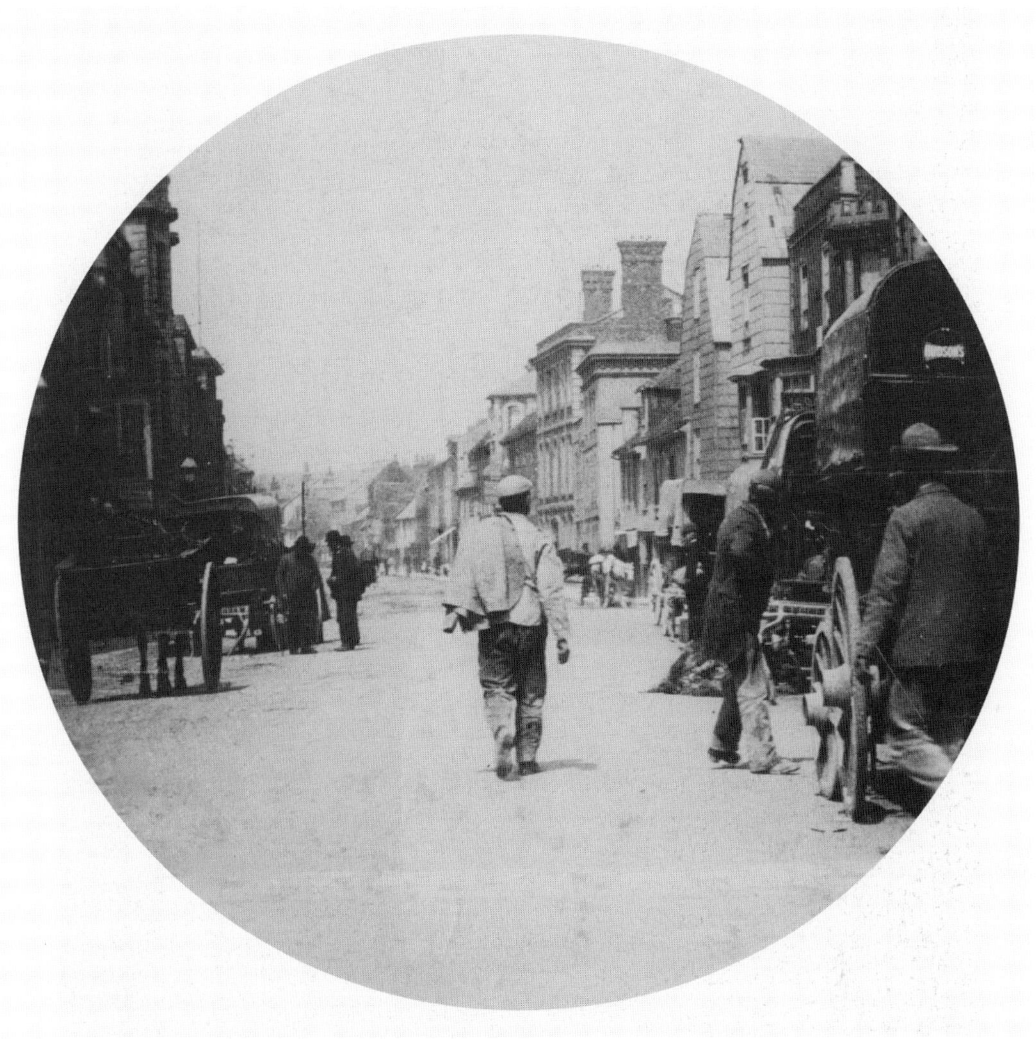

Castle Street on a Market Day in the Early 1900s
This circular photograph is one of a pair of slightly different images taken at the same time on a stereoscopic camera. The two photographs are mounted on card, known as a stereograph, which when viewed through a stereoscope can produce an impressive, three-dimensional picture. This particular stereograph was published by Theodore Brown, a pioneering Salisbury man who experimented with stereoscopic photography for many years. He lived in Portland House on the corner of Wilton Road and Devizes Road. On the right of the photograph we can see a number of country carriers vans parked by the side entrance of the Chough Hotel in Castle Street.

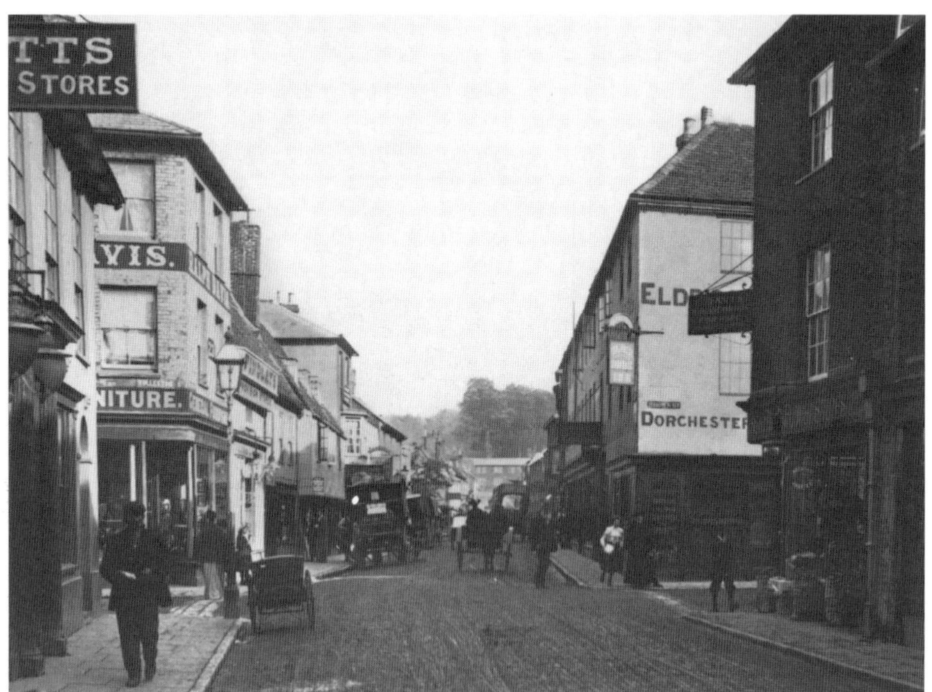

Winchester Street, 1911

Here, we can see the first intersection of Winchester Street at a time when it was a very busy thoroughfare, being the main route out of the city to London. On the corner of Rollestone Street, to the left, Ralph Davis's furniture store comes into view. This was later to become the site of Goddard's garage, and then followed residential development. On the corner of Brown Street, to the right of the photograph, stood the Black Horse Inn, an Eldridge Pope pub. Arthur J. Gould was the licensee.

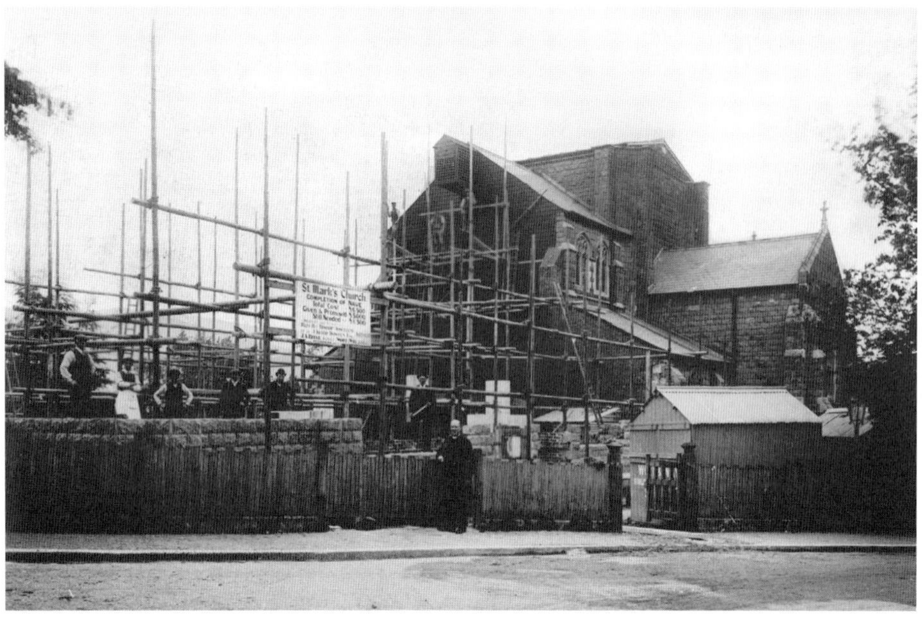

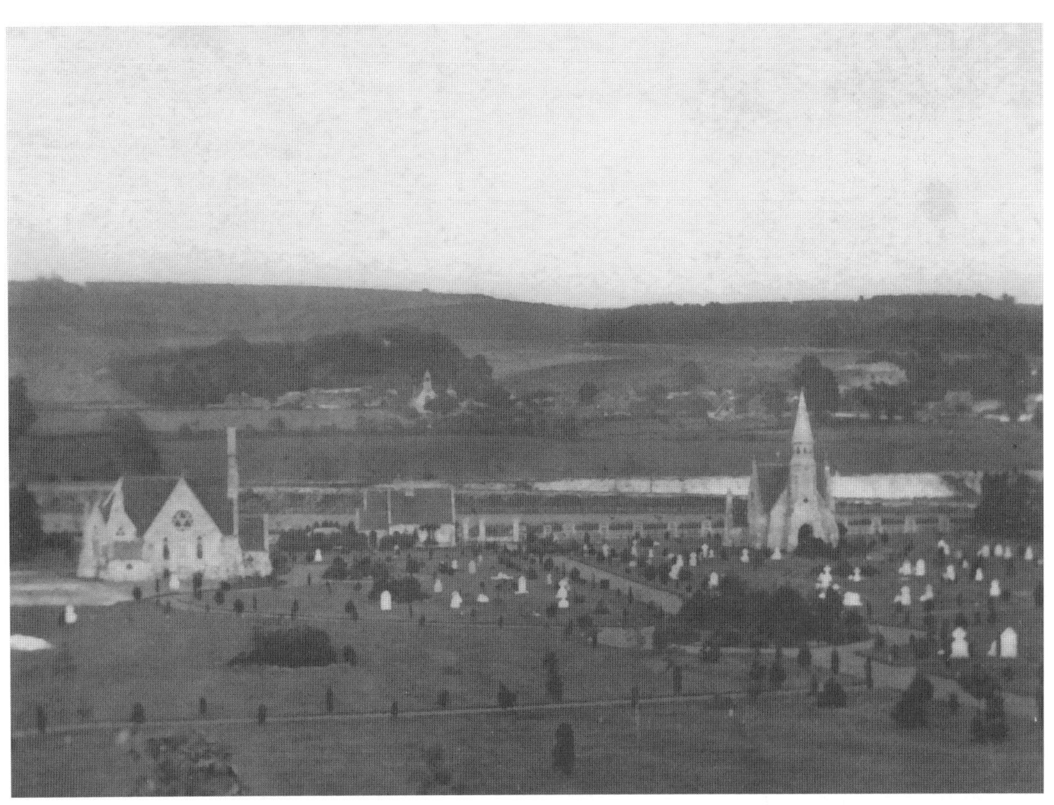

London Road Cemetery, 1860

The photographer stands in St Mark's Avenue, looking across the London road towards the village of Laverstock, where the parish church and asylum can just be seen. The London Road cemetery was consecrated of 29 January 1857, with a second plot of 8 acres being opened in October 1888, doubling the size of the cemetery. The two mortuary chapels and lodge house were demolished in the twentieth century.

A Building Project at St Mark's Church, 1915

Opposite bottom: A sign-written information board attached to the wooden scaffolding provides a few details about the project: 'Completion of Nave. Total cost: £6,500. Given and Promised: £5,000. Still Needed: £1,500. Donations please to the Right Rev. Bishop Joscelyne c/o The Vicarage, St Mark's Avenue. Or to Keith Dowden Esq. Architect: J. A. Reeve. Contractor: Wort & Way.' The wooden shed pictured to the right of the gate is not part of the development, it is Wort and Way's hut.

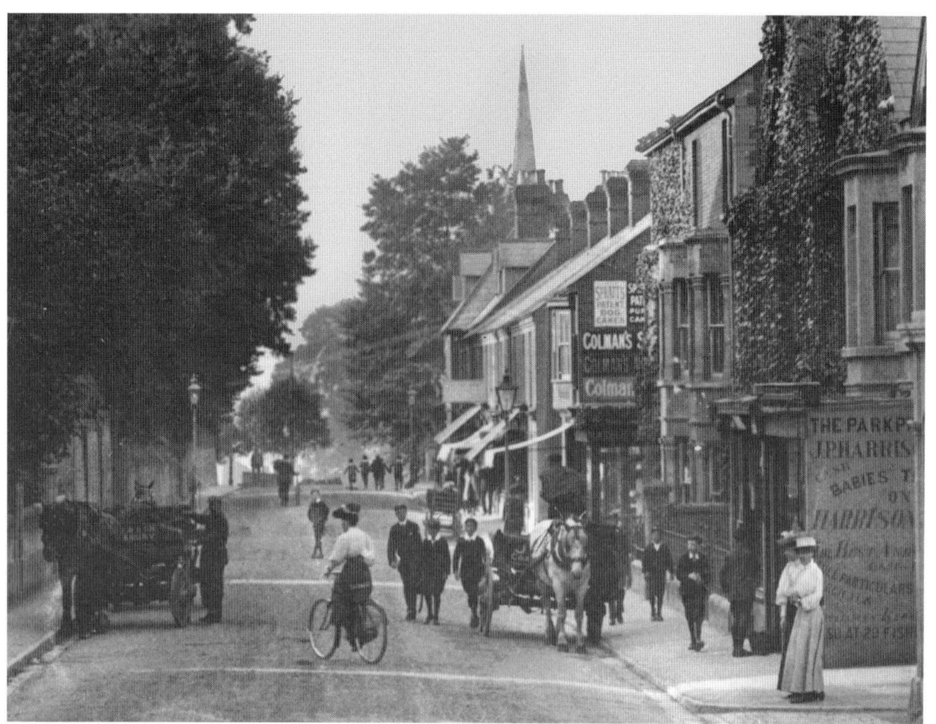

London Road, 1907

Before the Churchill Way East dual carriageway could be constructed in 1972, the properties numbered 46–54 London Road had to be demolished, including the walled gardens and trees pictured here to the left. The houses and shops to the right survived, but the thoroughfare was given a new name, Estcourt Road. Here we can see two horse-drawn carts delivering coal, they were from competing firms J. Lush and Read & Son.

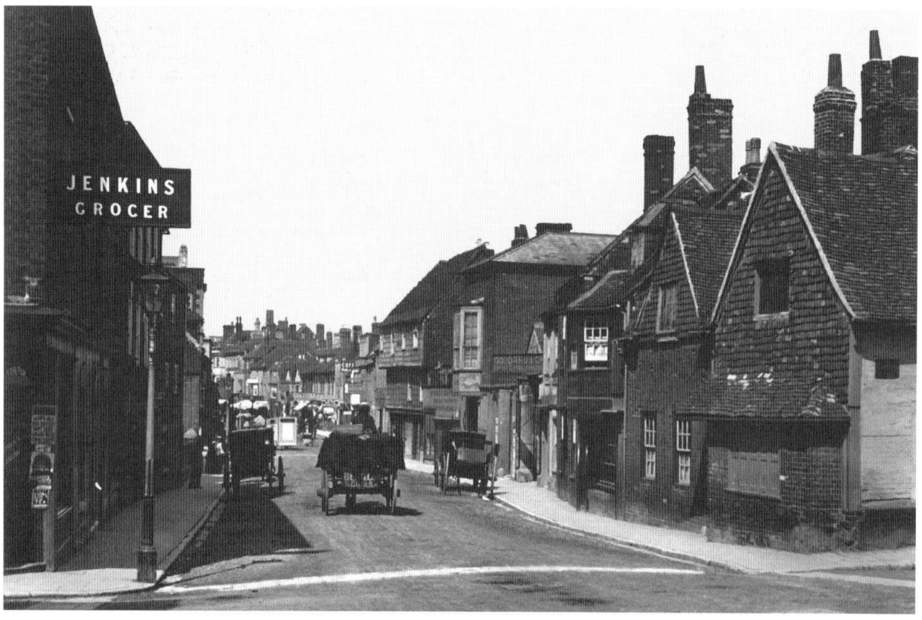

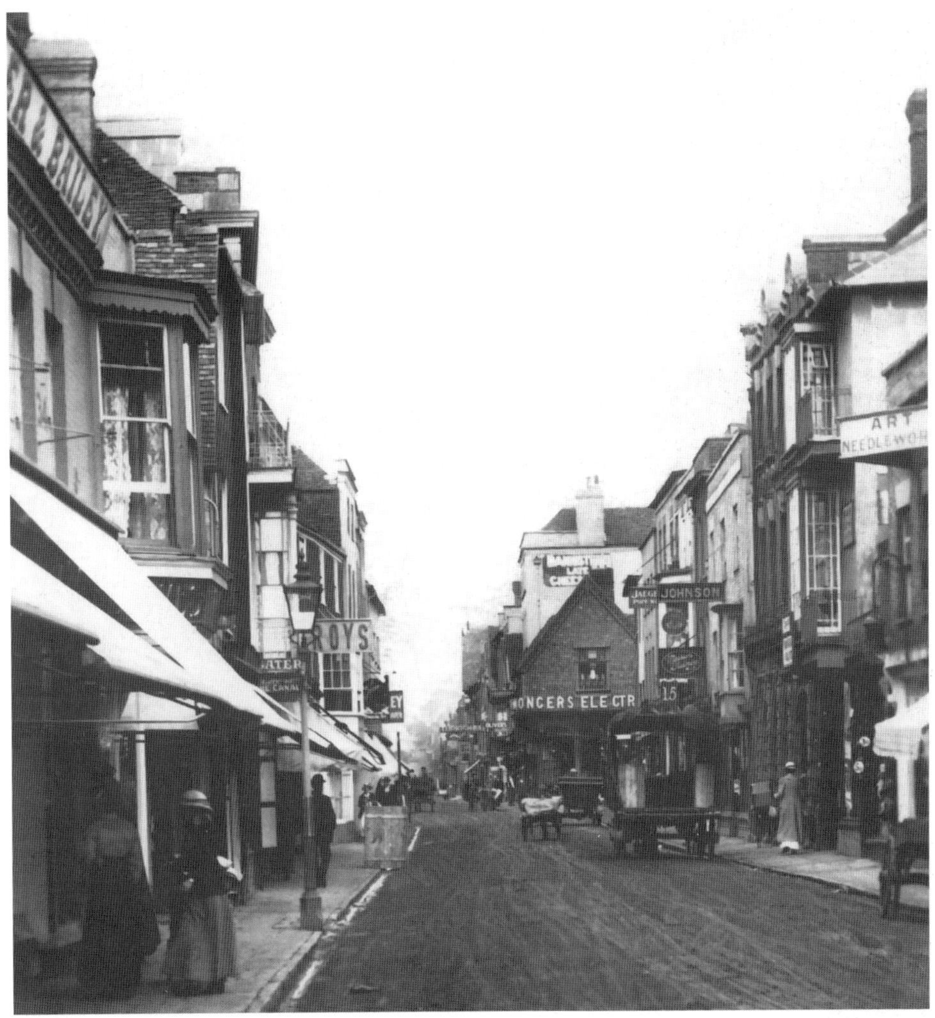

Catherine Street at the Time of the First World War, 1915

We are looking north, towards the intersection of the Canal, Milford Street and Queen Street. Most of the buildings in this thoroughfare have survived the passage of time, with two exceptions. The Tudor shop on the corner of Queen Street and Milford was badly damaged by fire in September 1937 and had to be taken down. It was a Co-operative furniture shop at the time. A photograph of the blaze can be seen on page eighty-two. When this photograph was taken, however, it was occupied by Wilkes, Son and Cassey ironmongers and electricians. The second building that seems to have gone was at No. 21 Catherine Street; the tall, dark, ornate building on the right with a woman walking by.

Milford Street, 1910

Opposite bottom: Coming into view on the left of the photo is Mrs R. Jenkins' grocery shop, on the corner of Culver Street, and further along on that side is Penn & Sons (collar and harness maker), James Talbot (dry salter), Milford Street Free School, James Maton (fish dealer) and Henry Richardson (bootmaker). Among the businesses on the opposite side of the street you would find W. Goddard & Co. (job and posting masters, and receiving office for the GWR), and William Rowland and Sons (engineers, iron founders and cycle manufacturers).

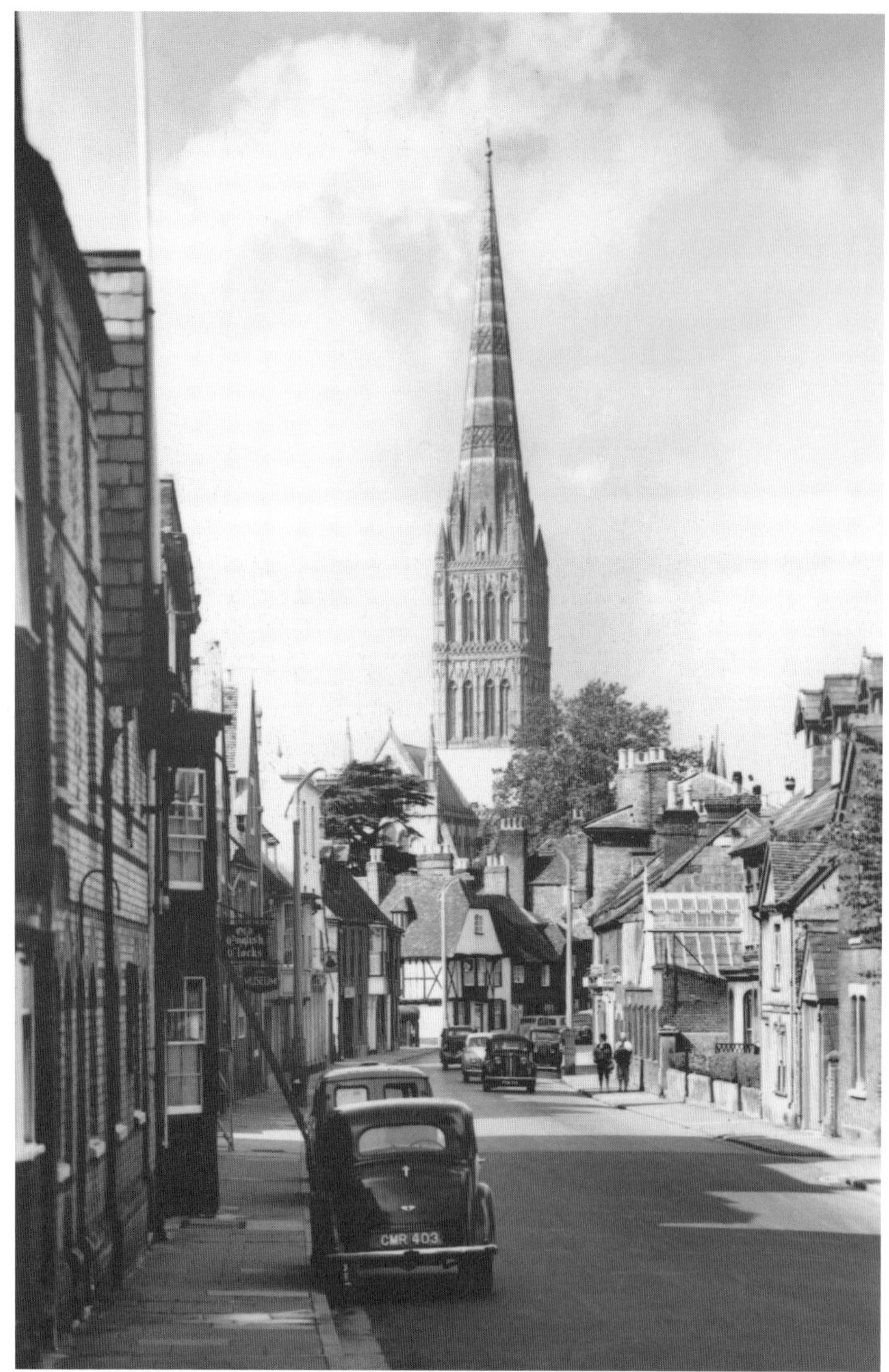

St Ann's Street, Looking West, 1952
Two-way traffic is still a feature of this street but it is no longer a through route to the Southampton road, having been blocked off when the Churchill Way inner relief road was built.

Chapter 3
Memorable Occasions

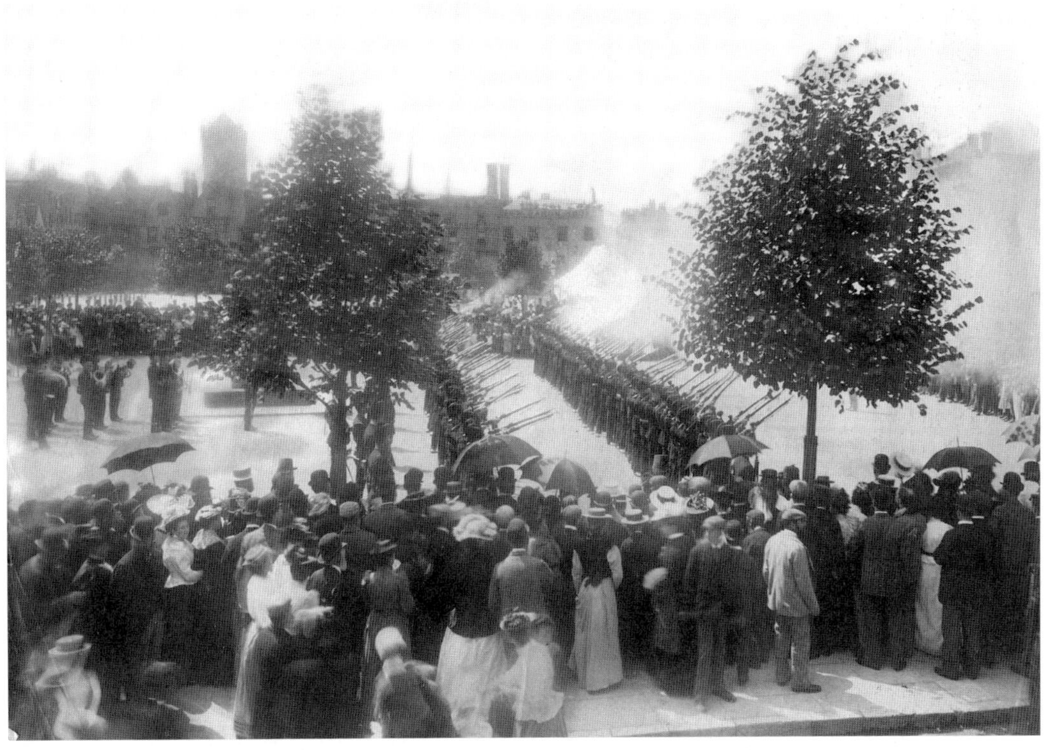

First Wilts Rifle Volunteers Firing a *Feu De Joie*, 1893
On the occasion of the marriage of the Duke of York and Princess Mary of Teck on 6 July 1893, a celebratory running fire of guns, a *feu de joie* (French: fire of joy), was performed in Market Place. We can see the riflemen assembled in front of the Sydney Herbert statue with the first Wilts Rifle Volunteer band behind them.

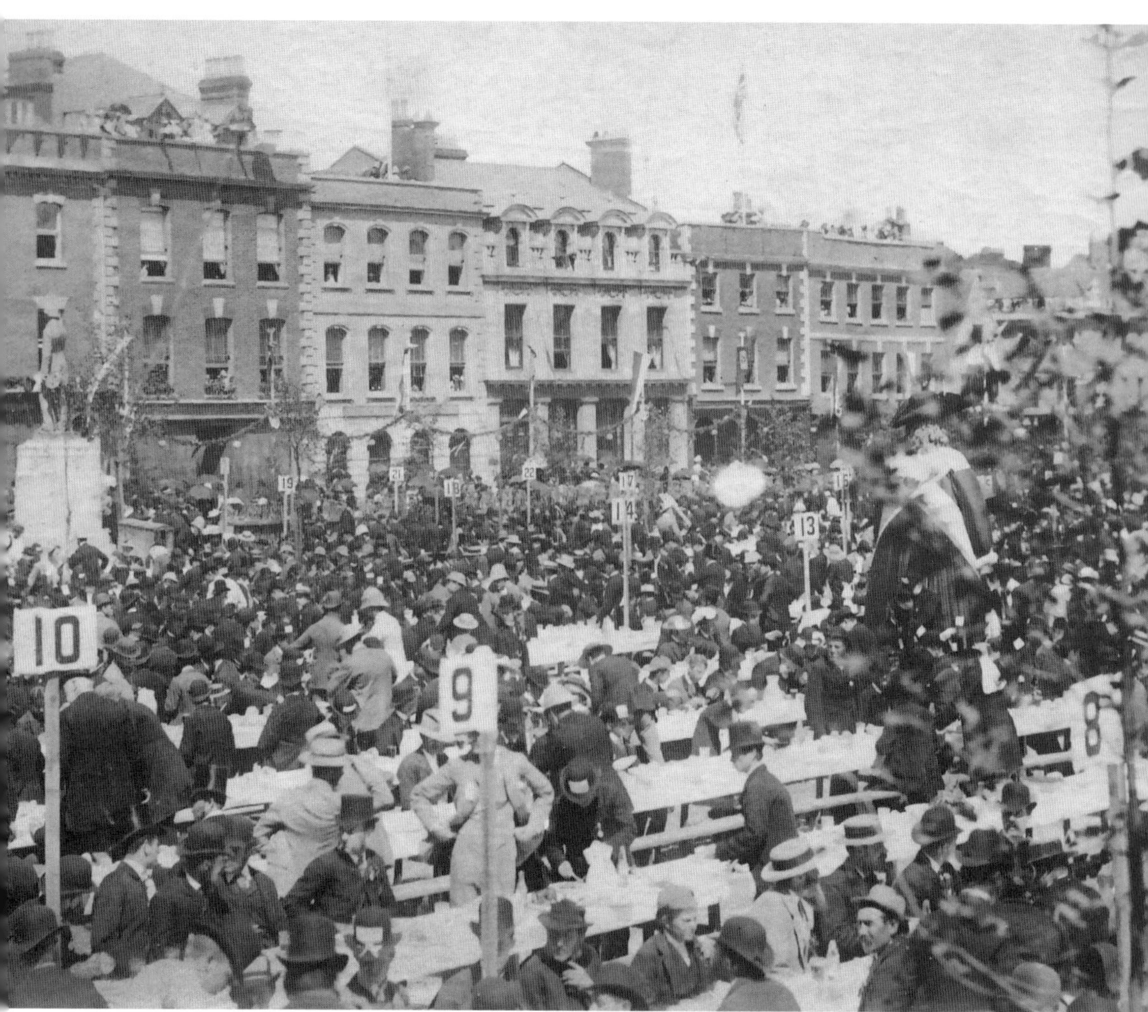

Public Celebratory Feast in Market Place, June 1887

The Golden Jubilee of Queen Victoria was celebrated with great enthusiasm in Salisbury on Wednesday 22 June 1887. 3,500 men sat down to a public dinner in the market place, where they consumed around 2½ tons of meat, 25 gallons of bread and 1,500 pounds of plum pudding, along with twenty barrels of ale and 1,800 bottles of ginger pop. The Salisbury Giant comes into view to the right, with his back to us, and the statue of Henry Fawcett is to the left. Blue Boar Row appears in the background, where women and children can be seen overlooking the scene from roof tops and upper storey windows.

A Ferocious Fire Devastates the Woolpack Inn, 1901

Opposite bottom: The skill, dedication and determination of the members of Salisbury Volunteer Fire Brigade were tested to the limit on 24 May 1901, when the men struggled to cope with the worst outbreaks of fire Salisbury had ever experienced. Having started at Ware Brothers Leather Works in Three Swans Chequer, the blaze spread surprisingly quickly and within a very short space of time the factory and several other neighbouring buildings were well alight. Horse-drawn and steam fire engines, hose carts, ladder carts and firemen began to arrive in Salisbury from fire brigades across the region. A number of buildings were seriously damaged and several had to later be demolished.

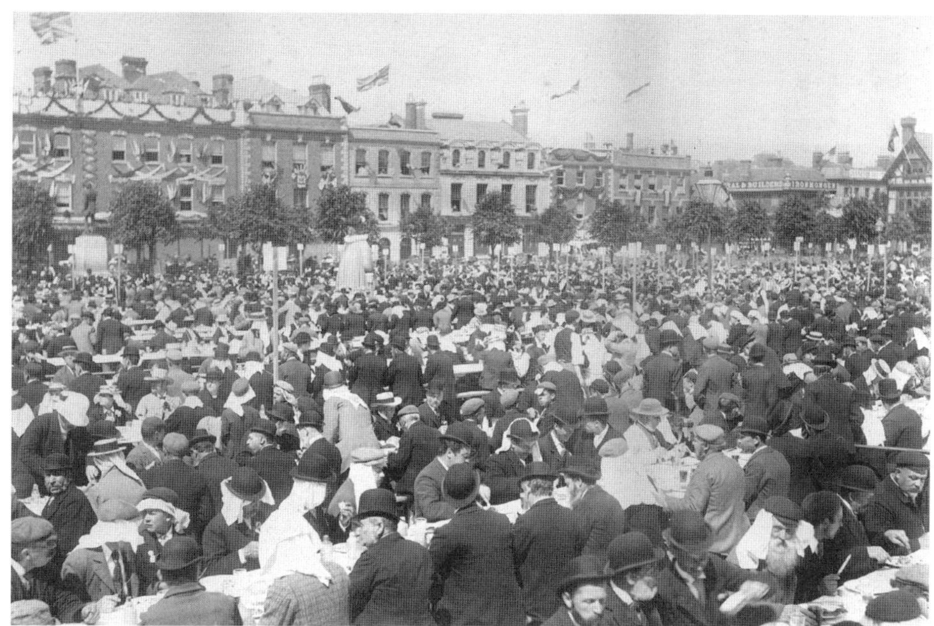

The Diamond Jubilee of Queen Victoria, 1897
This and the Golden Jubilee photograph on the opposite page make an interesting comparison, they are so similar and yet so different. The needs of the 3,500 or so guests who purchased a ticket for the feast were attended to by a team of around 400 carvers. Behind the tables can be seen the ten-year-old trees that were planted around the market place by the Mayor of Salisbury, Councillor Fred Griffin, in the year 1887 – they are conspicuous by their absence in the previous photograph.

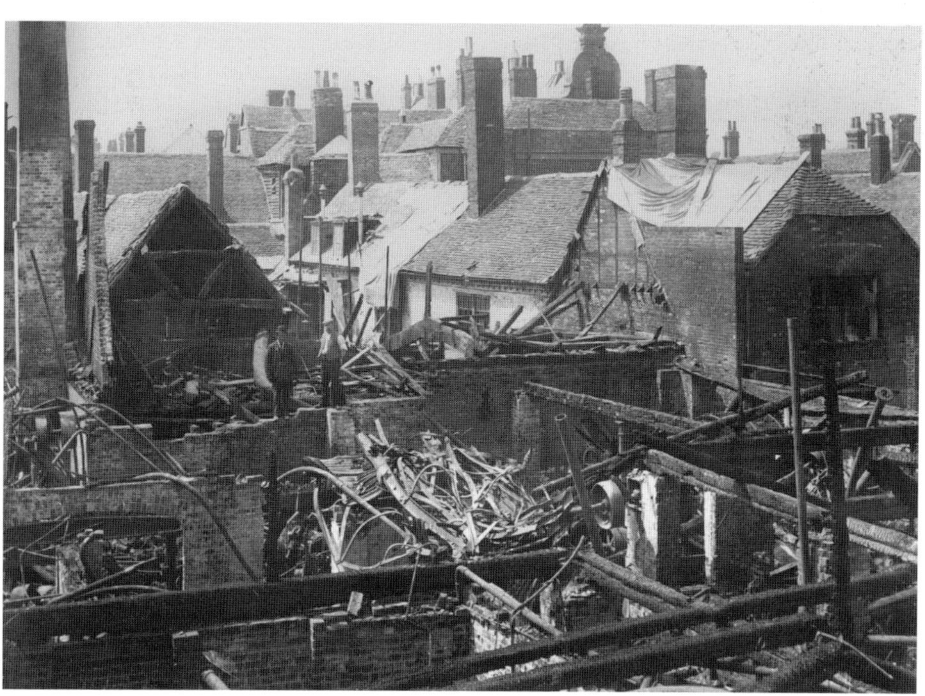

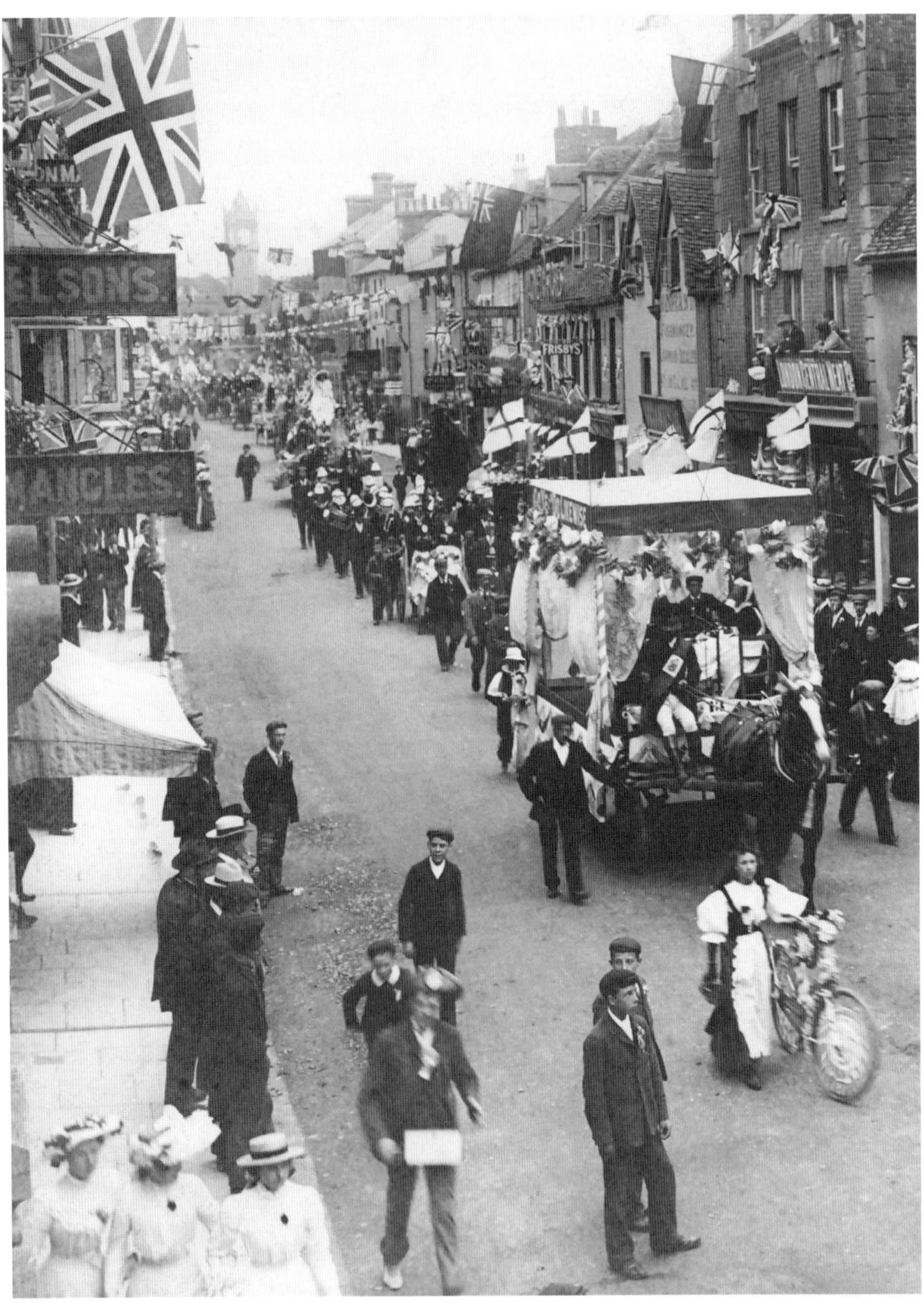

Coronation Procession in Fisherton Street, 1902

A huge parade was organised on Saturday 9 August 1902 to celebrate the Coronation of Edward VII. This was the scene as the procession made its way along Fisherton Street. The float in the foreground of the picture was entered by the juvenile section of the Egerton and Wyndham Court of the Order of Foresters. Depicting a nursing scene, a sick child was to be seen in bed, attended by a nurse and two visitors of the court. On one side of the car were the words 'I was sick and ye visited me' and on the other, 'Go ye and do likewise'. The float was followed by Alderbury brass band and numerous other tableaux.

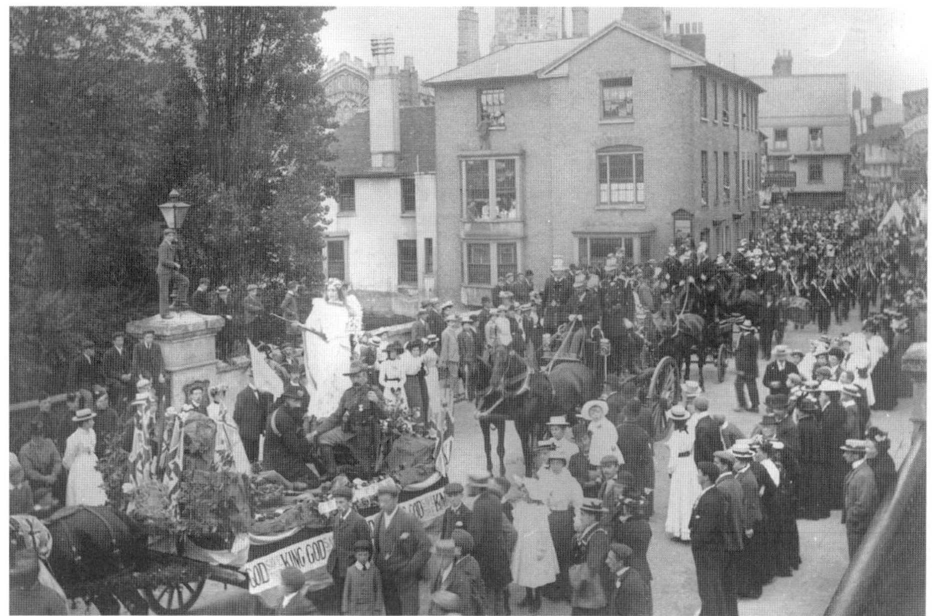

Salisbury Volunteer Fire Brigade on Parade, 1902
Here we can see the Merryweather steam fire engine 'Alert' taking part in the Coronation procession on 9 August 1902. Following their colleagues are crews of firemen with the brigade's horse-drawn fire escape and manual fire pump, and behind them appears to be members of the Sarum Battalion of the Church Lads Brigade, accompanied by a base drummer.

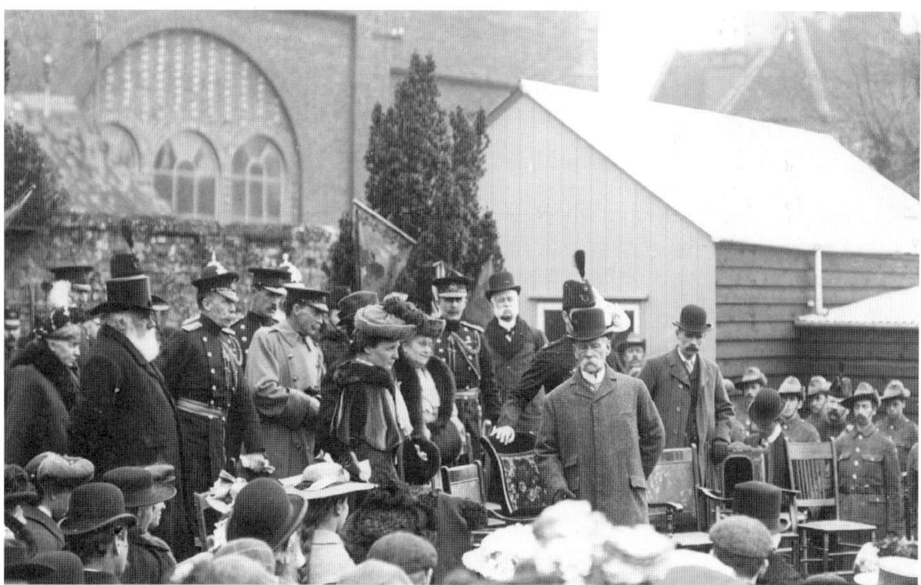

New Shooting Range Opens in Salisbury, April 1906
Field Marshall Lord Roberts can be seen just right of centre as he officially opens the new rifle range behind the Market House (later Salisbury Division Library), where the Maltings shopping precinct pleasure gardens were later created. The new facility was to become the headquarters of Salisbury and District Rifle Club.

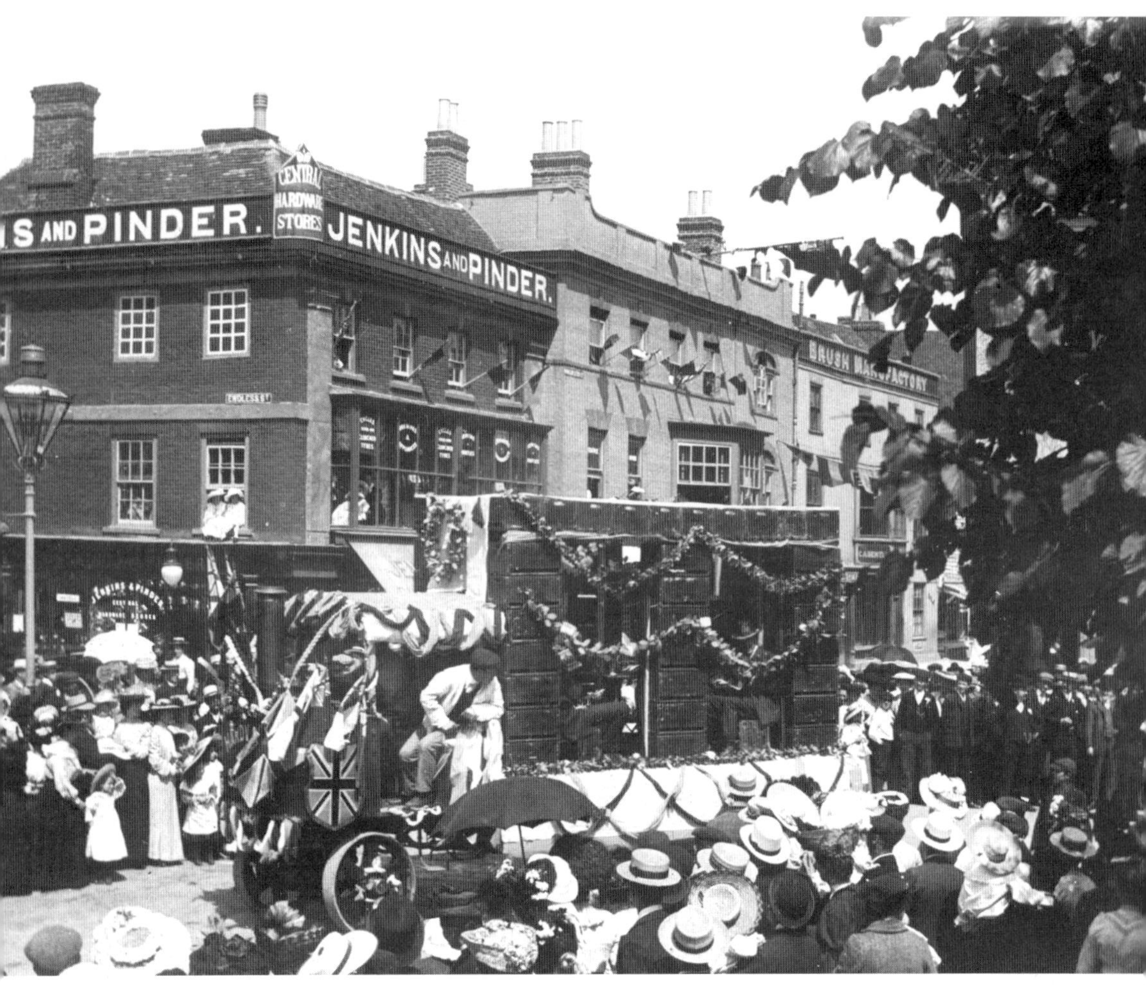

The First Salisbury Hospital Carnival Procession, 20 June 1906
This was the view in the north east corner of Market Place, with the buildings of Endless Street and
Winchester Street forming a backdrop to this busy scene. Hardy & Son's, mineral water manufacturers,
had dressed up their brand-new, coal-fired, Straker-Squire steam lorry (AM 426) with multi-coloured
tissue paper, ribbons and flags. The contraption is pictured here turning from Queen Street into Blue
Boar Row. The procession terminated at Victoria Park, where a fete was already in progress. Prizes were
presented there for the best floats or tableaux in the carnival procession. Hardy & Son's green and red
coloured steam lorry was awarded one of the prizes. Despite its success, the event was not staged again
until the year 1930.

The Great Salisbury Train Disaster, 1 July 1906
Opposite bottom: Fourty-three passengers from the transatlantic liner SS *United States* disembarked
at Plymouth on 30 June 1906 and boarded the London and South Western Railway 'Ocean Express'
train for London. At 2.40 a.m. the train entered Salisbury station travelling at more than twice the
recommended speed of 30 mph. With its whistle blasting continuously, the train leaned over and
collided with a milk train coming on the opposite direction. The impact was devastating. The carriages
of the express train piled up behind their locomotive and disintegrated. Twenty-four passengers were
killed in addition to the driver and fireman of the express, and the fireman and guard of the milk train.

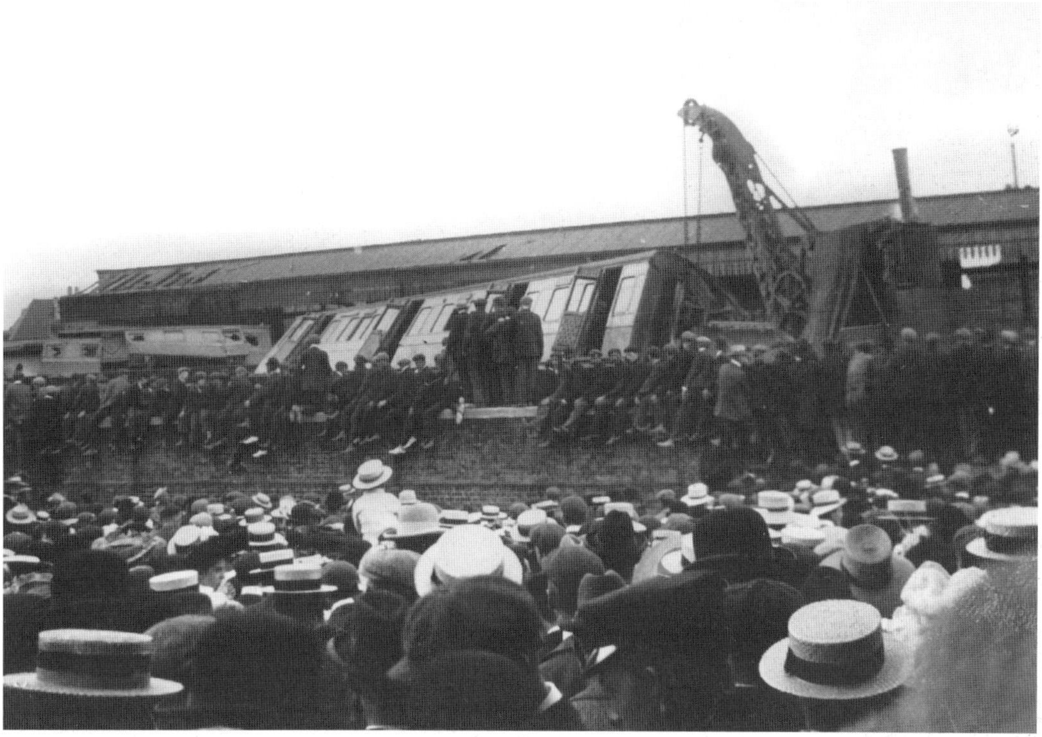

A Scene of Devastation at Salisbury Station, 1 July 1906
The disaster attracted a large number of on-lookers, some of whom can be seen here watching a steam crane remove the wrecked carriages.

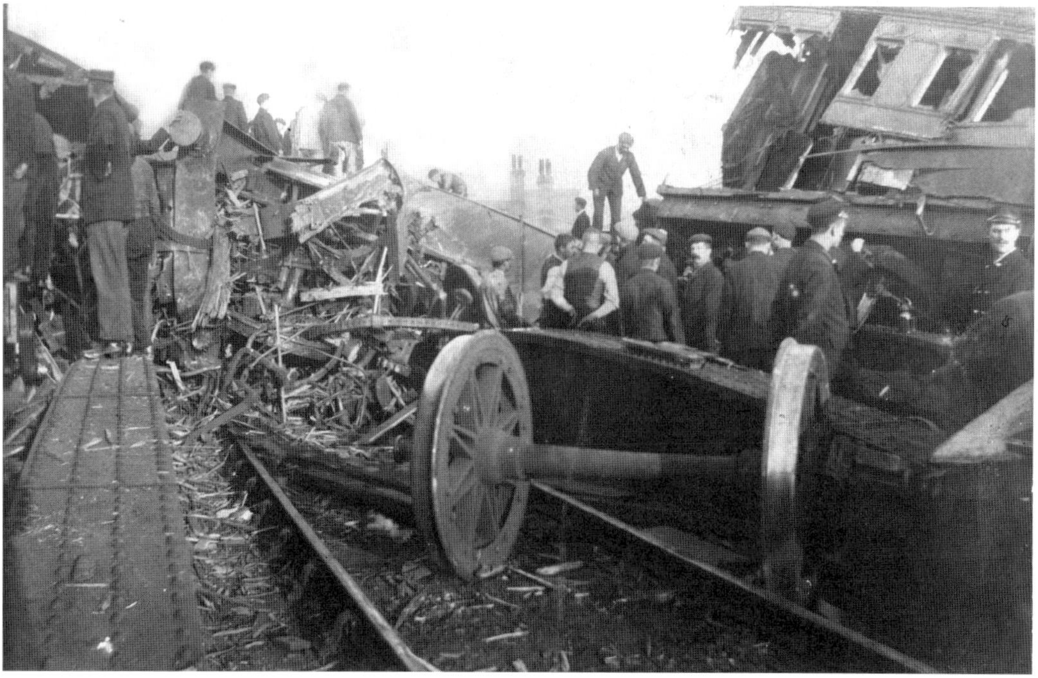

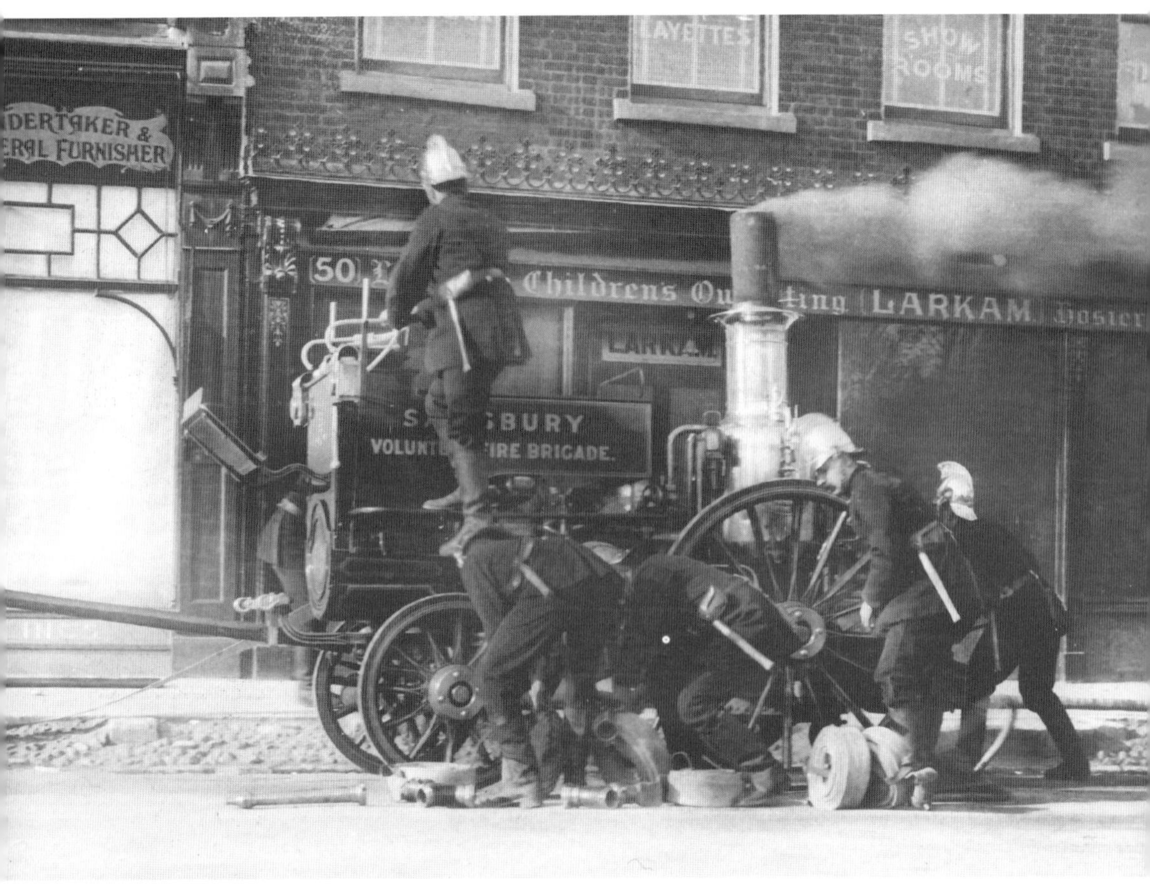

Salisbury Volunteer Fire Brigade Demonstration, 1907

Pictured here in front of Larkam's shop at 50 Blue Boar Row is the steam fire engine 'Alert' that was purchased by public subscription in 1891 at a cost of £585 11s. Manufactured by Merryweather & Sons Ltd, of Greenwich, this double-cylinder appliance was capable of pumping 360 gallons of water per minute. The engine displayed the Brigade's motto *semper paratus* (Always prepared). Following the official opening of the new fire station in Salt Lane, a crew of six Salisbury firemen attached lengths of hose to the pump and then sprayed water jets high into the air, much to the delight of the spectators.

Lifeboat Fund Day, 1907

Opposite bottom: Boys from the Sarum Battalion of the Church Lads Brigade can be seen marching down Castle Street ahead of the 'Mayor's Collecting Car' – the Chapel Lifeboat (D8). The lifeboat crew are using long poles with nets attached to encourage spectators to drop coins in – even those looking on from first-floor windows could contribute this way. Having been organised by the Mayor of Salisbury, Councillor Samuel Grove, Salisbury Lifeboat Fund was able to make a generous donation to the Royal National Lifeboat Institution. The procession terminated at East Harnham Meadows, where lifesaving demonstrations took place and the boat was launched into the river opposite The Swan Inn (later Greyfisher).

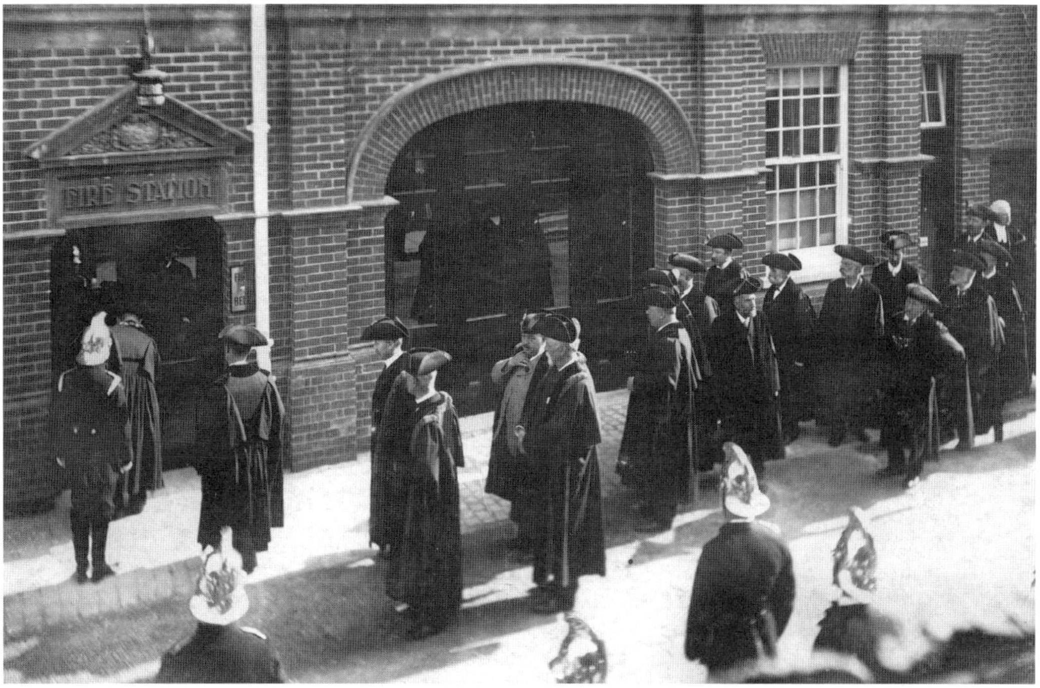

The Official Opening of a New Fire Station in Salt Lane, 1907
Having been erected on the site of the original engine house, the new fire station was commissioned by Salisbury Corporation at a cost of £1,700. It was officially opened on Wednesday 1 May 1907. The Mayor of Salisbury, Councillor Samuel Grove, can be seen ceremoniously unlocking the fire station door before handing the key to John M. Folliott, captain of Salisbury Volunteer Fire Brigade. The guests then joined thousands of spectators in the market place who had gathered there to watch some firefighting demonstrations.

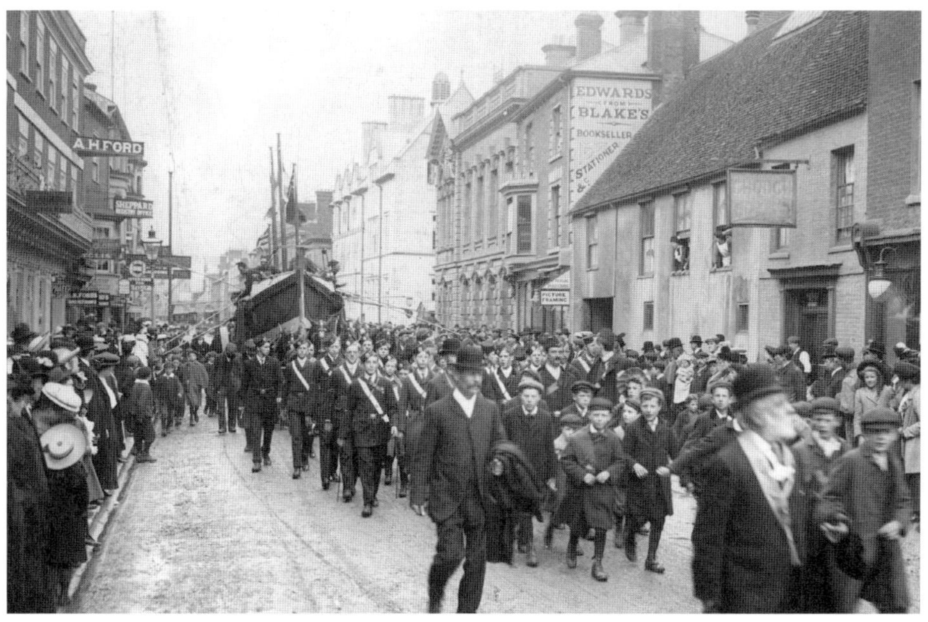

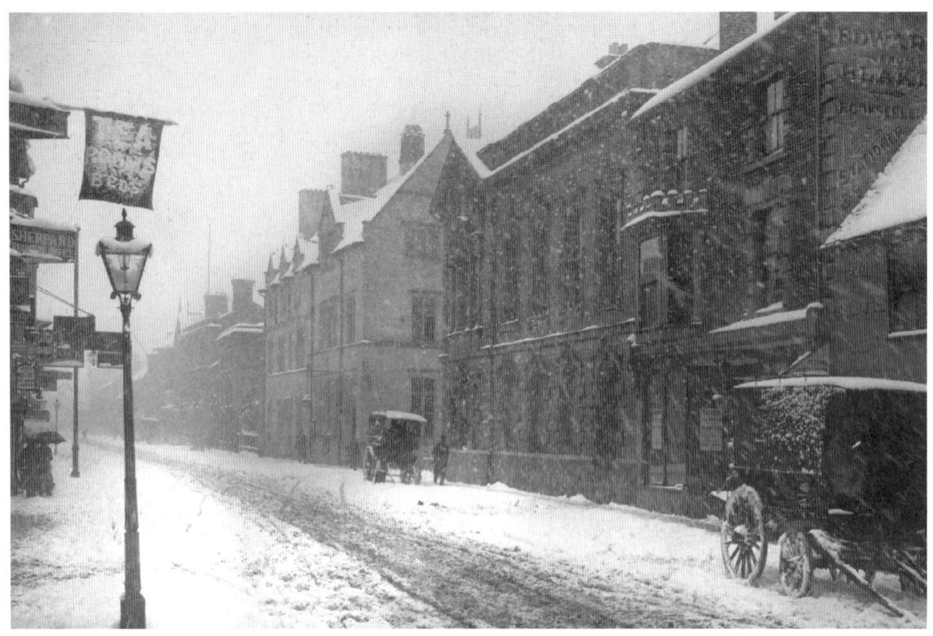

A Record Snowstorm, 1908

A relentless snow storm swept across South Wiltshire on Saturday 25 April 1908. It was an awe-inspiring sight and nothing like it had been experienced since the great snowstorm of January 1881. For twelve hours or more the snow was blown around by a fierce, bitterly cold wind, and for a time Salisbury was completely cut off from the rest of the county. The amount of snow in the streets was greater than many could remember, averaging 14 inches in places. Here we can see the southern end of Castle Street where two horse-drawn vans appear to have been abandoned.

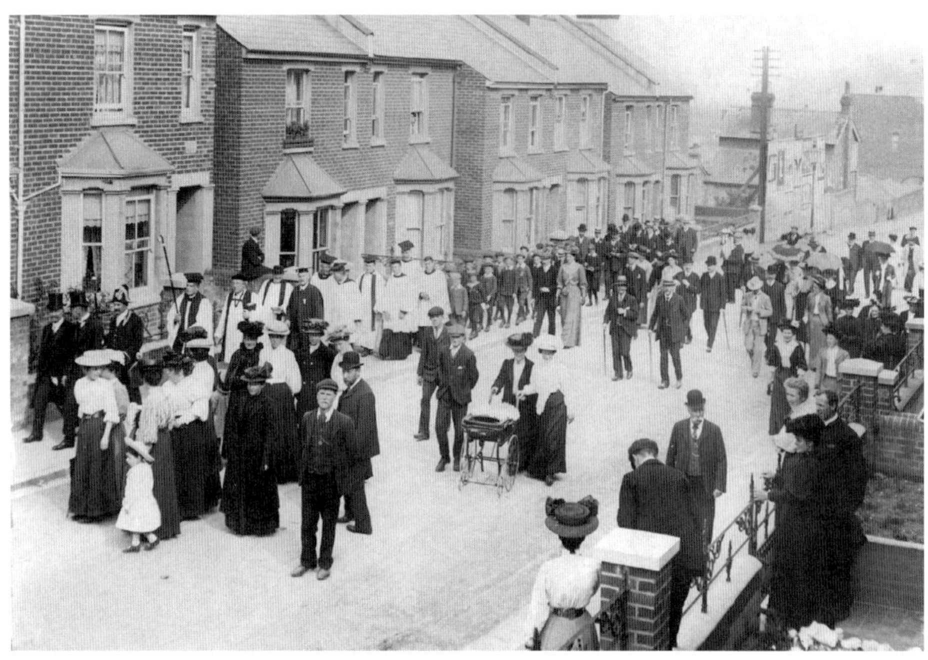

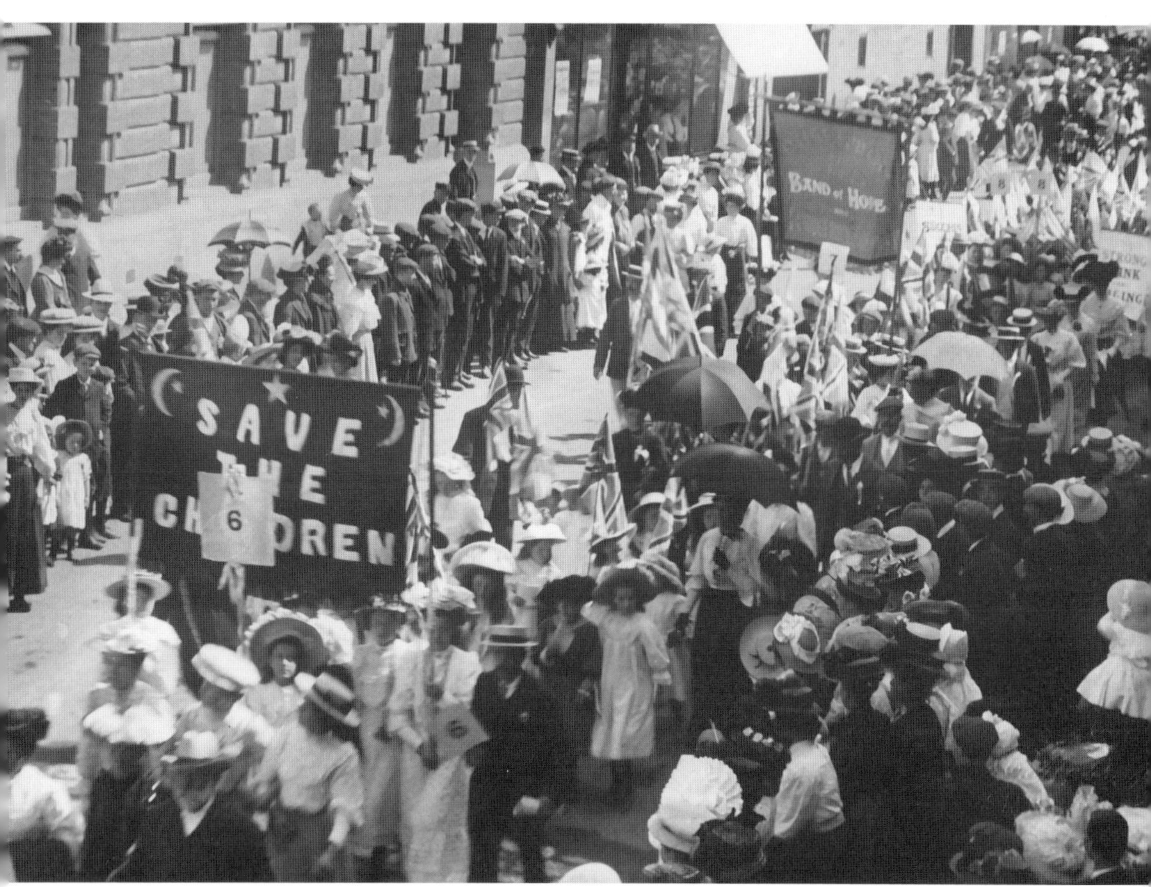

Band of Hope Demonstration, June 1908
Seen here marching along Castle Street are some of the 27 Bands of Hope (twelve groups from within the city, and fifteen from other parts of the county) who marched to a rally at Victoria Park on 10 June 1908. Organised by Salisbury and District Temperance Society, the event was intentionally held on a Wednesday to take full advantage of the half-day closing scheme adopted by many of the city centre shops at that time. Around twenty-five Band of Hope banners were carried through the central streets of Salisbury, accompanied by a large number of children, many of whom were transported on horse-drawn wagons lavishly decorated with ribbons and tissue paper to add colour and gaiety to the procession. One particular banner carried the message 'Drink Like a Fish, Water Only'.

Clergymen Walk to Devizes Road Cemetery, 5 May 1908
Opposite bottom: This was the scene in Devizes Road when the bishop of Salisbury, Right Revd John Wordsworth, and Revd Canon Charles Myres, of St Martin's Rectory, Southampton Road, lead a group of clergymen to the Devizes Road Cemetery, where a new extension of the burial ground was to be consecrated.

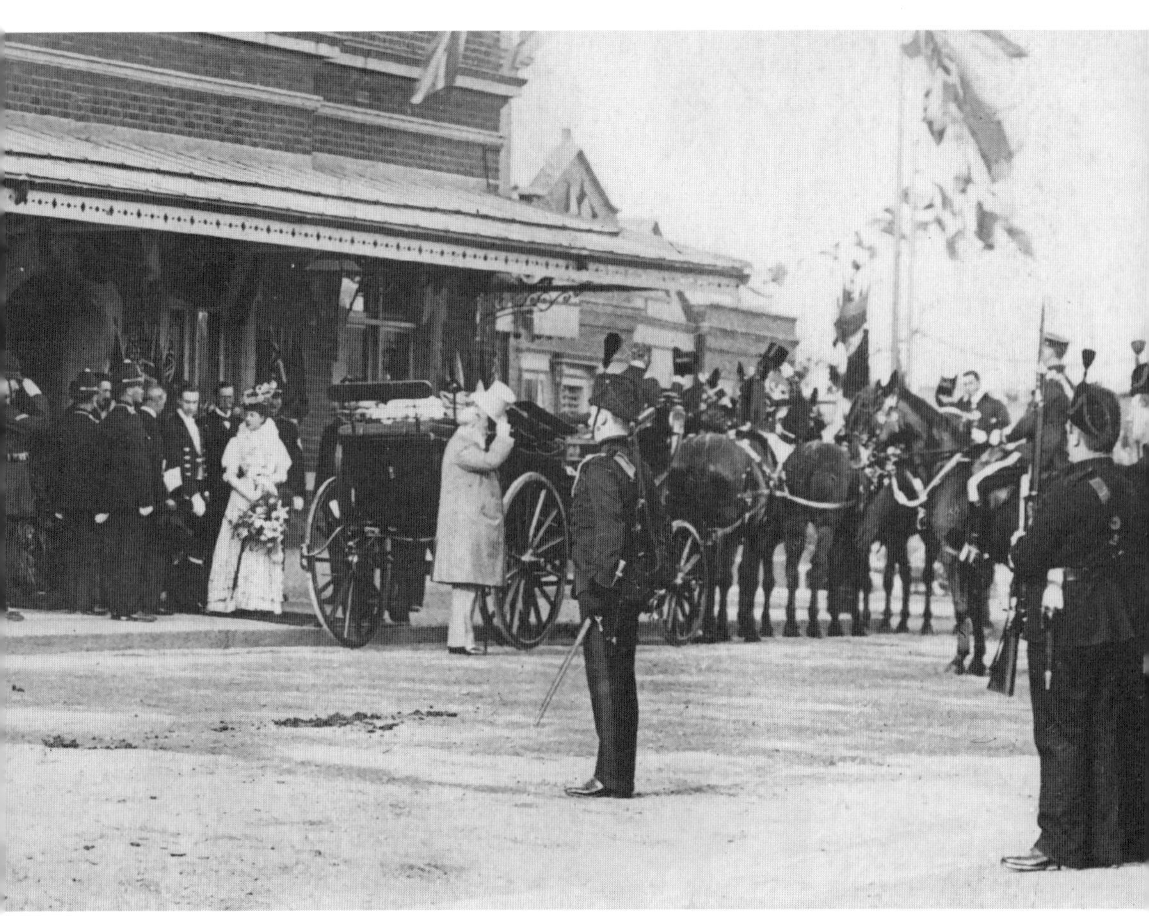

The King and Queen Arrive at Salisbury Station, 27 June 1908
The royal visitors were met at the London and South Western railway station by the Earl and Countess of Pembroke; the Mayor of Salisbury, Councillor R. M. Hall and his wife; members of the corporation; representatives of the Church, and numerous other privileged guests. Standing at the back of the horse-drawn landaulette, Edward VII can be seen doffing his top hat as a greeting to the spectators. The royal couple then left the station with a military escort and proceeded in the open carriage along South Western Road (then part of Fisherton Street), under Fisherton railway bridge, past St Paul's church and on into Wilton Road. There were red, white and blue flags, bunting, ribbons and banners displayed in abundance along the route to Wilton House, where the king and queen were to spend the weekend with the Pembroke family.

The Grave of Teddy Haskell in Devizes Road Cemetery, 1908
Opposite bottom: A tender tribute from the directors of Salisbury Football Club can be seen on the grave – a football created from small white flowers and purple violets with the words 'In Loving Memory'. The card on another pretty wreath reads 'Darling Little Teddy, from your Loving Mother and Grandmother'.

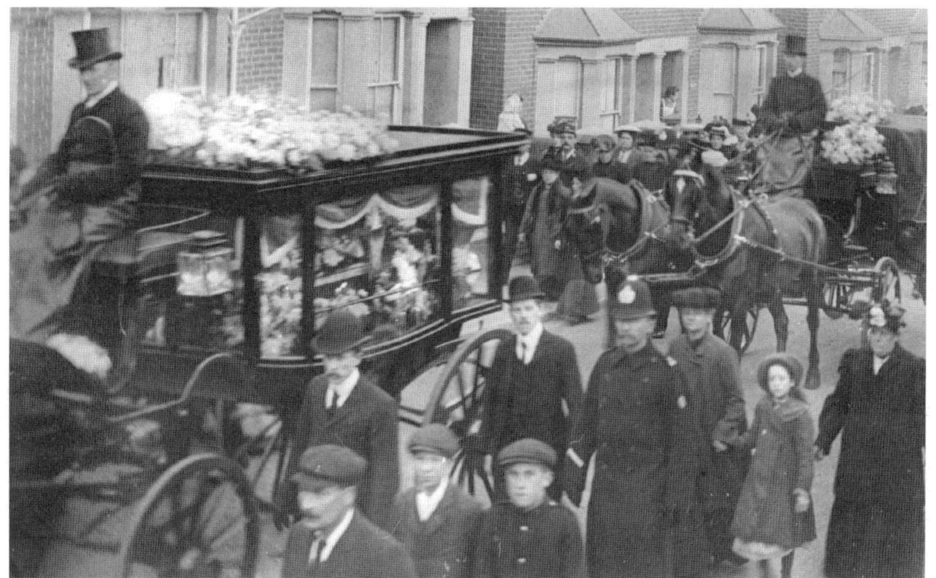

The Funeral Cortege of Edwin Richard Haskell, 1908

The twelve-year-old schoolboy was found dead in bed at his Meadow Road home on Saturday 31 October 1908. A blood-stained kitchen knife was discovered in the house, which was at that time occupied by the boy and his mother. A very likeable child with many friends, he was affectionately known as Teddy. At around the age of seven his right leg was amputated as a result of a bone disease, and yet despite such a severe handicap he was a remarkably good footballer. The boy's mother, Flora Fanny Haskell was arrested and twice charged with the felonious and wilful killing of her son but due to lack of evidence was found not guilty on both occasions. The case remains unsolved. A horse-drawn hearse and mourning carriages proceed at a sedate pace on Devizes Road. A large number of people followed the cortege, many of whom also witnessed the interment at Devizes Road Cemetery.

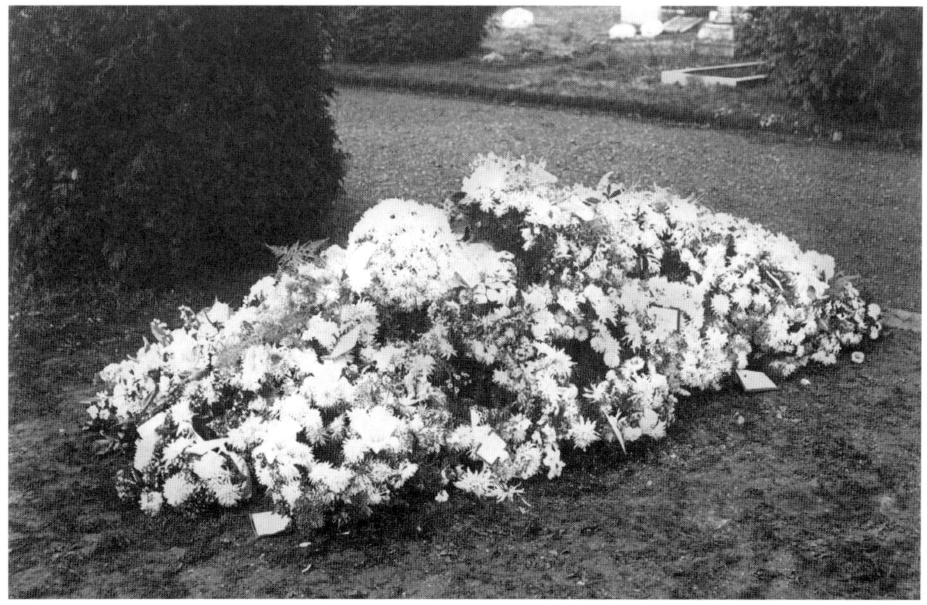

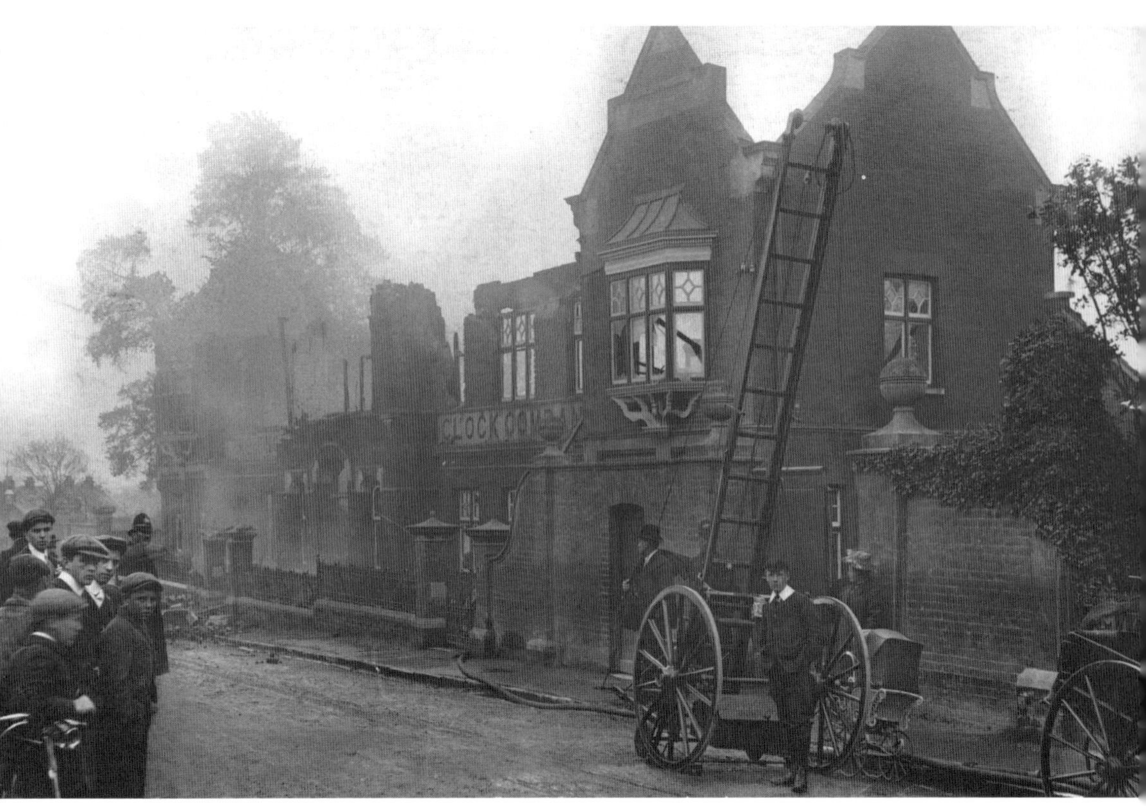

Fire at the Clock Factory in Southampton Road, 1909

H. Williamson Ltd started manufacturing clock mechanisms at the English Clock Factory in Southampton Road (later renamed Tollgate Road), Salisbury in 1902. It was a very successful business, supplying a number of concerns with clock movements including the rapidly expanding S. Smiths & Sons. Unfortunately production came to an abrupt end on Friday 27 May 1909 when fire took hold. Despite the best efforts of the Salisbury Volunteer Fire Brigade, the building was so severely damaged that what little remained of it was thought to be a safety hazard so it had to be demolished. None of the manufacturing machinery could be saved. Production was transferred to Williamson's factory in Coventry. A disaster fund was launched in Salisbury to benefit the eighty-one employees who lost their jobs, and numerous local firms took on extra workers to lessen their hardship – brothers Frederick and George Roper were among them.

Presentation of Trophies at Victoria Park, 1909

Opposite bottom: The first Wiltshire Marathon Race took place in Salisbury on Whit-Monday, 31 May 1909. Having been started by Salisbury MP, Mr Godfrey Tennyson Locker Lampson, thirty-seven competitors headed for Scammell's Bridge, in Nelson Road, and then on to the Devizes Road. Passing the Druids Lodge military training area, they turned right towards Stonehenge and then continued on into Amesbury. Leaving the town by way of Workhouse Hill (now known as Salisbury Road), the runners passed Old Sarum before finding their way back to Victoria Park. It is estimated that 15,000 spectators were spread around the 20-mile route. Here we can see the Duchess of Albany presenting a cup to Fred Monk, whose family were residents of Exeter Street. He finished the race with a time of two hours and twenty-four minutes. Councillor Frank Perkins, the Mayor of Salisbury at that time, can be seen on the stage wearing his chain of office.

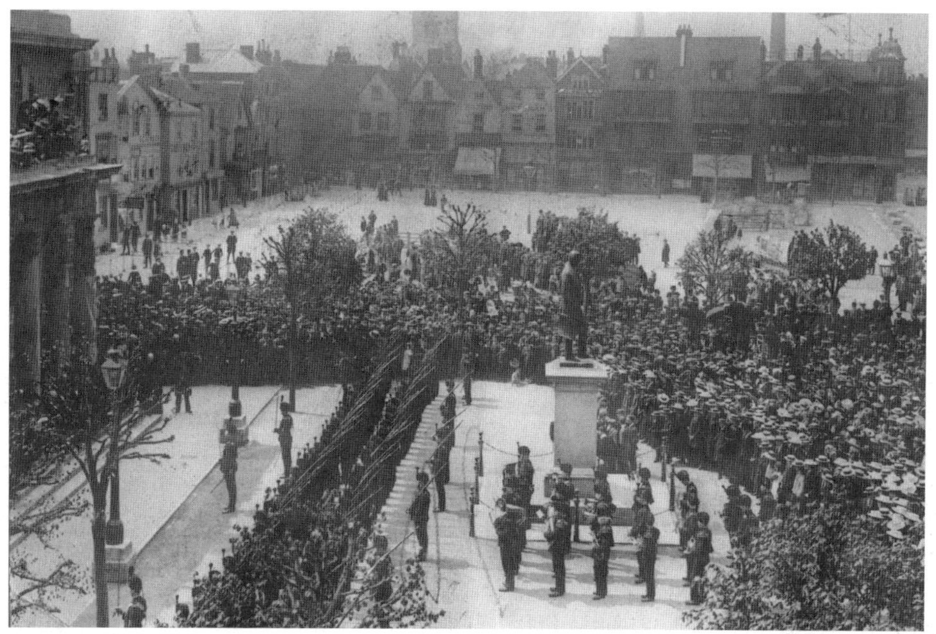

A Royal Proclamation on the Steps of the Council Chamber, 1910

The accession of George V to the throne was proclaimed in Salisbury on Monday 9 May 1910. Two rows of local territorial soldiers and a military band can be seen here on the gravelled market square. A large crowd of schoolchildren and adults had also assembled to hear the announcement that the mayor, Councillor Frank Shepherd, was to make from the steps of the Council House (later to become Guildhall). There was unfortunately a problem with the wording of the proclamation document and a few days later it had to be read out again, but this time to include the phrase 'Emperor Beyond the Seas'.

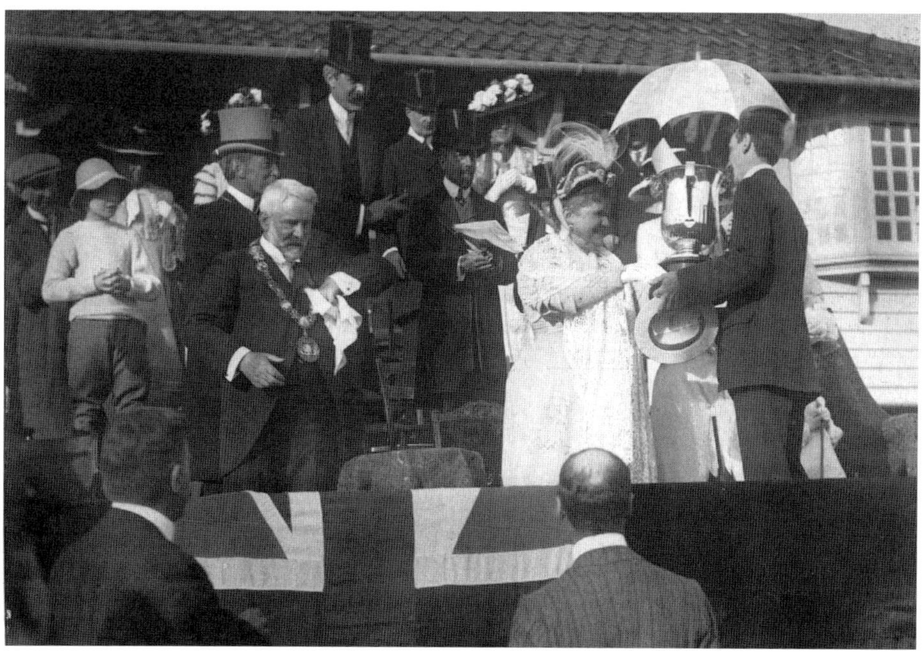

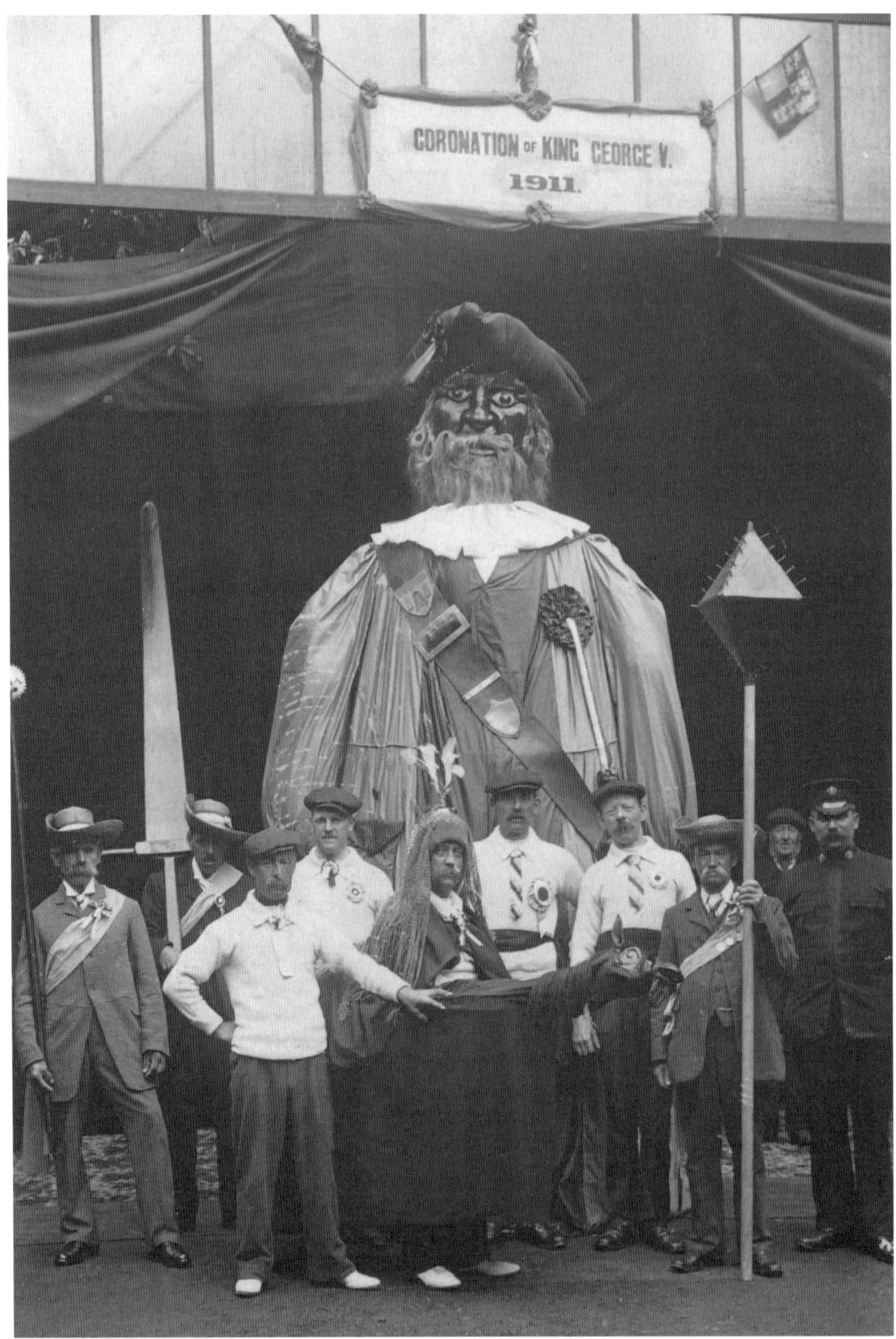

The Salisbury Giant, Hob-Nob and Friends, June 1911
This is an official photograph taken by F. Futcher & Son, commercial photographers, of Fisherton Street, Salisbury on the occasion of the Coronation of George V in June 1911. The morris dancers pictured here accompanied the giant and his mischievous little friend Hob-Nob when they were in procession.

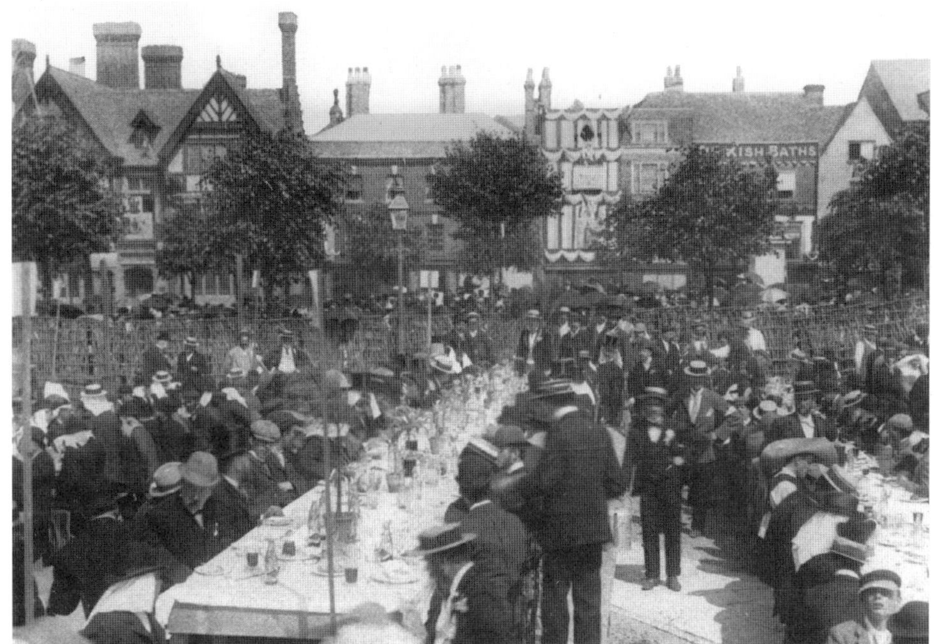

King George V's Coronation Feast in Market Place, June 1911
It was a tradition on occasions of national rejoicing that only the male citizens of the city would assemble in Market Place for a midday feast of meat, beer and plum pudding. The women and children were not invited, they could only look on from upper storey windows, rooftop balconies, or by peeping through the hurdle fencing that had been temporality erected around the dining area. Queen Street forms the backdrop in this scene.

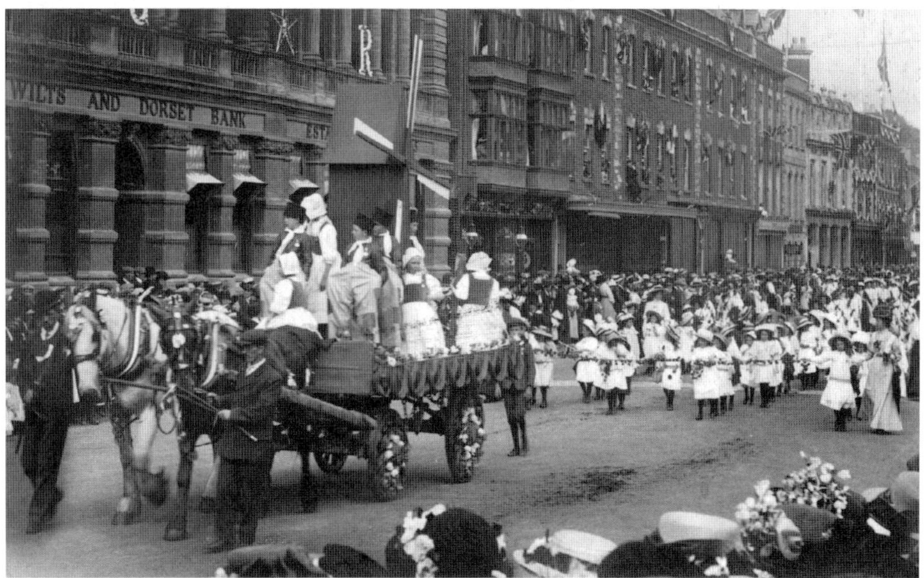

The 'Dutch Car' in the Coronation Street Procession, 23 June 1911
Seen here in Blue Boar Row while taking part in the children's procession is a group of boys and girls from Fisherton School. Their float, or car as they were called at that time, has a Dutch theme.

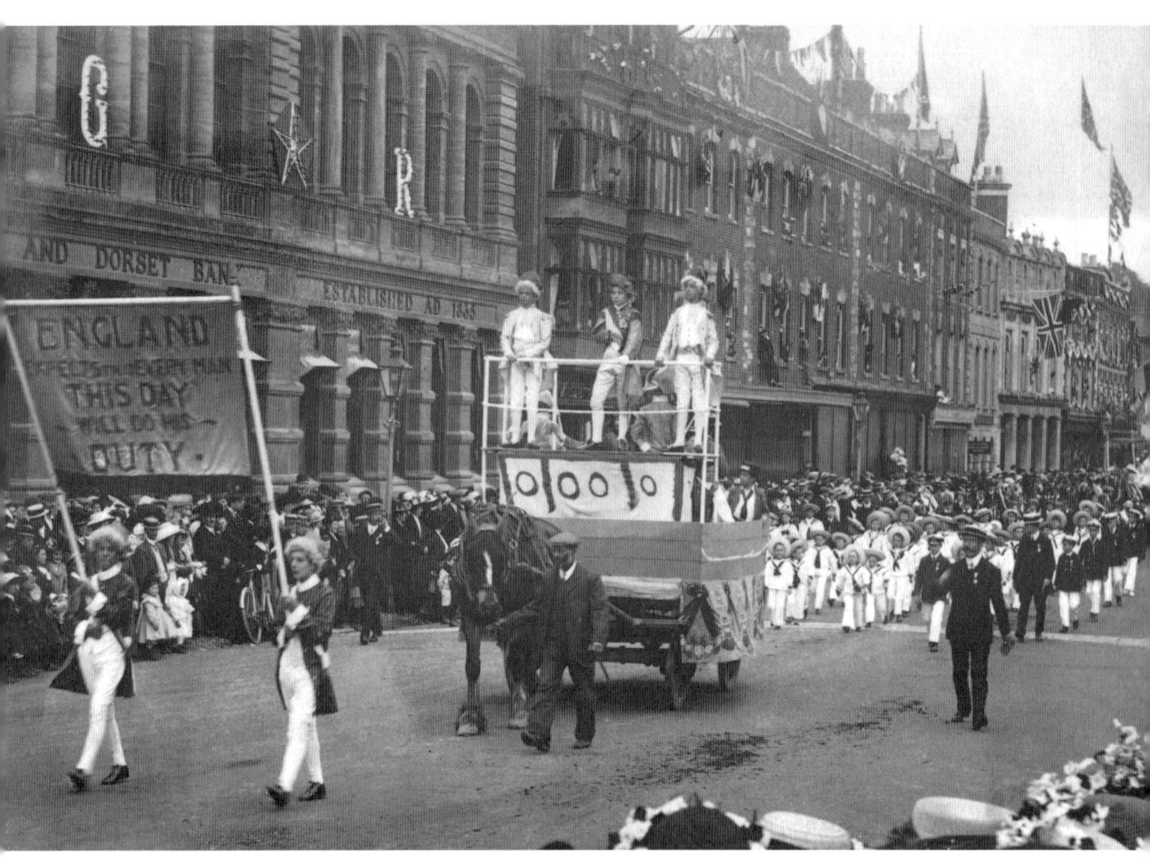

An Iconic Moment in History Re-Enacted, June 1911

'England expects that every man will do his duty' was the signal sent by Admiral Horatio Nelson from his flagship HMS *Victory* as the Battle of Trafalgar was about to commence on Monday 21 October 1805. That iconic moment in history was re-enacted in Salisbury 106 years later, on the occasion of the Coronation of King George V when a 'Children's Procession and Fete' took place in the city, involving all the local schools. Here, at the head of a group from St Thomas's School, we can see a representation of Lord Nelson standing on the deck of HMS *Victory*, and following on behind the horse-drawn car are about fifty boys dressed in sailor suits. On Thursday 23 June 1911, more than 4,000 children joined the parade through the city streets, starting in Exeter Street and proceeding along Catherine Street, Queen Street, Blue Boar Row (pictured), Castle Street and Castle Road, terminating at Victoria Park. Every child was asked to wear their Coronation medal.

Presentation of Badges to Salisbury National Reservists, 1912

Opposite bottom: Shortly after 2 p.m. on Sunday 13 October, a contingent of 152 local volunteers from the National Reserve marched from the Market House (Salisbury Library) to the square in front of the Council Chamber (now known as Guildhall) where they were to be each presented with a badge. The presentations were made by Lieutenant-Colonel the Earl of Radnor, who can be seen standing nearest the camera with the Mayor of Salisbury, Councillor Mr W. Pritchard beside him.

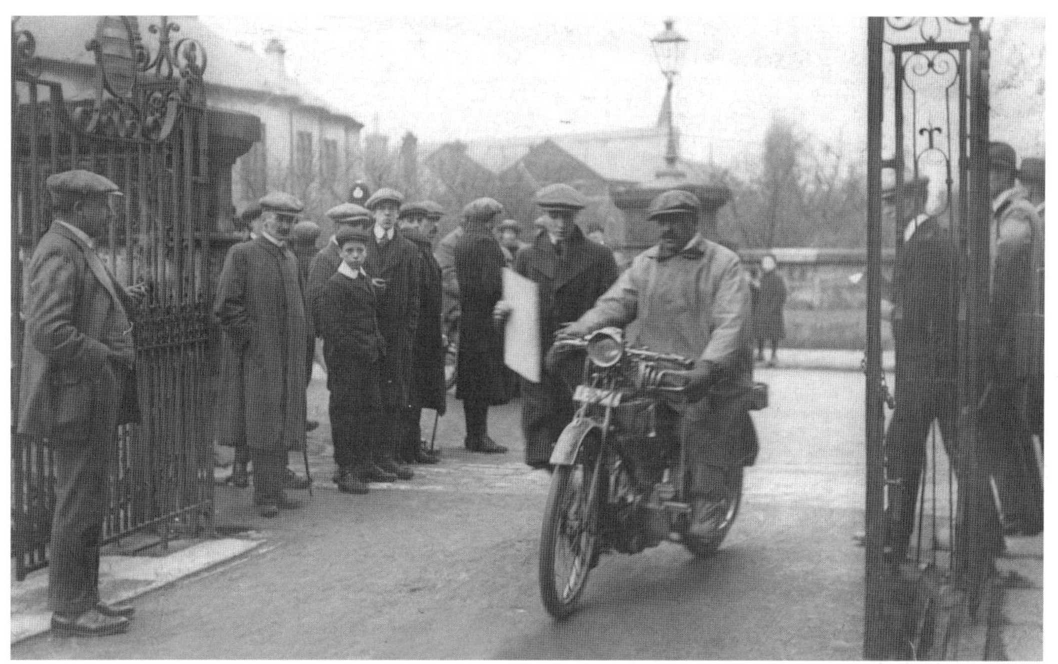

London Motorcycle Club's Winter Run to Salisbury, December 1911
Members of the London Motorcycle Club (known as Wheelers) and guest riders from around the country took part in the Annual Winter Run, which in this particular year was a round trip from London to Exeter and back with stops at the County Hotel in Salisbury on both the outward and return journeys. Nearly a hundred Wheelers took part, some of them accompanied by a friend in a sidecar. Here we can see the first motorcycle to arrive at the County Hotel.

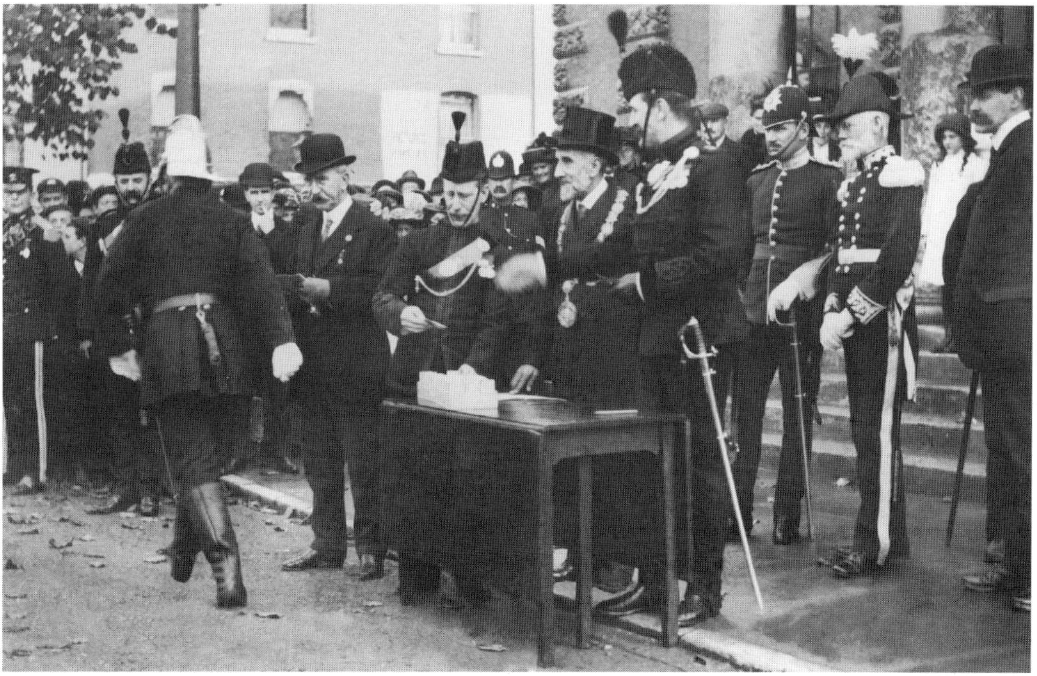

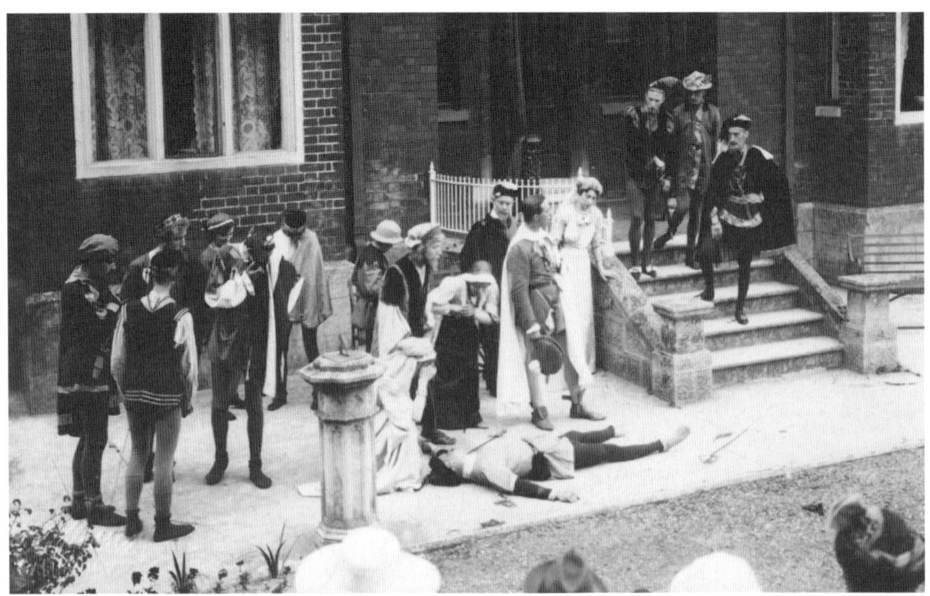

The Avon Players Perform at the Brambles, London Road, July 1913

Fundraising events were often held at The Brambles between the years 1910 and the start of the First World War in 1914. A series of open-air plays were performed there by Basil Gummer and his Avon Players. *Alice through the Looking Glass* and *Romeo and Juliet* seem to have been two of the more successful presentations. The Brambles, 80 London Road, was the residence of Mr and Mrs F. Alexander, who were keen supporters of St Mark's church.

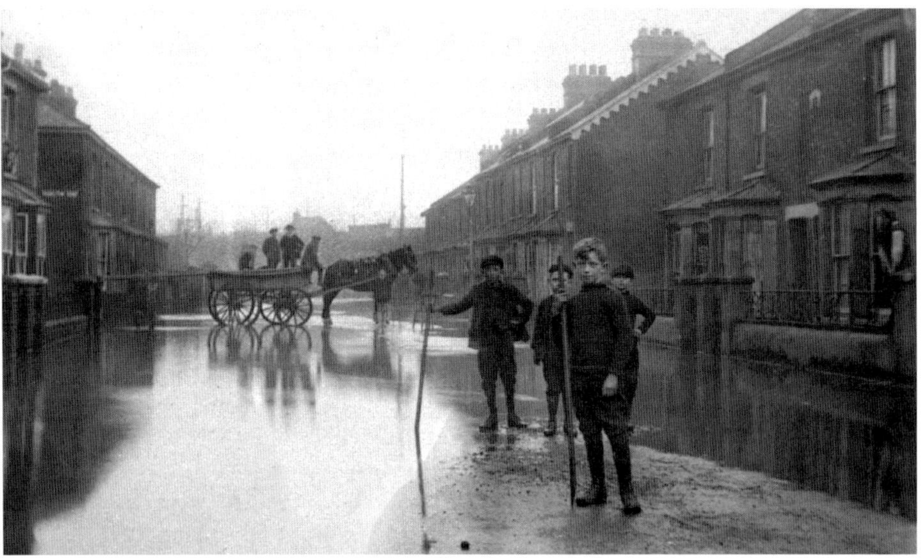

St Paul's Road Flooded In January 1915

On Saturday 4 January, Salisbury City Engineer, W. J. Goodwin, started to inspect the local rivers several times each day and on the fourteenth of the month he warned about the imminent risk of serious flooding. He commented that 1914 had ended with rain falling almost incessantly, which continued on into the new year. And, just as Mr Godwin had predicted, the Rivers Avon and Nadder overflowed and millions of gallons of water poured into the streets.

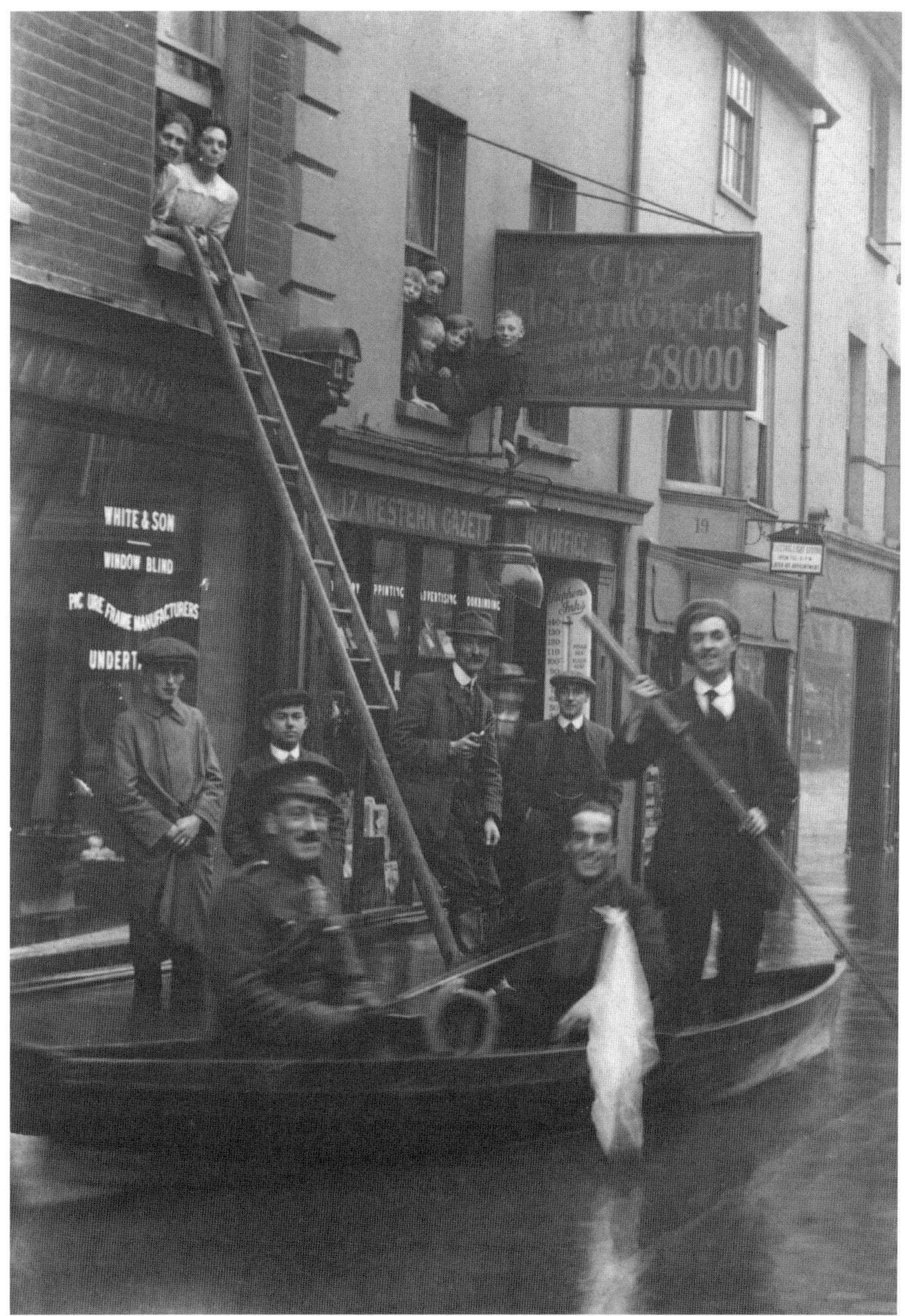

Boating in Fisherton Street, 15 January 1915

Disasters do seem to bring out the best in people: Percy Elliott offered the free use of his boats to ferry pedestrians up and down Fisherton Street, where the water was up to 14 inches deep in places. Ordinarily, the boats were hired out for pleasure trips up the River Avon from the Castle Street Boathouse. A number of local firms also made their horse-drawn carts and delivery wagons available to carry people through the flooded parts of the thoroughfare.

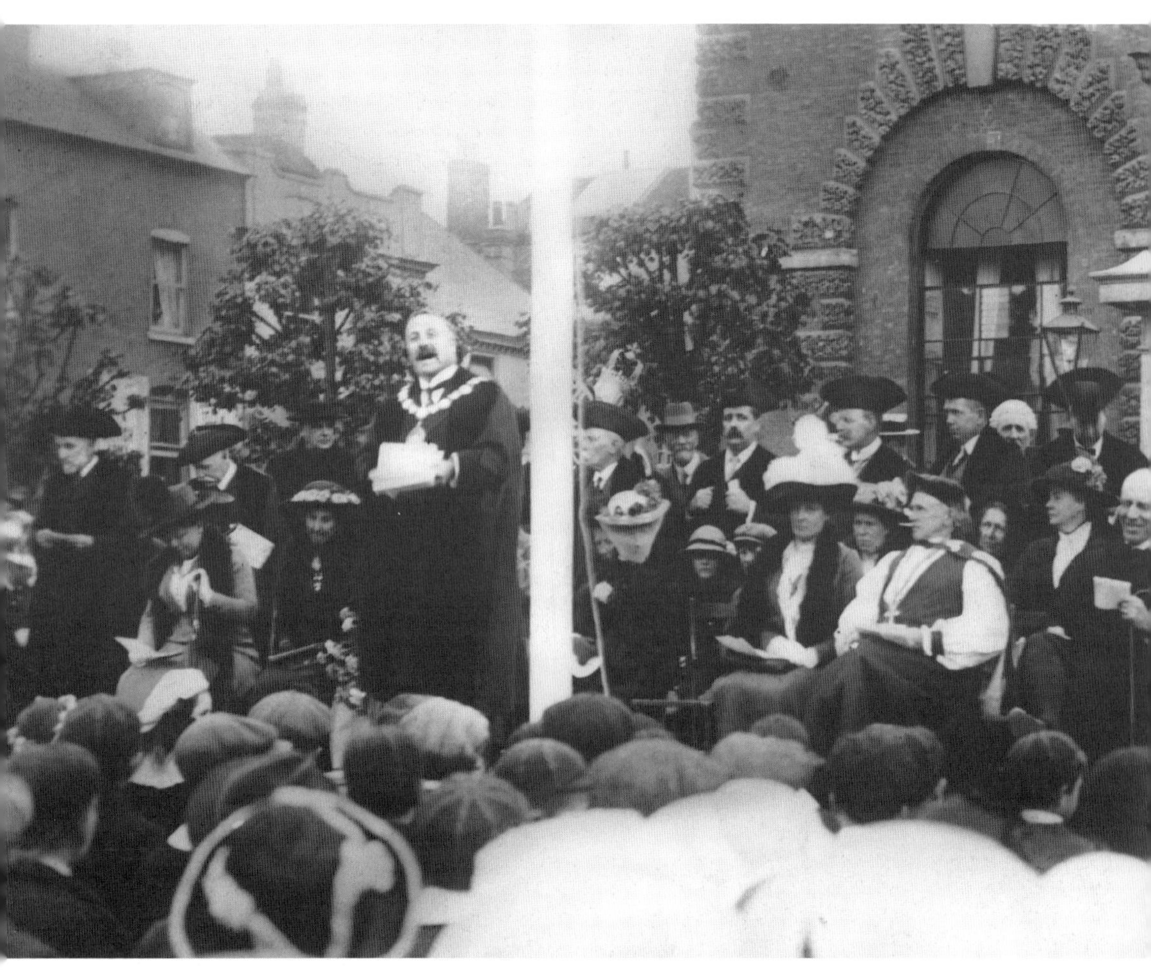

Salisbury's Longest-Serving Mayor Gives a Speech on Empire Day, 1916
On a platform set up in front of the Council Chamber (Guildhall), the Mayor of Salisbury, Councillor James Macklin, was accompanied by the Countess of Pembroke, Lady Hulse, the mayoress, officers from Southern Command, representatives of the church and members of the town council. Throughout the years of the First World War, it was felt that the usual process of appointing a new mayor every year should be postponed. Mr Macklin, mayor elect for the year 1913–1914, remained in office for six consecutive terms, until 1919. He was knighted in 1920 for his public services, and granted the freedom of the city of Salisbury in 1921. Macklin Road was named in his honour.

A Magical Scene in the Cathedral Close, April 1917
Opposite bottom: It was very cold on this particular day and definitely not ideal weather for anyone to be out ganderflanking (an old Wiltshire word meaning 'walking around aimlessly'). The young man seen here by the gate near the west walk of Salisbury Cathedral appears to have accompanied the artist and professional photographer Henry Brooks as he took a series of awe-inspiring photographs of the snow in the Cathedral Close. Mr Brooks had a studio at 45 High Street.

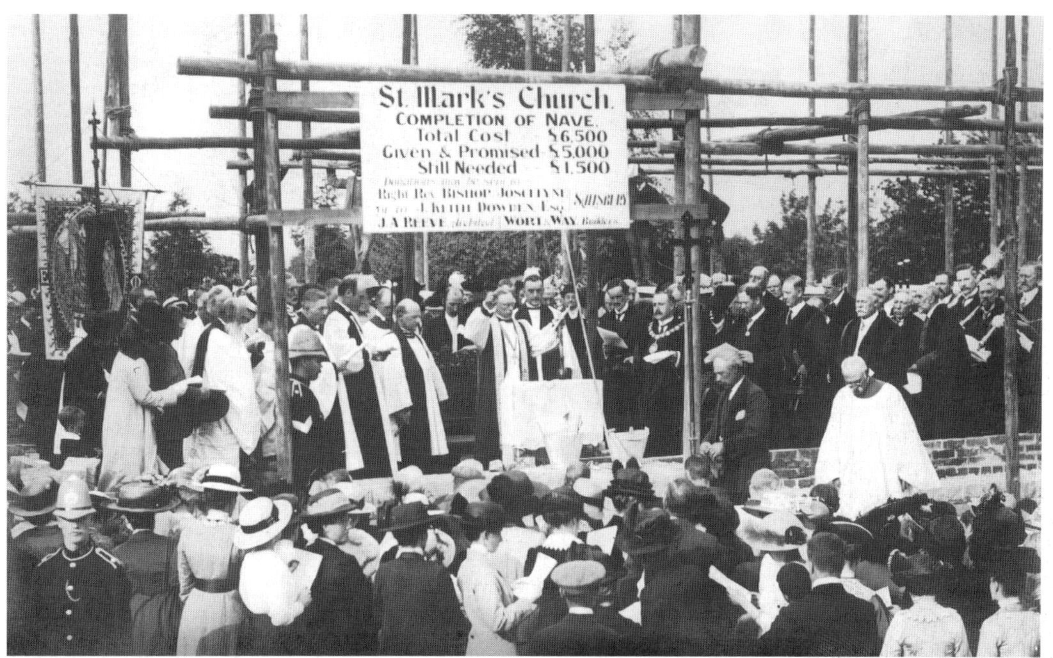

Bishop Ridgeway Dedicates the Nave Of St Marks' Church, 1915

The competition of the Nave was commenced in 1915, some twenty-four years after the foundations of the church were laid in October 1891. The church continued to be built in phases throughout 1892 and 1893, and Bishop Wordsworth dedicated the completed parts of the church on 28 April 1894. Sadly, having passed away suddenly in 1911, he never got to see the end of the project.

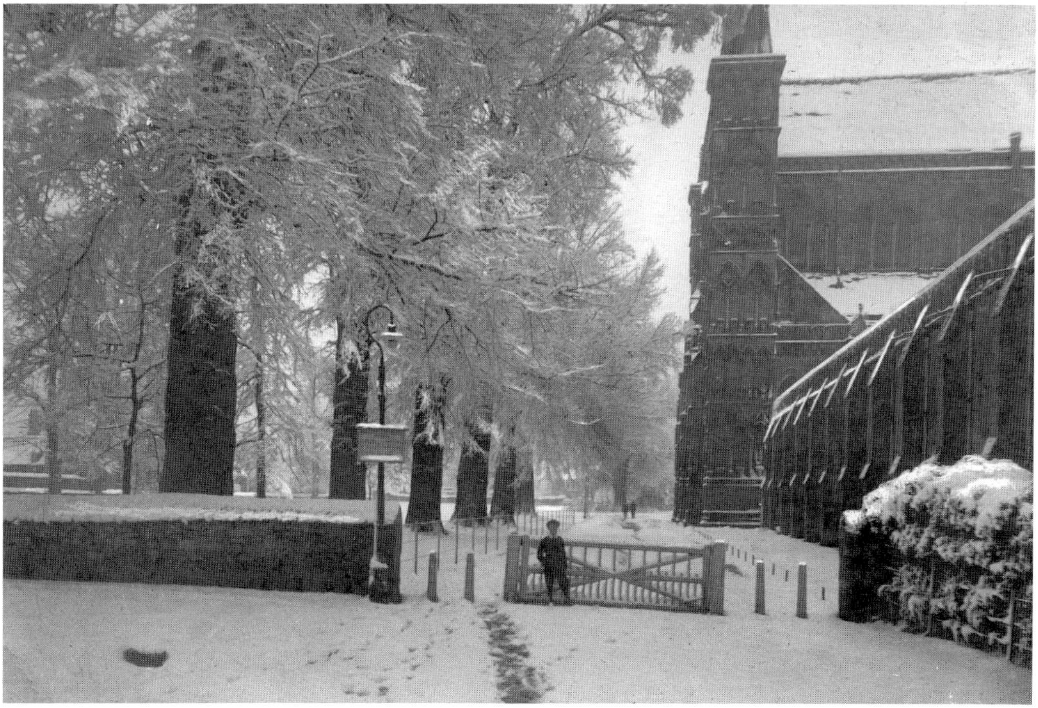

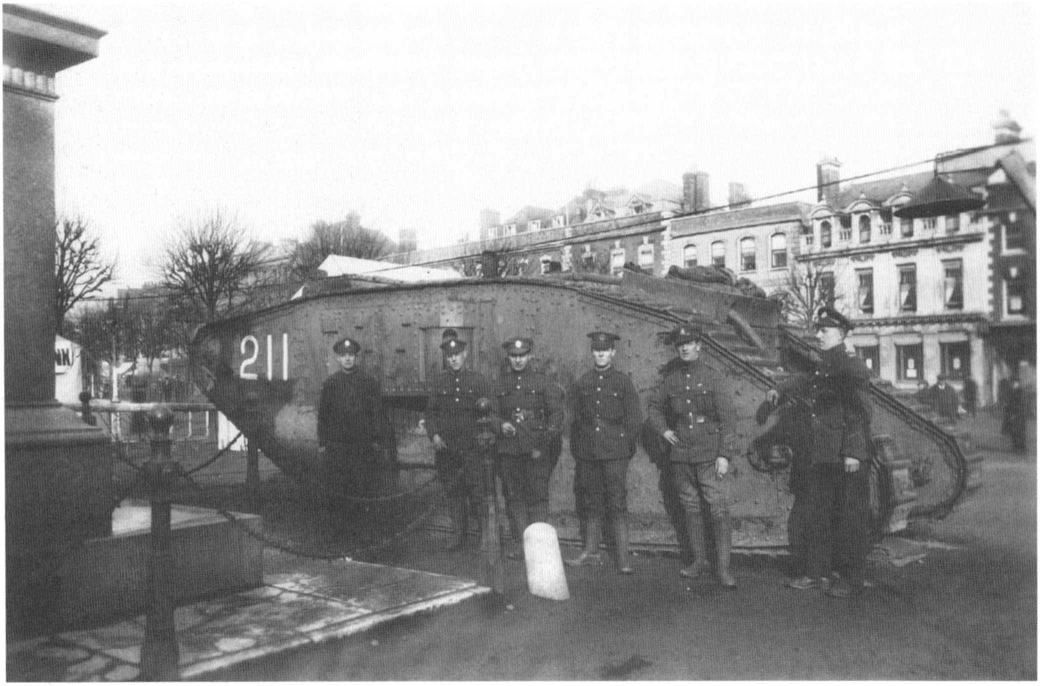

First World War Battle Tank in Market Place, 1918

Salisbury Tank Week, officially known as War Bond Week, took place from 4 to 9 March as part of a national campaign to raise money for the war effort. Tank No. 211 was put on display in front of the Sidney Herbert statue in Market Place. A banner stretched across the front of the Council House (Guildhall) was asking people to contribute by buying war bonds and depositing them in the battle tank. A target of £52,500 was set to purchase a number of aeroplanes. On several occasions during the week the tank was taken out, so it could be seen and heard rumbling around the city streets.

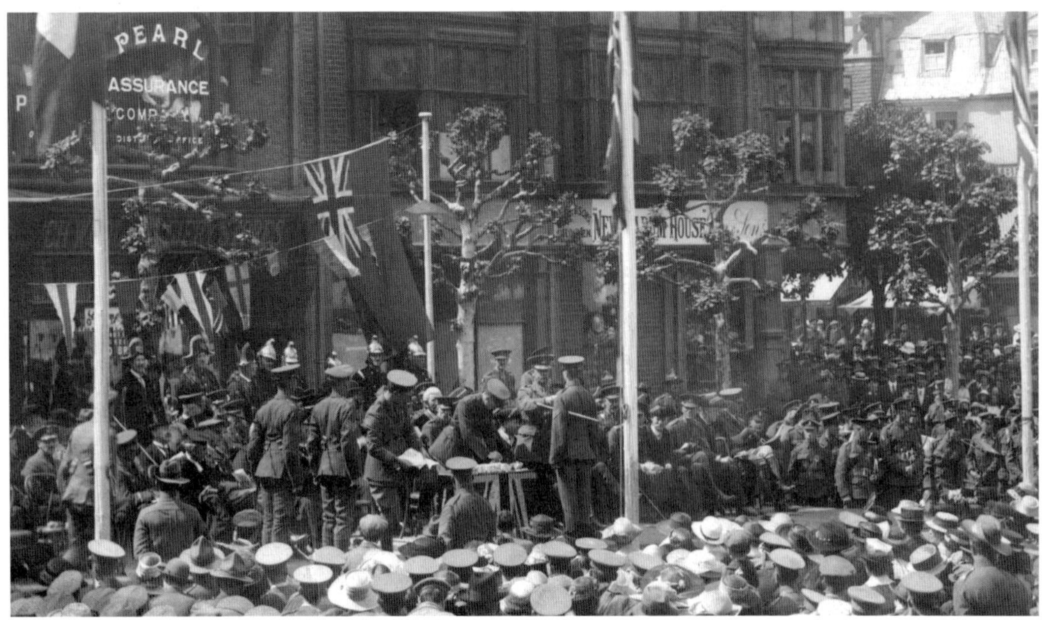

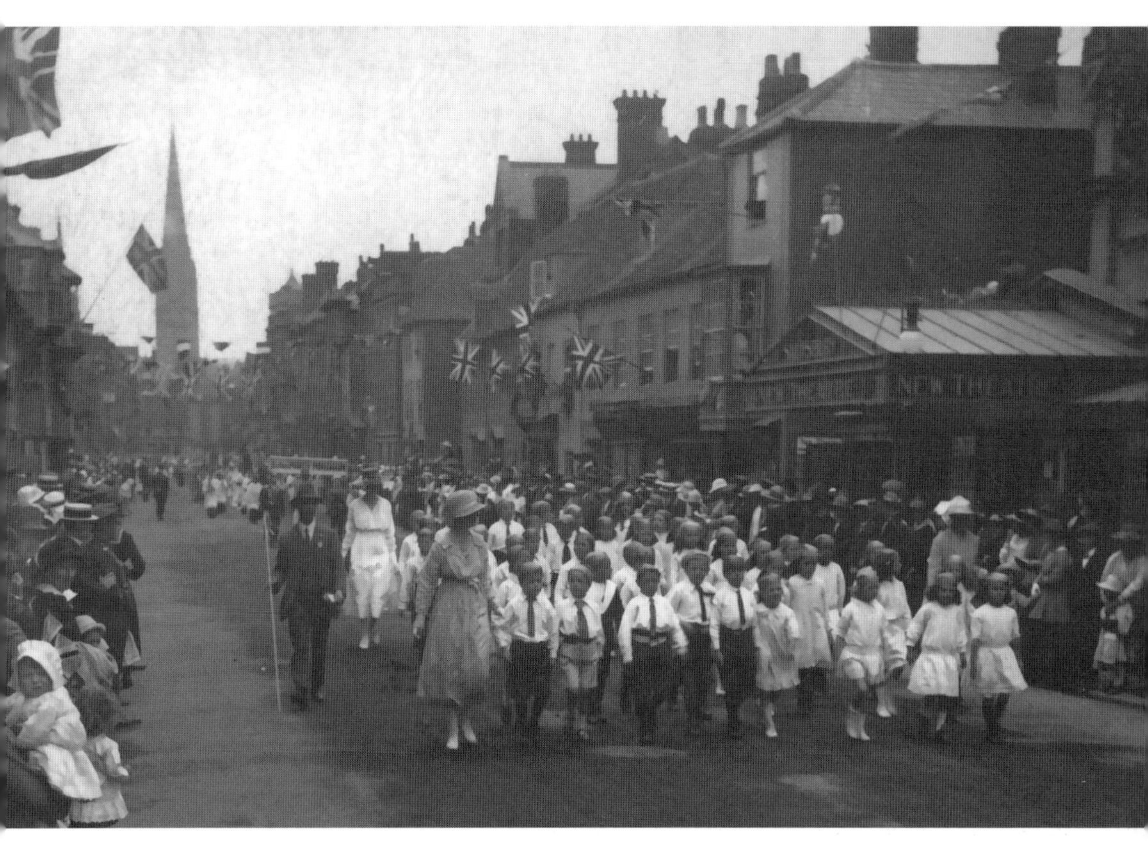

Children's Peace Festival – Salisbury Through the Ages, 1919

Seen here in Castle Street are the children of St Osmund's School who are making their way to Victoria Park to portray 'Doomsday at Old Sarum' in the children's peace pageant. Having taken place on Monday 28 July 1919, it was a triumph, with around 4,000 children from Salisbury schools taking part. After the event the mayor, Councillor James Macklin, wrote: 'Kings, Queens, Lords, Ladies, Jesters, Soldiers, Bishops and Peasants have laid down their Sceptres and their Crowns, their Swords, their Baubles and their Staves. The Pageant has become a memory, something to look back upon, and always to carry in our thoughts.'

Presentation of Medals in Market Place on Empire Day, 1919

Opposite bottom: The mayor, Councillor James Macklin was accompanied on stage by the band of the Durham Light Infantry, and men of the 2nd Wiltshire Regiment formed the Guard of Honour. The Salisbury City Sergeant at Mace and Beadles can be seen at the back of the stage, and also four members of Salisbury Volunteer Fire Brigade.

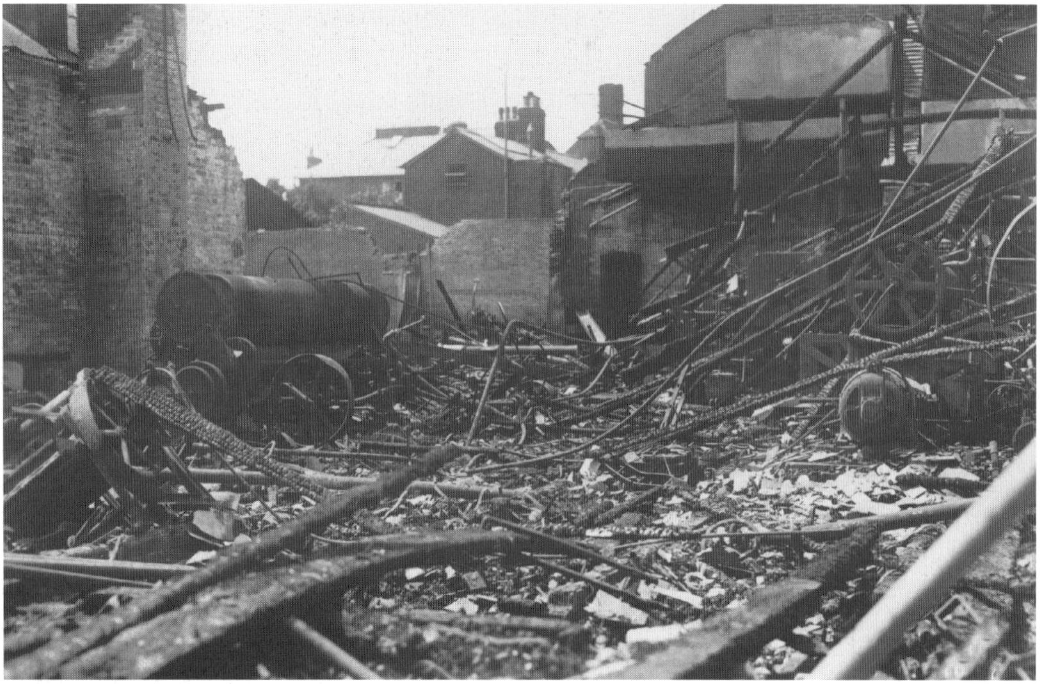

Salisbury Steam Laundry Destroyed by Fire, 1922
The full extent of the horror is vividly revealed in this archive photograph taken on 12 June 1922. Charred wood and twisted metal pipes lying everywhere – items of equipment damaged beyond repair. To the right appears a large bed linen rotary iron that will never be used again. Damage to the factory and loss of customers' goods was estimated to be around £40,000. There was, coincidentally, a fire at the laundry exactly fifty years earlier, in June 1892.

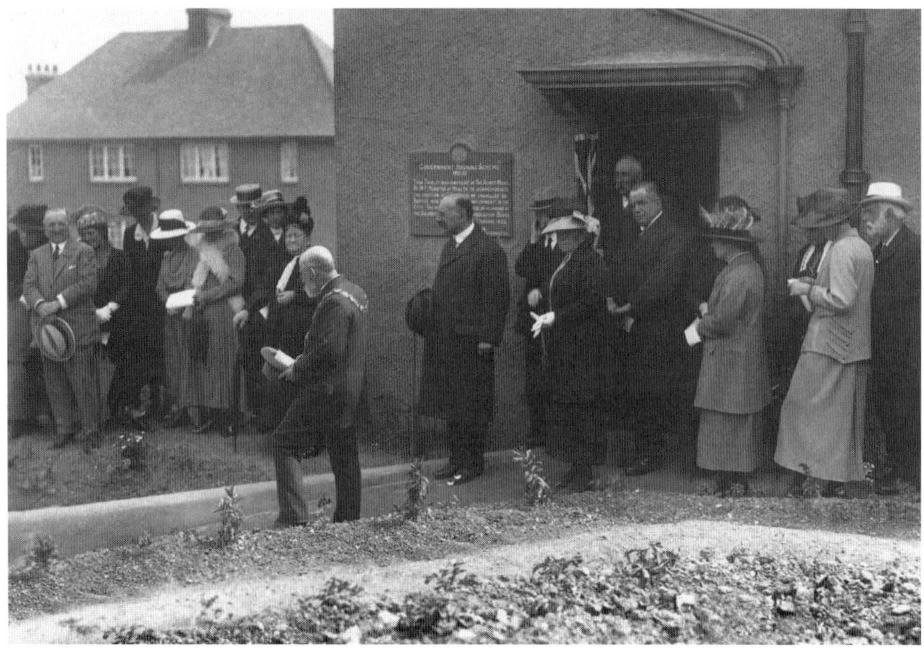

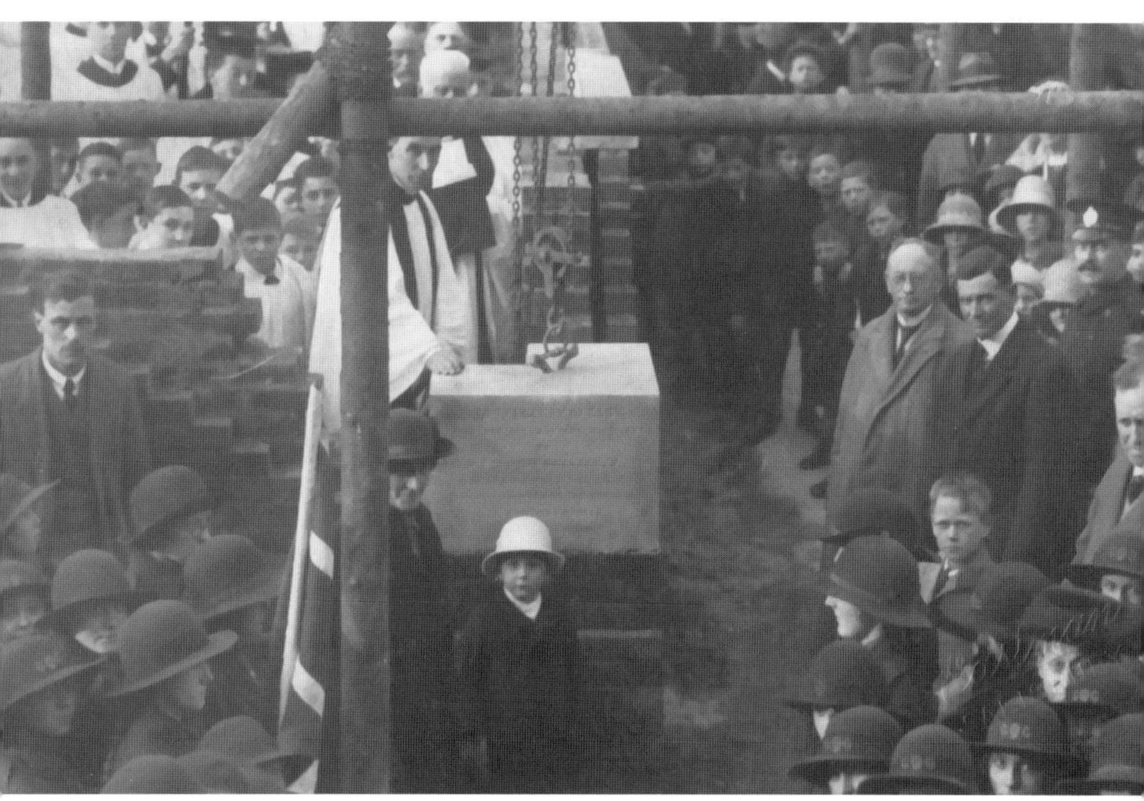

Laying a Foundation Stone at St Edmund's House, 1927
The foundation stone can still be seen on the corner of the building at the entrance to School Lane. It has two inscriptions. On the Bedwin Street façade it reads: 'To the Glory of God. This stone was laid on 16 March 1927 by W. H. Yeatman-Biggs Esq. J. P. Son of Bishop Yeatman-Biggs who was founder of the original St Edmund's house in 1873.' And on the School Lane façade: 'Saint Edmund's House erected by voluntary contributions on the site of the Vine Inn. Alfred Roles and Edwin Guy, churchwardens. Rupert P. Shiner, rector'. Constructed at a cost of £2,340, the building was designed by architects H. and R. Messenger, and the contractor was E. Lindsey and Sons of Trowbridge.

New Council Houses Opened in Wain-A-Long Road, May 1922
Opposite bottom: One solution to the problem of housing and employment shortages in Salisbury after the First World War was the construction of council houses by unskilled ex-servicemen. In this official opening ceremony photograph taken at 22 Wain-a-Long Road we can see Sir Alfred Moritz Mond MP standing in front of a plaque commemorating the project. The Mayor of Salisbury, Councillor Harry B. Medway is making a speech.

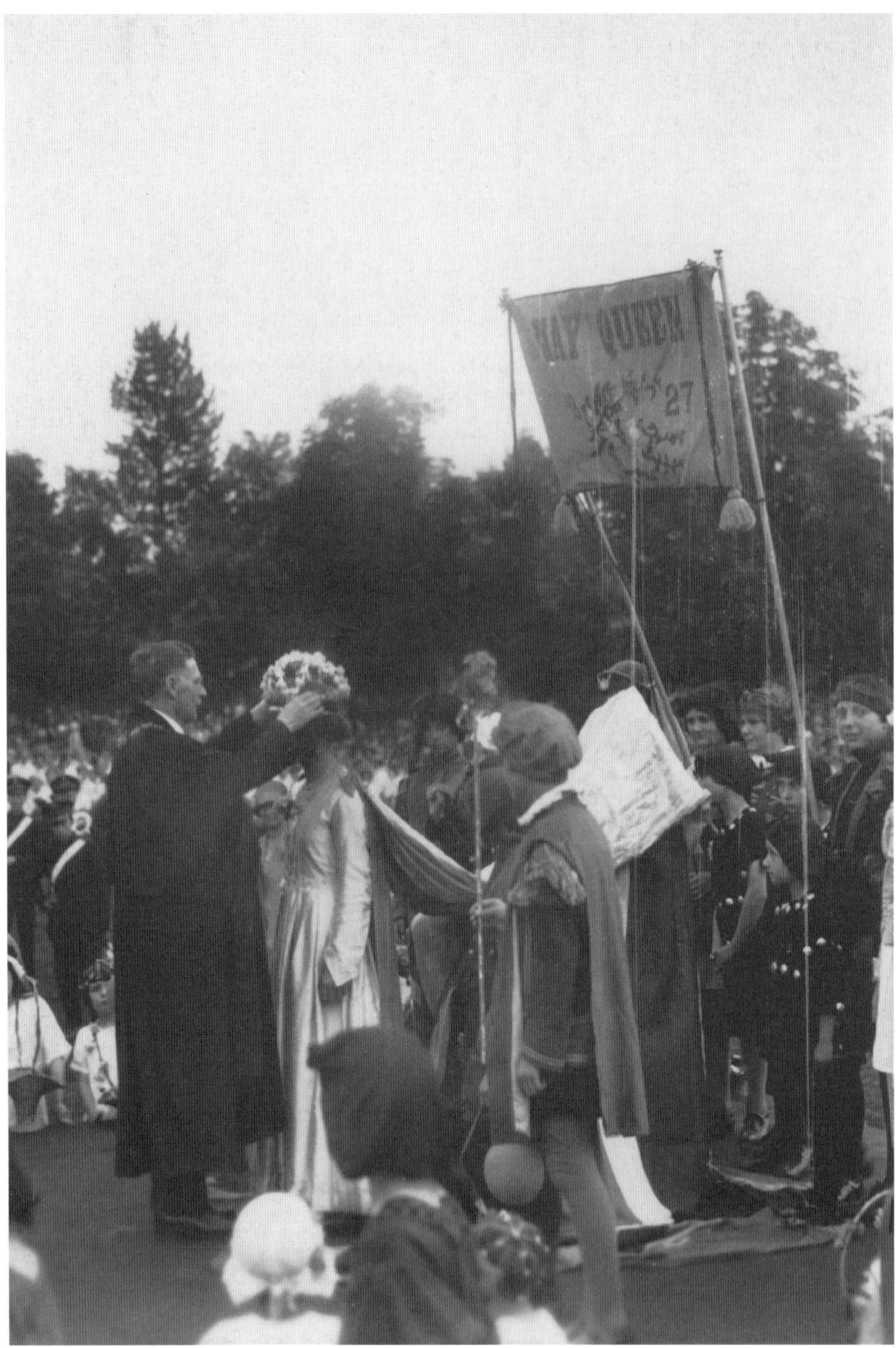

Mayor John Hudson Crowning the May Queen at Victoria Park, 30 June 1927
Just one of many events that took place during Salisbury's 700th anniversary celebrations, which commenced on 22 June and ended on 2 July 1927. Here we can see Muriel Bath receiving her May Queen crown from the mayor. The crown was made of flowers, which unfortunately was ruined by rain so Gullick's florists were asked to quickly make Miss Bath a new one.

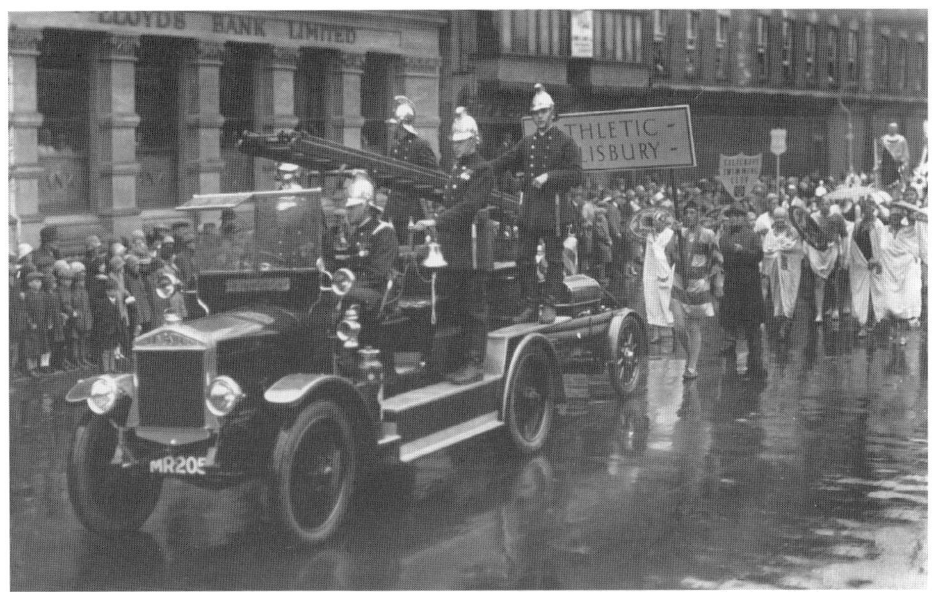

Salisbury's 700th Anniversary 'Centenary Procession', 29 June 1927
A crew of six fireman from Salisbury Volunteer Fire Brigade are pictured here in Blue Boar Row
with their shining new Tilling Stevens motor fire tender and trailer pump (named Frank Baker
after the chairman of the Fire Brigade Committee). Closely following the appliance is the 'Athletic
Salisbury' group of sports enthusiasts from local badminton, bowling, boxing, cricket, football
and tennis clubs. A banner from Salisbury Swimming Club can be seen among them.

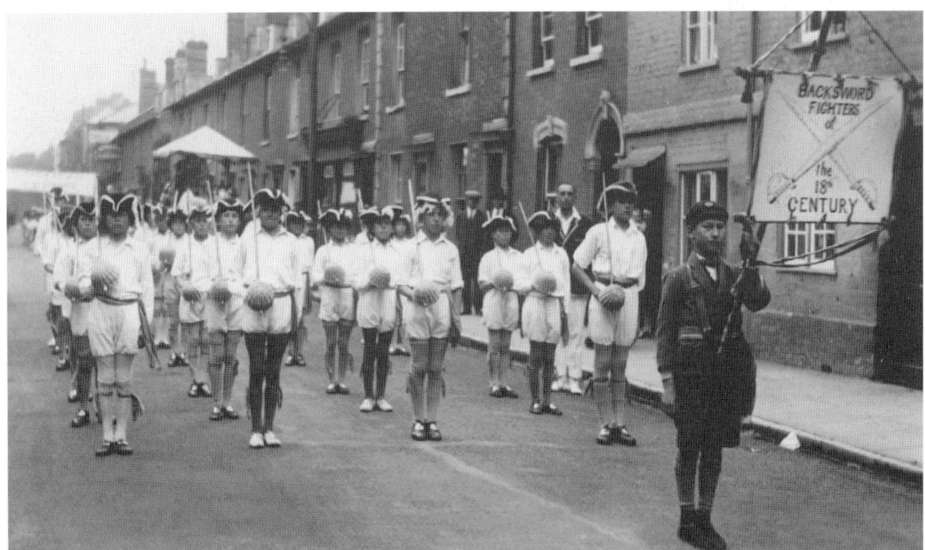

Eighteenth-Century Backsword Fighters From St Thomas's School, 30 June 1927
One of the main attractions of Salisbury's 700th anniversary celebrations was a very impressive
and extensive street procession involving many of Salisbury's schoolchildren – each school
depicting a different period in the city's history. Seen here in New Street is a group of boys
from St Thomas's school. The terraced houses in the background were demolished prior to the
development of Old George Mall.

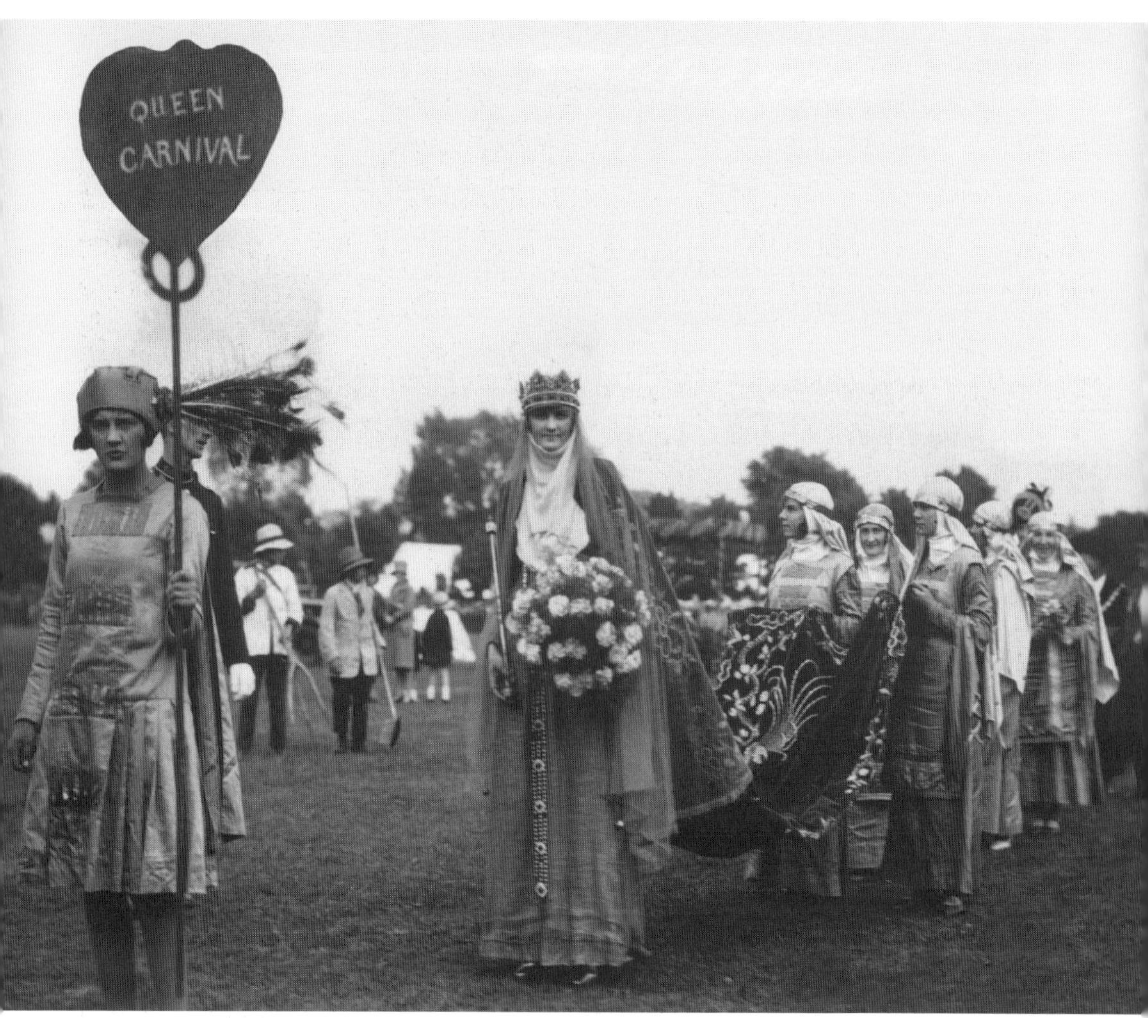

Salisbury Hospital Carnival Queen and Court, 28 June 1930
Miss Guendolen Wilkinson was Carnival Queen for Salisbury Carnival Week, 1930. Her court was as follows. Maids of Honour: Miss Joan Edwards, Miss Doreen Hopkins, Miss Edith Major, Miss Barbara Sant, Miss Kathleen Sargent, Miss Ruth Sims, Miss Estmin Smith and Miss Barbara Snelgar. Herald: Mr Hedley G. Coombes. Jester: Mr Francis U. Pullen. Page: Miss Patricia Sant. This was only the second appearance of this event, the first one having taken place twenty-four years earlier in June 1906. Both events were organised to raise much needed funds for Salisbury General Infirmary.

Aunty Smiler in the Hospital Carnival Procession, 2 July 1930
Opposite bottom: The giant mechanical nurse was conceived and assembled by Salisbury Steam Laundry as a special attraction for the Hospital Carnival procession. An Austin Seven car had been adapted by W. Goddard & Co. Ltd (motor engineers) of St Edmund's Church Street to portray the nurse's pram. Arthur Edward Davis, and his uncle Arthur 'Sonny' Davis, were the babies in the pram. Auntie Smiler's legs were attached by cams to the wheels of an undercarriage, so when pulled along behind the little Austin it appeared that she was walking. This was the scene in Milford Street where a large number of spectators were watching her turn into Catherine Street.

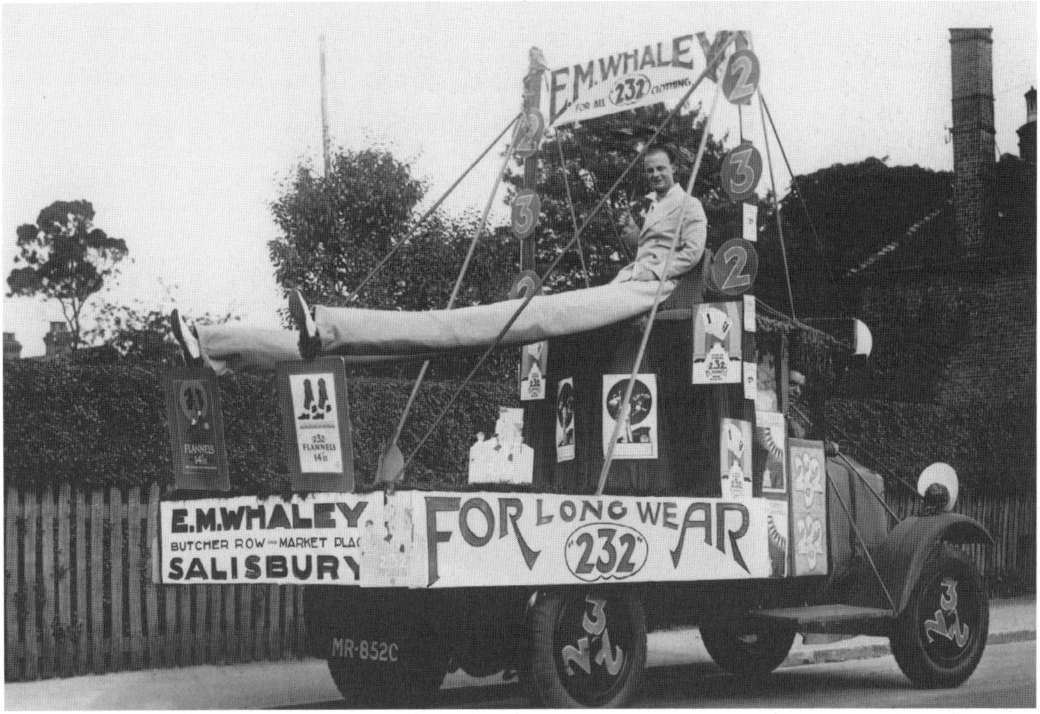

Prize-winning Float in the Hospital Carnival Procession, 2 July 1930

The decorations on E. M. Whaley's float was red and green. It won third prize in the Trade Class (Class A) – 30 shillings worth of lubricating oil (five gallons) donated by Lowther's Garage of 27 Canal. The float was built around a 1927 Bean lorry (made by Harper, Sons & Bean Ltd, of Tipton) that was loaned by the Building Material Company of 52 Fisherton Street. The theme was based on a range of hardwearing men's grey flannel trousers known as '232s'.

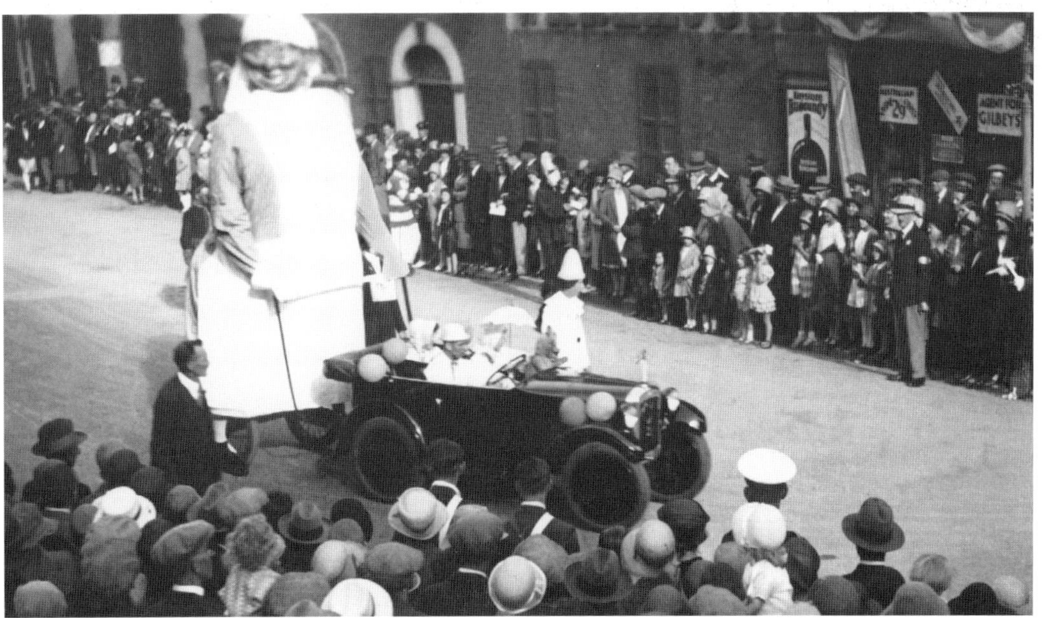

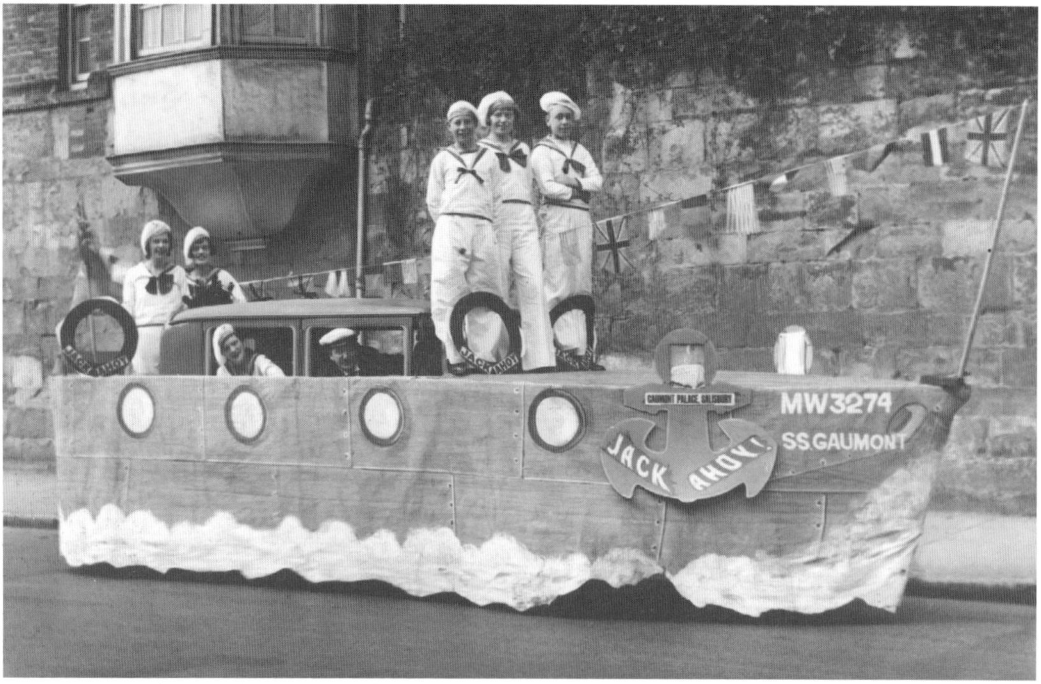

SS *Gaumont* Sails Along St John Street, 1934

This would seem to be a publicity stunt organised by the Gaumont Palace cinema in The Canal (very appropriate street name) to advertise the film *Jack Ahoy*, starring John Norman 'Jack' Hulbert, released by Gaumont-British in 1934. The car on which the float (again very appropriate) was built was an Essex Super Six saloon (MW3274) owned by Victor Haydn, an employee at the Gaumont Palace in Salisbury.

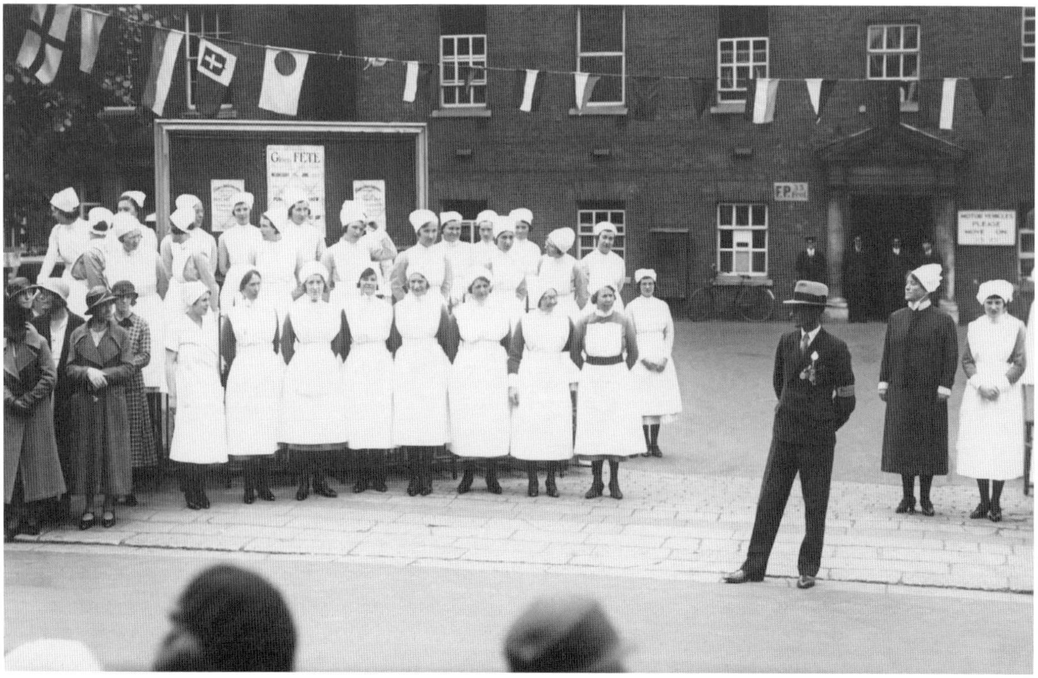

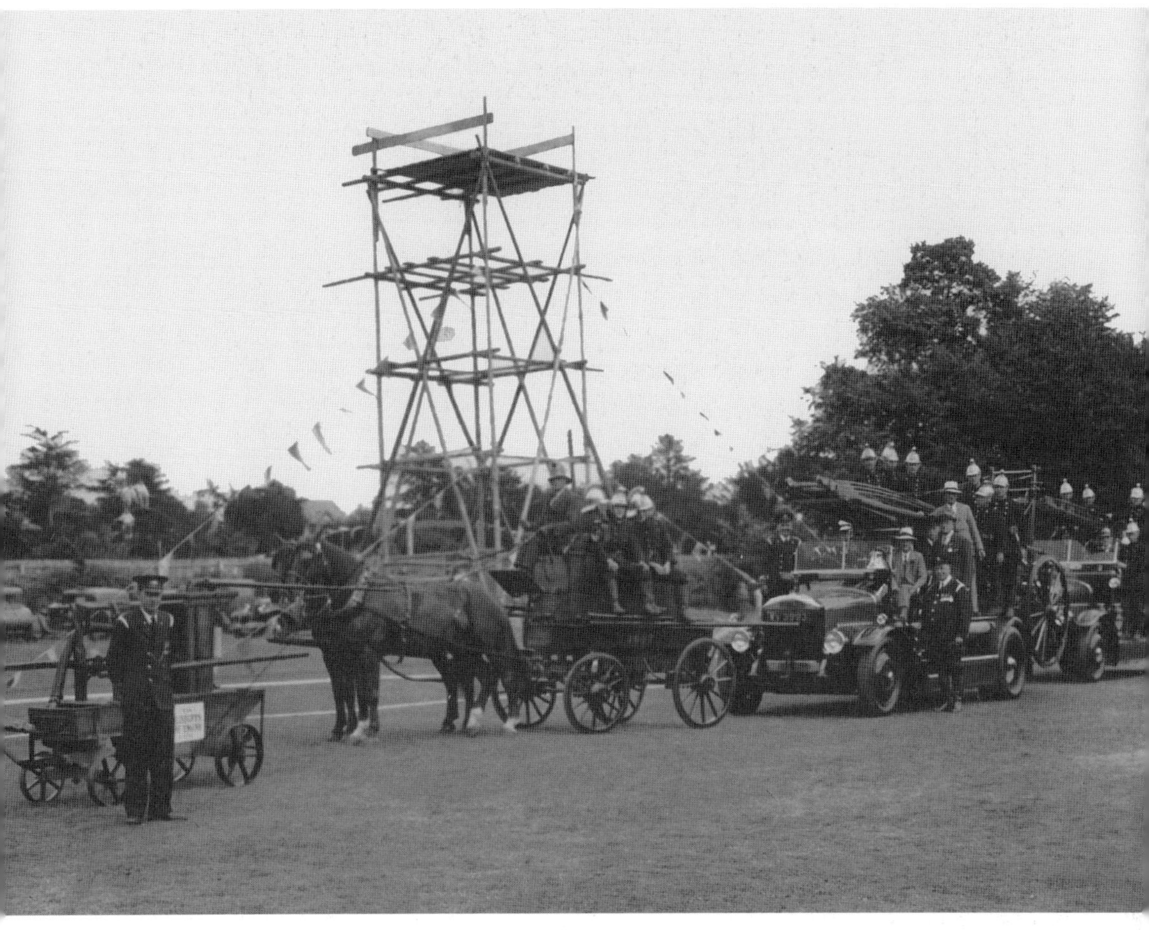

Fire Brigade Completions, 1934

Following a thanksgiving service at the cathedral on 29 July, a number of retired and serving firemen from the Salisbury Volunteer Fire Brigade marched behind an assortment of old and new fire engines as they paraded around the city streets. The procession was just one of several events arranged to celebrate the brigade's golden jubilee. This was the scene at the Bemerton Cricket Ground, near Skew Bridge, where firefighting demonstrations and pump and ladder drills were performed. Two very early manual fire engines are pictured here ahead of two modern Dennis fire engines, *The Chairman* (WV 3883) and *The Chief* (MW 6125).

Public Appeal Launched to Re-Build the Infirmary, 1934

Opposite bottom: The appeal for £85,000 generated great enthusiasm locally and in the first few months more than £1,000 was raised by nursing and domestic staff alone. The event presented an excellent photo opportunity for the matron, Miss Bishop, who can be seen standing on the right next to Nurse Hedderman. The matron was a strict disciplinarian whom the nurses rather cruelly named the Green Dragon. She is pictured here in front of Salisbury General Infirmary, wearing a dark-green uniform.

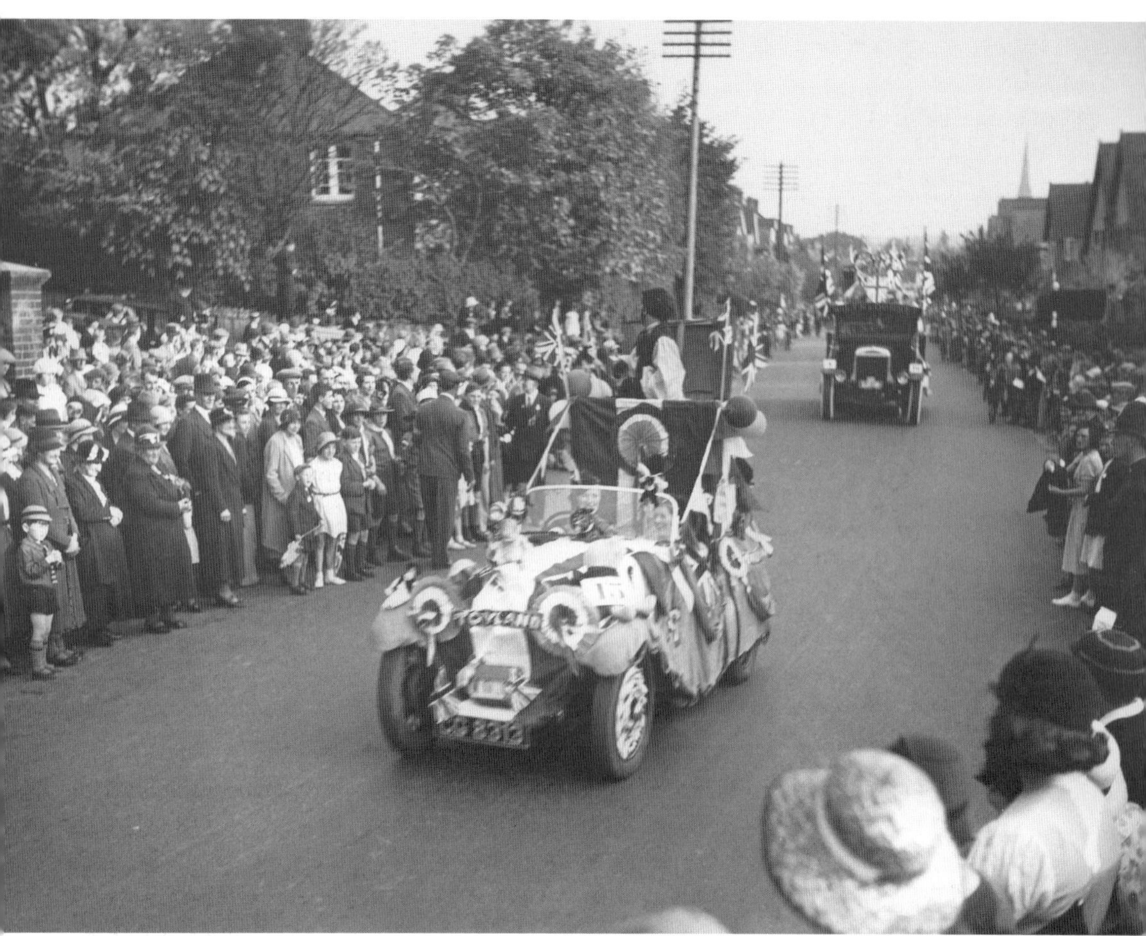

The Silver Jubilee Parade in Castle Street, May 1935

The 25th anniversary of the Coronation of George V was celebrated with great enthusiasm by the people of Salisbury. The street procession and party in the park were very well supported, as can be seen by the huge number of spectators assembled here in Castle Street as the parade approaches Victoria Park. Madge Mankin comes into view in the foreground of the picture at the wheel of her Singer Car (CG-8313) that had been colourfully decorated on the theme of 'Toyland'. The float following on behind was entered by the Wilts & Dorset Motor Services.

City Streets Lavishly Decorated for the Coronation, 1937

Opposite bottom: The decorations in Catherine Street were described by the *Salisbury Times* as the prettiest in the city. Red, white and blue streamers were draped from building to building, and strings of high-level coloured lights were carried the whole length of the street, which when illuminated at night created a truly magical scene.

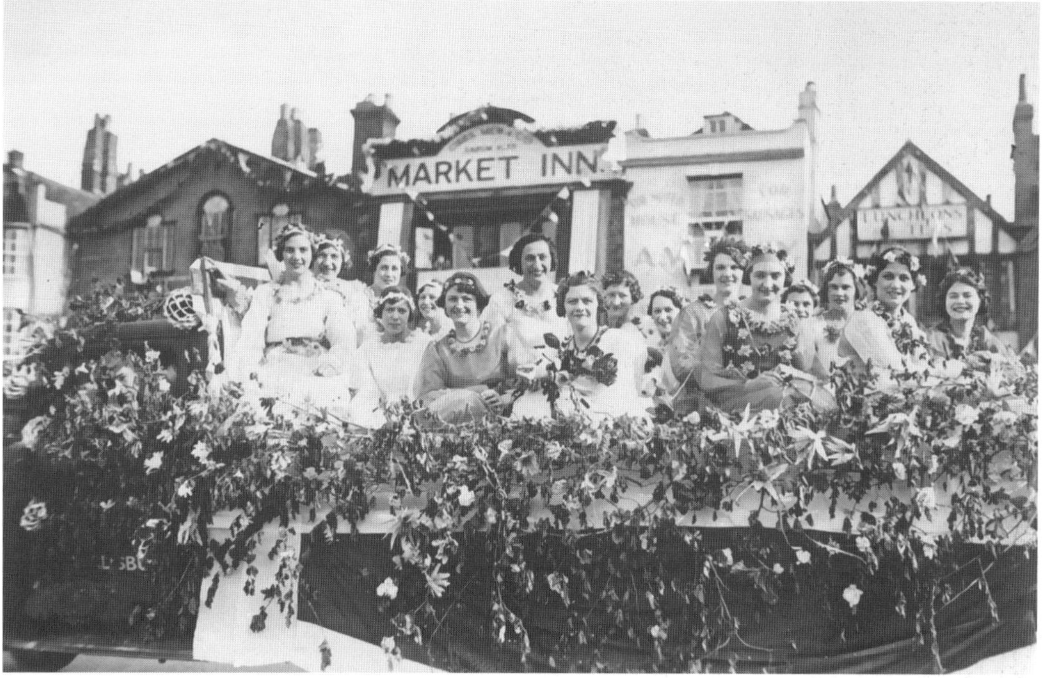

The Flower Girls' Jubilee Carnival Float in Market Place, 1935
The Market Inn and other buildings along Ox Row appear to be adorned with red, white and blue decorations, forming a colourful backdrop to this photograph of the flower girls. Joyce and Mary Bridle can just be seen peeping through from the back of the group. The girls are seated on the back of a lorry loaned by James Dolman, builder, of St Ann Street.

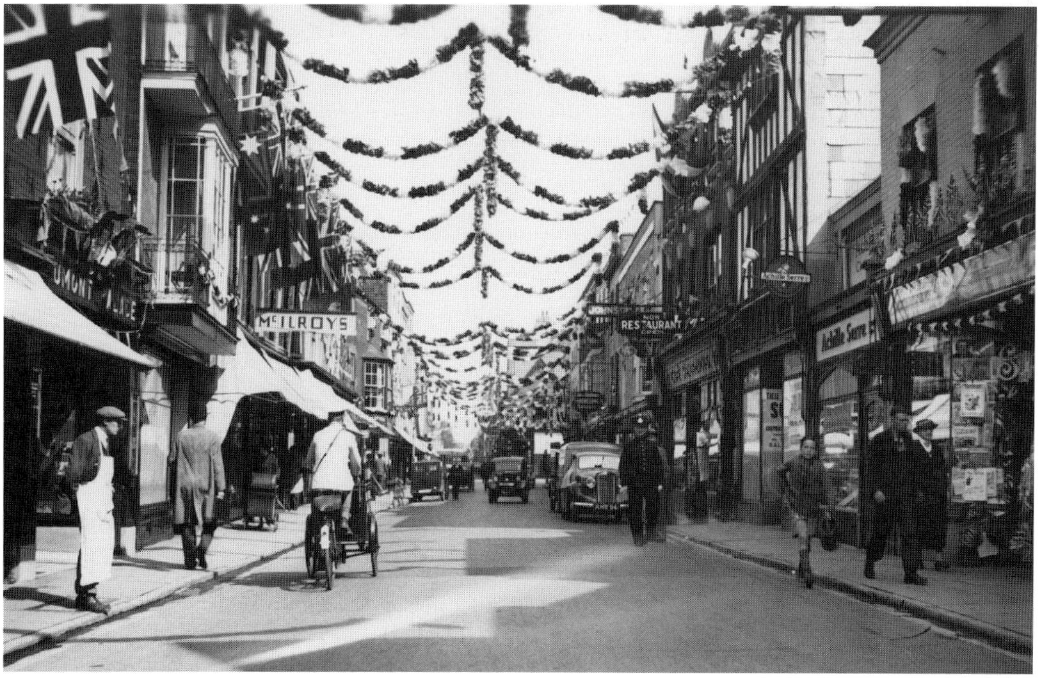

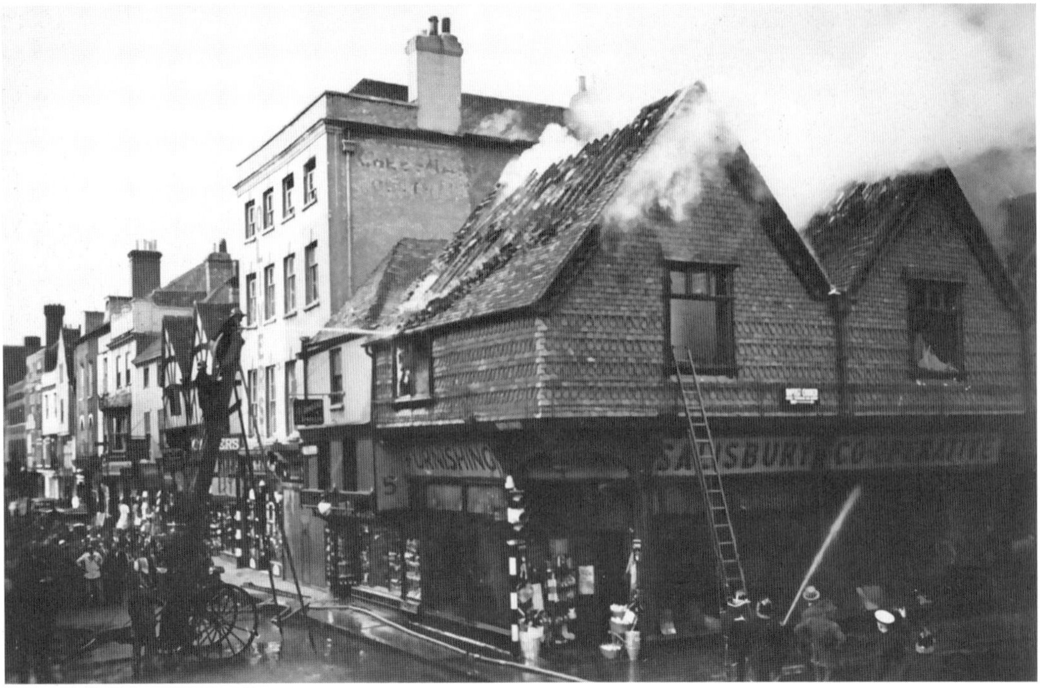

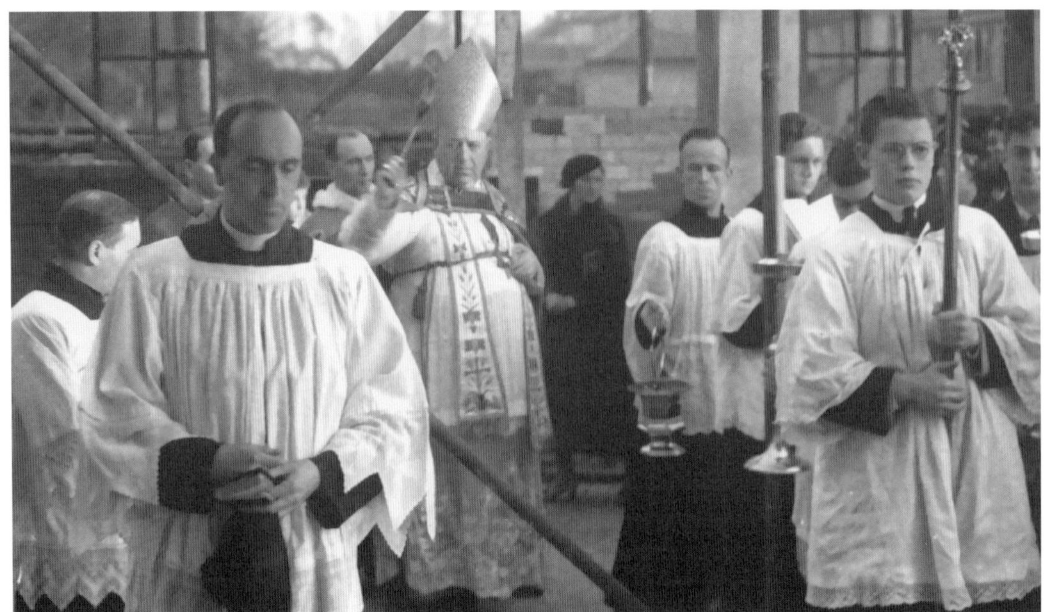

Fire Destroys Co-Operative Furnishing Store, 1937

A fire broke out at the Co-operative furnishing store on Monday 13 September 1937. Having received an emergency call, the Salisbury Volunteer Fire Brigade responded immediately and dispatched two motor fire engines that arrived at the incident within minutes, but despite the best efforts of the firemen, the Tudor building that had been externally refaced late in the nineteenth century could not be saved. Damage to the furnishing store and two neighbouring properties, Constad's Jewellers in Queen Street and Cathedral Hotel in Milford Street, was estimated to be around £15,000 pounds.

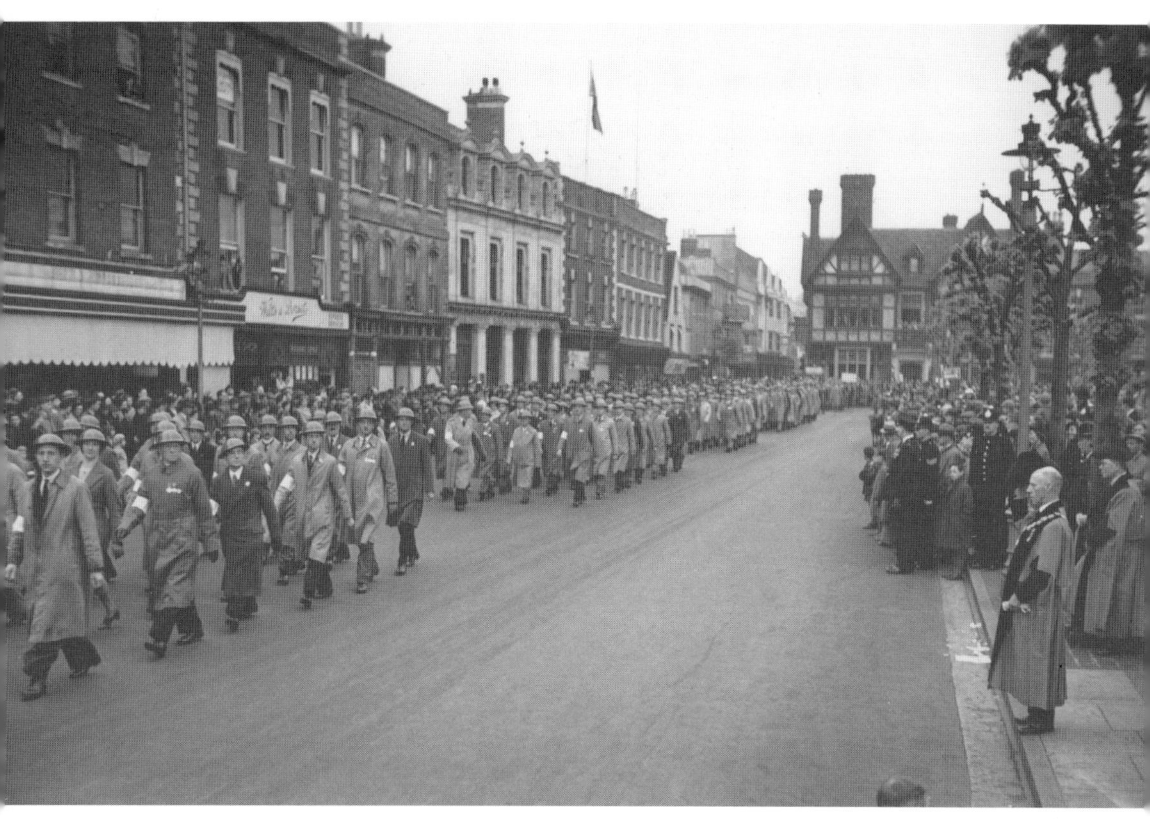

National Service Parade in Market Place, 1939
The Mayor of Salisbury, Councillor William C. Bridge, comes into view on the right of the picture, where he can be seen doffing his hat while ranks of civil defence volunteers march along Blue Boar Row. Having taken place on Sunday 14 May 1939, the event was attended by members of Salisbury Volunteer Fire Brigade, Auxiliary Fire Service, Special Constables, Wiltshire Police, First Aid Services, Air Raid Wardens, Decontamination Squads, Royal Navy, Royal Air Force, 4th Wilts Territorial Army, Sea Cadets, Boy Scouts and Girl Guides, and others. Following demonstrations of Civil Defence equipment in Market Place, around 1,500 individuals marched to the cathedral to attend a service – it was one of the largest parades Salisbury had ever seen.

Dedication of the Foundation Stone at St Gregory's Church, 1937
Opposite bottom: The Roman Catholic Church of St Gregory and the English Martyrs was opened by the Bishop of Clifton, Dr William Lee, on Wednesday 22 June 1938, following a stone laying ceremony the previous autumn. The church had been designed in a modernized Romanesque style by J. H. Williams, architects, of Taunton, featuring red bricks with stone dressings to harmonize with other buildings in the neighbourhood. Messrs Wort & Way, of Salisbury, were the contractors.

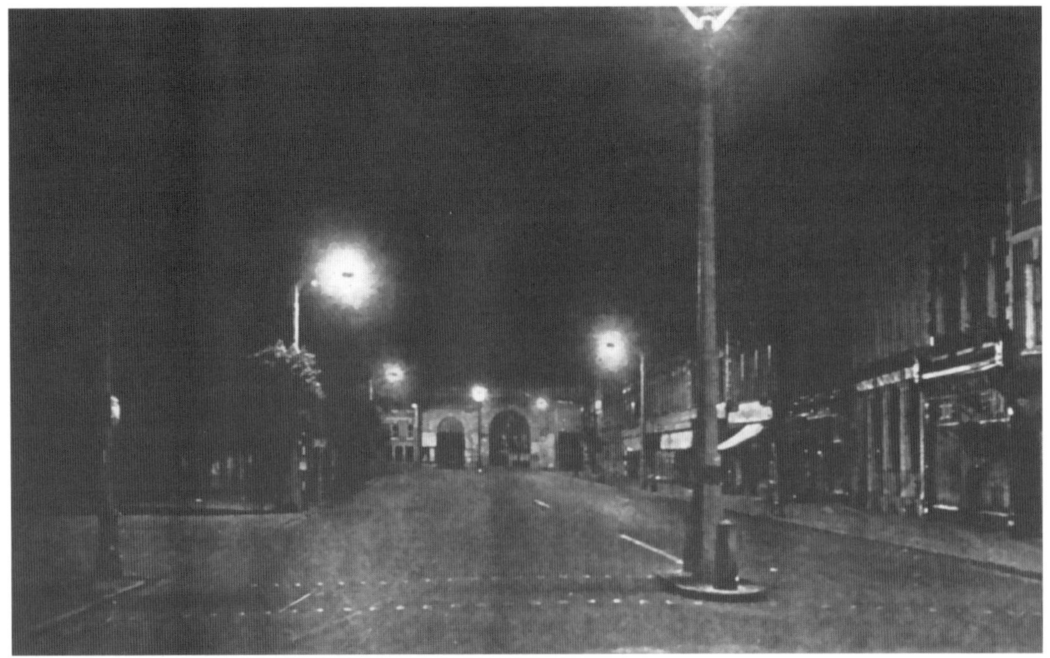

Sodium Electric Street Lighting Installed in the City, 1939

The question of removing the old gas lights and improving the public lighting in Salisbury was brought under review in 1937. The city engineer, S. R. Little, in consultation with the Salisbury Electric Light & Supply Co. Ltd, published a report and a new lighting scheme was adopted by the council. In this night photograph of Blue Boar Row can be seen the new concrete columns with Holophane Prismatic Panel Lanterns fitted with 140 Watt sodium lamps. The new public electric lighting was inaugurated by the mayor, Councillor William C. Bridge, at 8 p.m. on 25 August 1939.

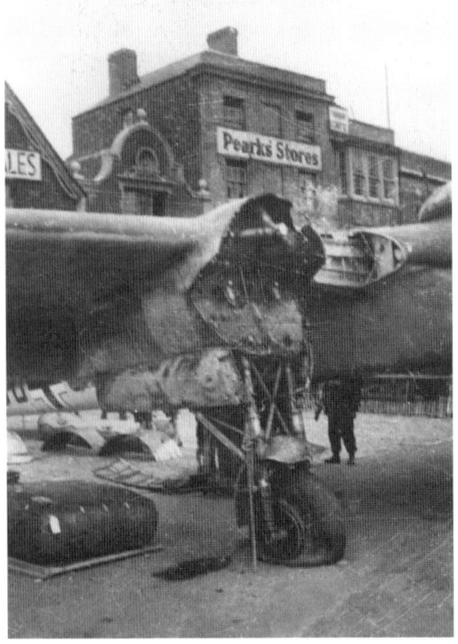

German Bombers Displayed in Market Place, 1940

As a means of promoting the South Wilts Spitfire Fund, and much to the astonishment of local sightseers, the RAF displayed a Luftwaffe Dornier 17 and a large section of a Heinkel in Salisbury market square. The Dornier was the same type of aircraft that targeted Buckingham Palace with a stick of five high-explosive bombs the week before. It was ironic that both German aircraft had been brought down by a Spitfire, and the number of bullet holes that could be seen on the wreckage was a clear indication of the skill of the Spitfire pilots.

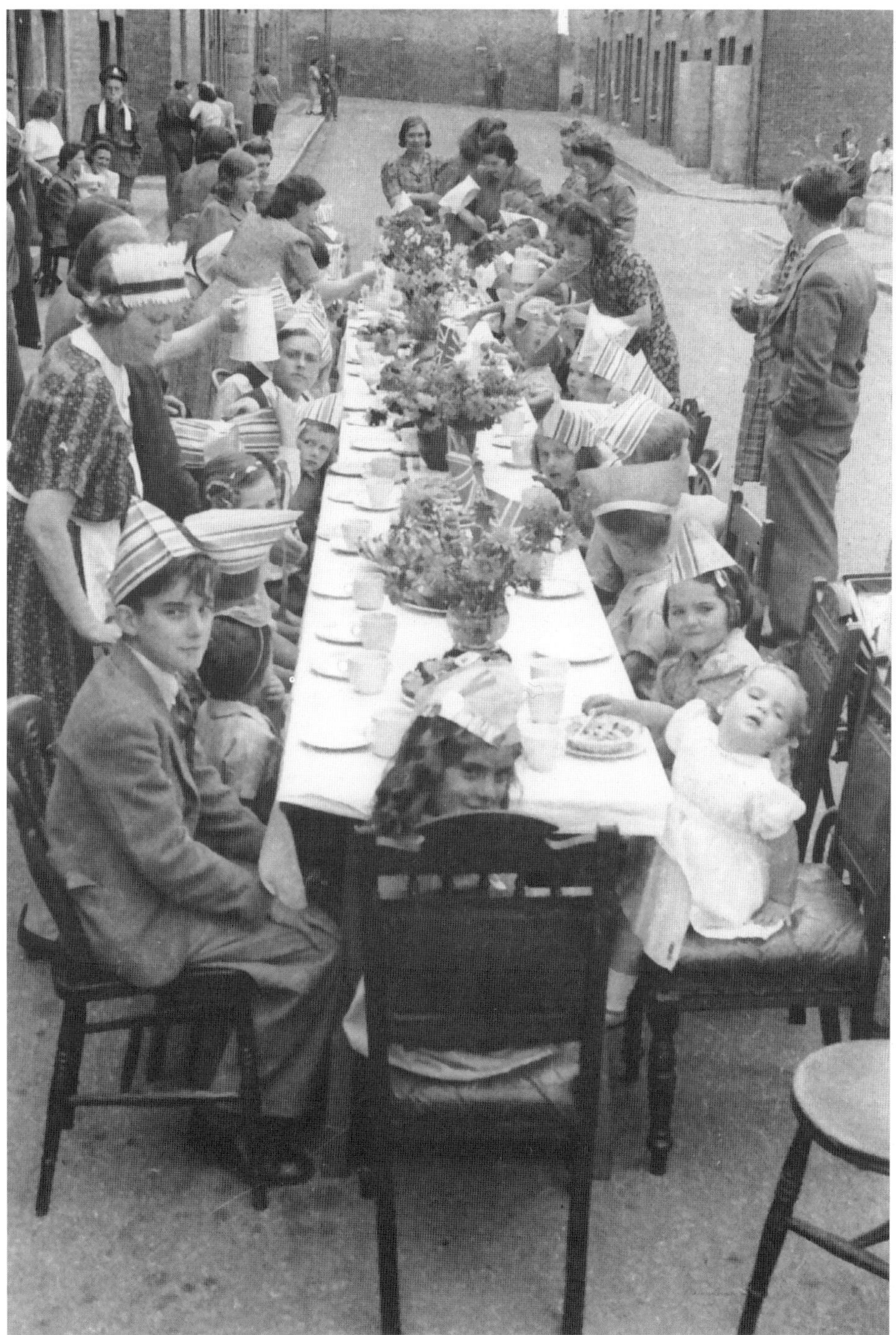

Sidney Street Children's Tea Party, 8 May 1945
The VE Day celebrations in the Meadow Road, Sidney Street and York Road area were very well organised and one of the liveliest events in the city. At E. Rigiani & Son's (Coca Cola concessionaires and ice merchants) shop at 50 Meadow Road free ice creams were given to the children.

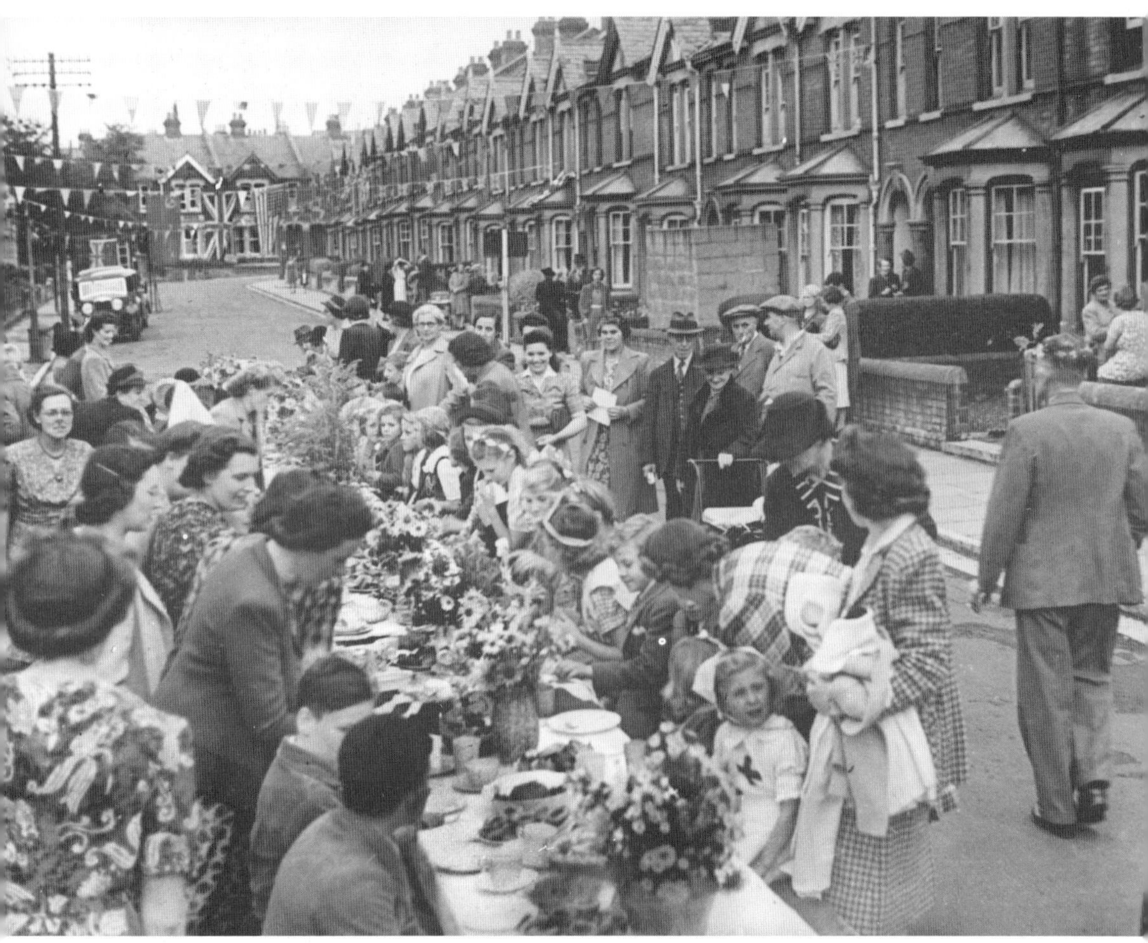

Albany Road V. E. Day Celebrations, Tuesday 8 May 1945
On VE Day church bells rang out all around Salisbury and there was dancing in the streets. The city exploded with joy as the people welcomed the news that the war with Germany had finally come to an end. Red, white and blue flags appeared everywhere, and the celebrations took many forms. Here we can see the celebrations in Albany Road, where the children were just about to start their party. There is a fine selection of sandwiches, biscuits, cakes and soft drinks for them to enjoy. Multicoloured pennants were strung across the street and some large Union flags were draped over the front of some houses. But even among all this colour, there were still a few reminders of darker days. On the right side of the photograph we can see a concrete block blast wall protecting the entrance of 'Belmont', No. 22 Albany Road, which at that time was the home of Joseph Bache.

Mayor Opens the Local Festival of Britain Celebrations, 1951
Opposite bottom: This was the scene on the steps of the west door of the cathedral on Sunday 3 June when the mayor, Councillor Sidney Chalke, officially opened the Salisbury Festival of the Arts. The festival was the city's contribution to the Festival of Britain. The council brightened up the city with rockeries and flower beds, the Guildhall was illuminated at night and between 10 p.m. and midnight the cathedral spire was floodlit. The event, organised by Salisbury and District Society of Arts, was to run for fourteen days, ending on 17 June.

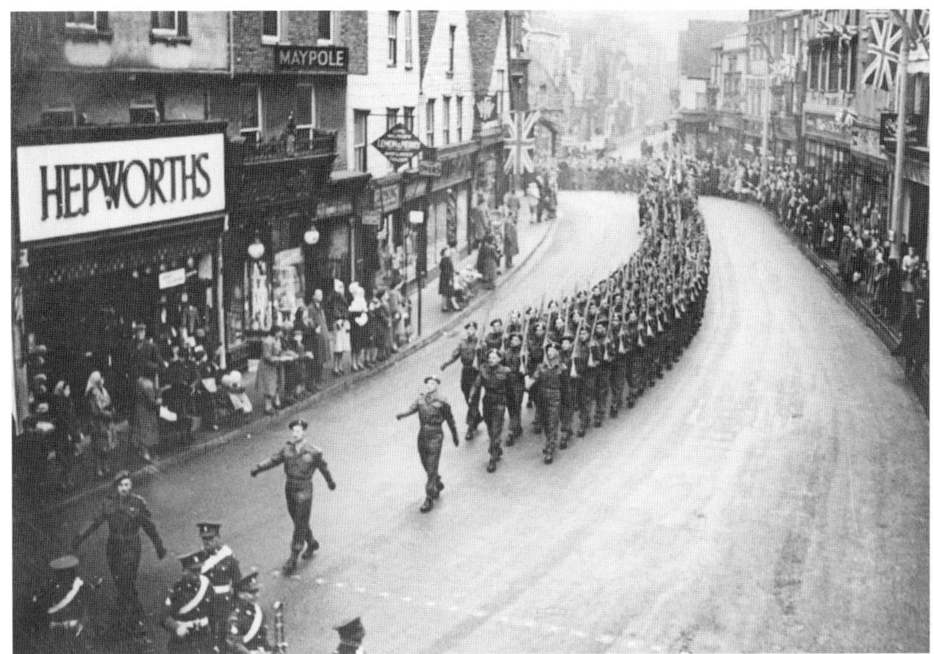

Honouring the Wiltshire Regiment, December 1947
On Wednesday 3 December, the Wiltshire Regiment marched through the streets of Salisbury with colours flying, drums beating, bands playing and bayonets fixed following a ceremony in Market Place where the mayor, Councillor Roland G. Gordon, presented the Regiment with the Freedom of the City of Salisbury. Some of the troops are pictured here in Silver Street as they march around the city streets before being entertained to high tea at the British Restaurant in Rollestone Street.

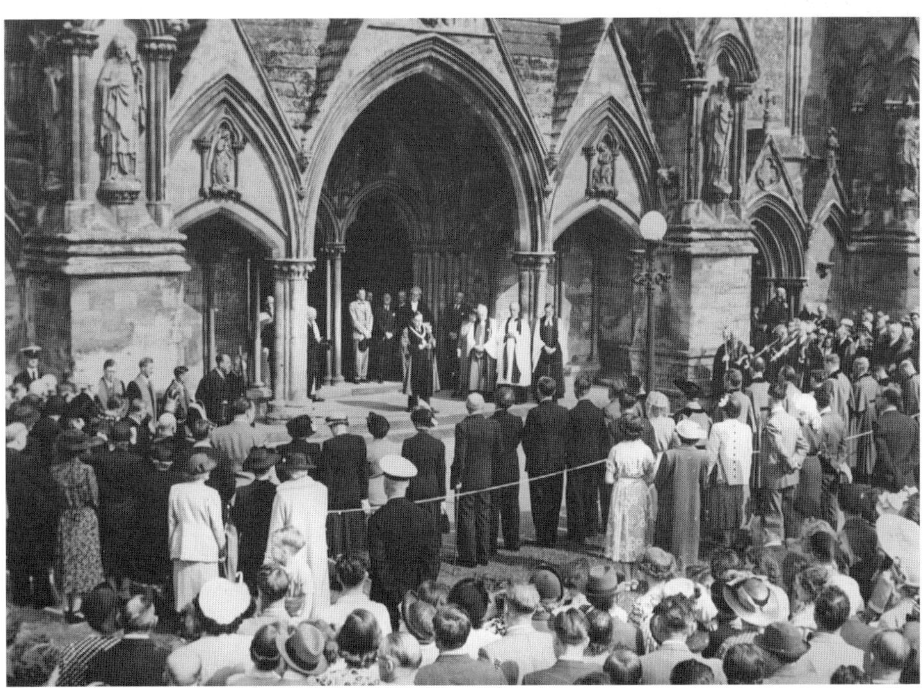

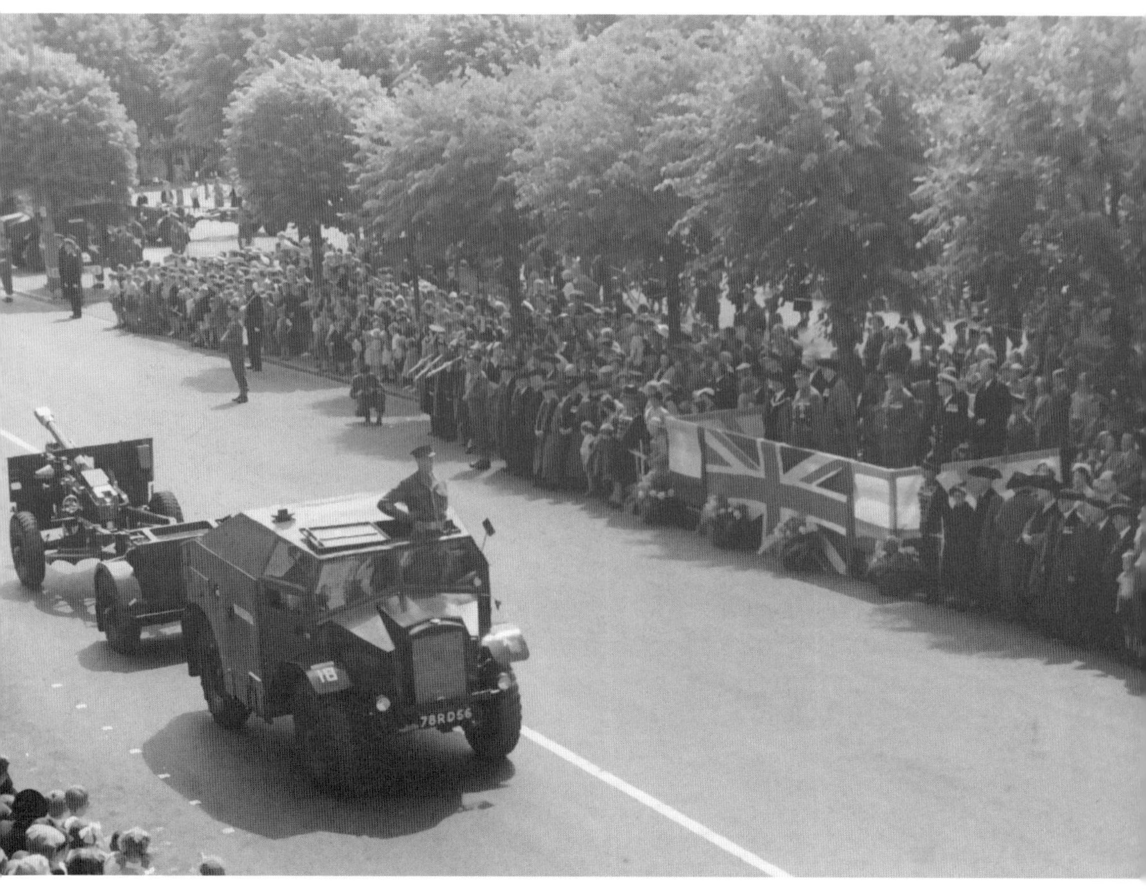

King's Birthday Parade in Blue Boar Row, 1952

On Thursday 5 June, on the occasion of the king's birthday, a large crowd gathered in Market Place to enjoy the spectacle of a military parade and march past. Here we see a Morris Commercial Q8 field artillery tractor with gun and limber passing the saluting base, which was occupied by a small number of VIPs, including the Mayor of Salisbury, Councillor George Whatley, and Commanding Officer of 6th Armoured Division, Major General G. E. Prior Palmer. There were about fifty vehicles of all descriptions involved in the parade, these were from 5 Royal Horse Artillery, the 2nd, 6th and 8th Royal Tank Regiment, the 27th Field Engineer Regiment, the Royal Signals, 2nd King's Royal Rifle Corps, and the Royal Electrical and Mechanical Engineers. On parade in the market square were 600 infantrymen from the 1st Battalion of the King's Own Royal Regiment and the Duke of Cornwall's Light Infantry, Bulford, and the Duke of Wellington's Regiment, Chiseldon. Schoolchildren were not given the usual holiday but it was arranged for 700 pupils from local schools to attend the event. A special enclosure was provided for them.

Coronation Decorations in Winchester Street, June 1953

Opposite bottom: In publicity material published by Salisbury City Council at the time, it states that the ancient city has never looked more attractive and beautiful than on the occasion of the Coronation of Elizabeth II. The businesses in Winchester Street helped fund the spectacular decorations pictured here. The vertical banners hung on each side of the street were described as bannerettes, screen-printed by Maidment's Publicity. The clock that can just be seen on the Co-operative Society building on the left of the photograph was removed when the Co-op shop closed – a branch of McDonald's opened there in December 1988.

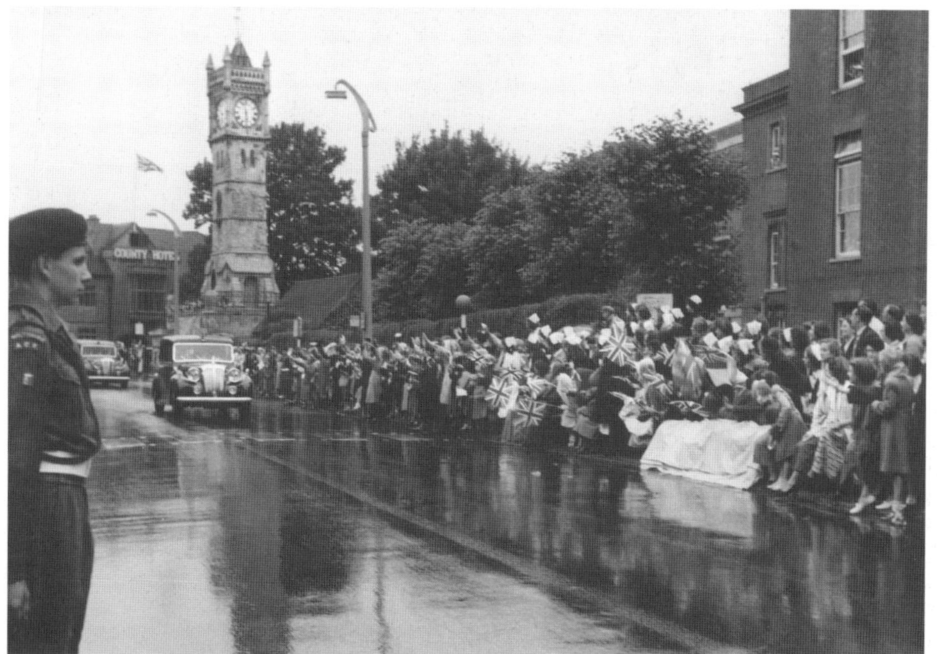

The Queen's Visit to Salisbury, 3 July 1952
The rain seems to have done little to dampen the spirits of the enthusiastic crowd of sightseers pictured here outside Salisbury General Infirmary where they hoped to get a wave from the queen as she is driven by in a royal Daimler. Before boarding the royal train, the queen shook hands with the Mayor of Salisbury, Councillor George Whatley; his wife, Mrs Whatley; and the Town Clerk, George Richardson. She expressed her gratitude for the warmth of her welcome, and also inquired about the families who suffered in the air disaster at Bemerton Heath the previous day (2 July 1952).

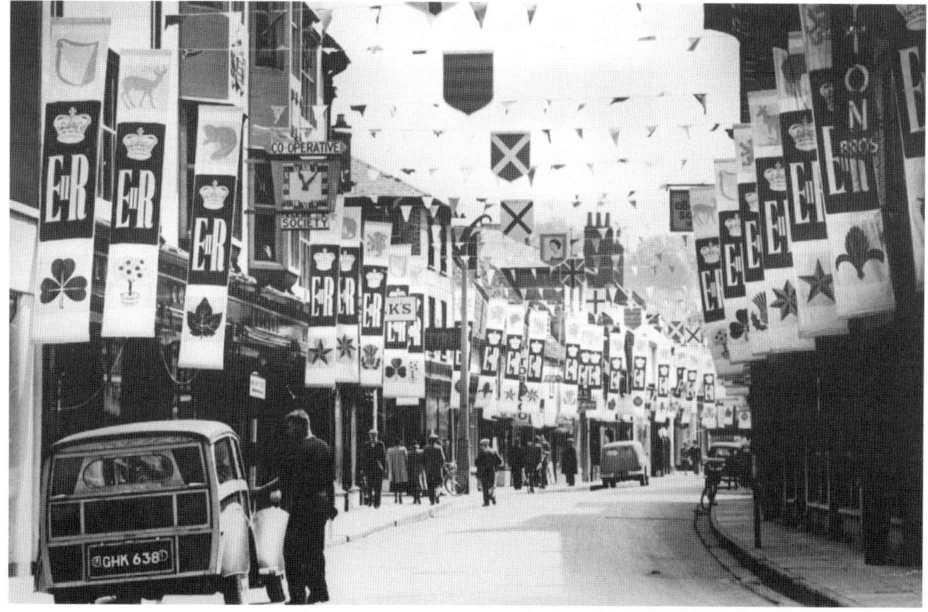

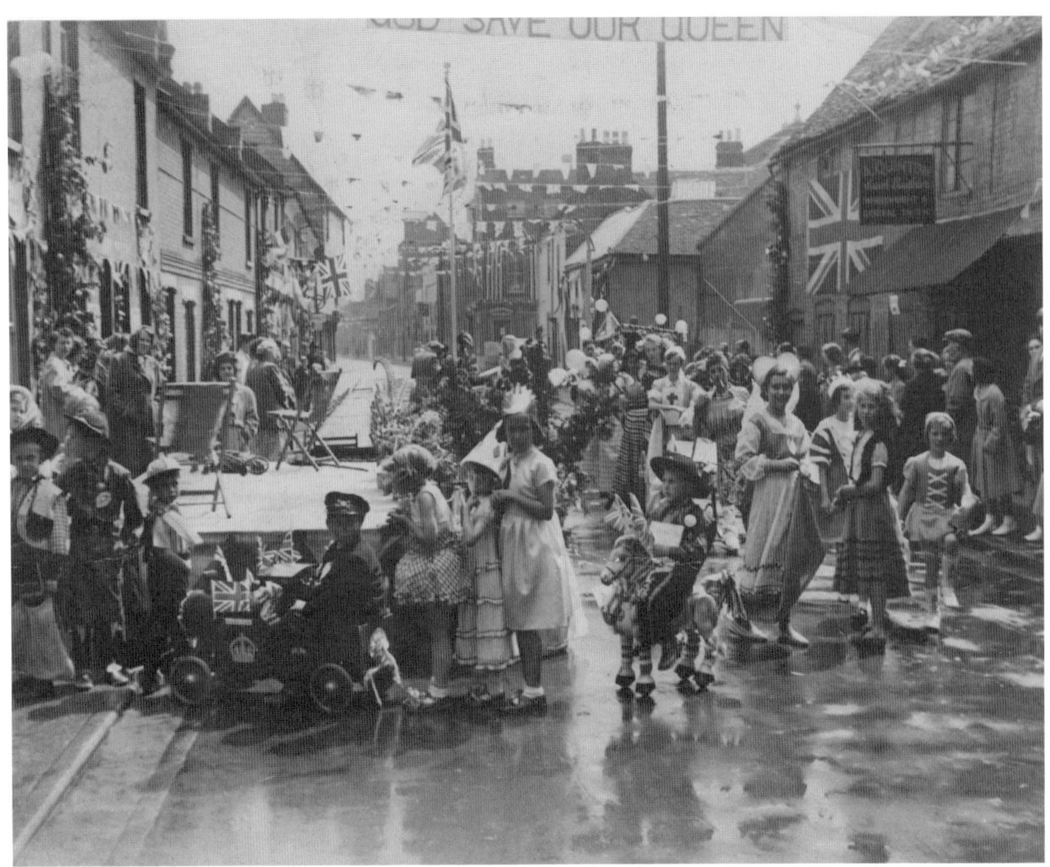

Coronation Party in Pennyfarthing Street, 2 June 1953

The Mayor of Salisbury, Councillor H. J. Annetts, said, 'I cordially invite my fellow citizens, men, women and children to a worthy and appropriate celebration of Coronation Day on Tuesday, June 2nd.' Street parties were arranged around the city, including Bedwin Street, The Greencroft, Hill View Road, Kingsland Road, Milford Street, North Street, Nursery Road, St Mark's Road, St Paul's Road, Salt Lane, Wain-a-Long Road, Waters Road, Wiltshire Road, Winding Way, Woodside Road and more. Here we see some of the partygoers in Pennyfarthing Street where a makeshift stage seems to have been set up (for live musical entertainment no doubt). A large union flag was displayed on the front of A. Quinton coach builders' workshop. Many of the houses in the street were adorned with red, white and blue decorations. This particular party was organised by Dennis G. Stainer.

Chapter 4
From Above

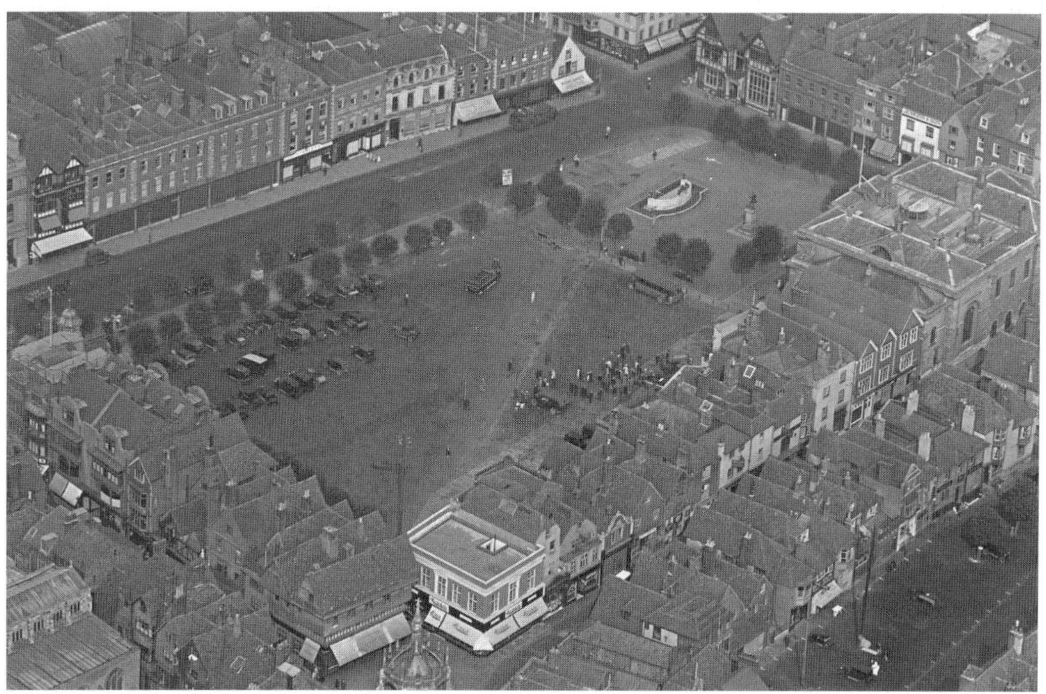

The Market Place, Mid-1930s
In the upper right corner of the image is the area of Market Place that is now known as Guildhall Square, within which can be seen the war memorial, and also the statue of Sidney Herbert that was removed to Victoria Park on 12 May 1953. The trees planted around the market place by Mayor Fred Griffin on the occasion of Queen Victoria's Golden Jubilee in 1885 have grown considerably in the intervening years. Blue Boar Row comes into view in the upper part of the picture, and Poultry Cross is at the bottom.

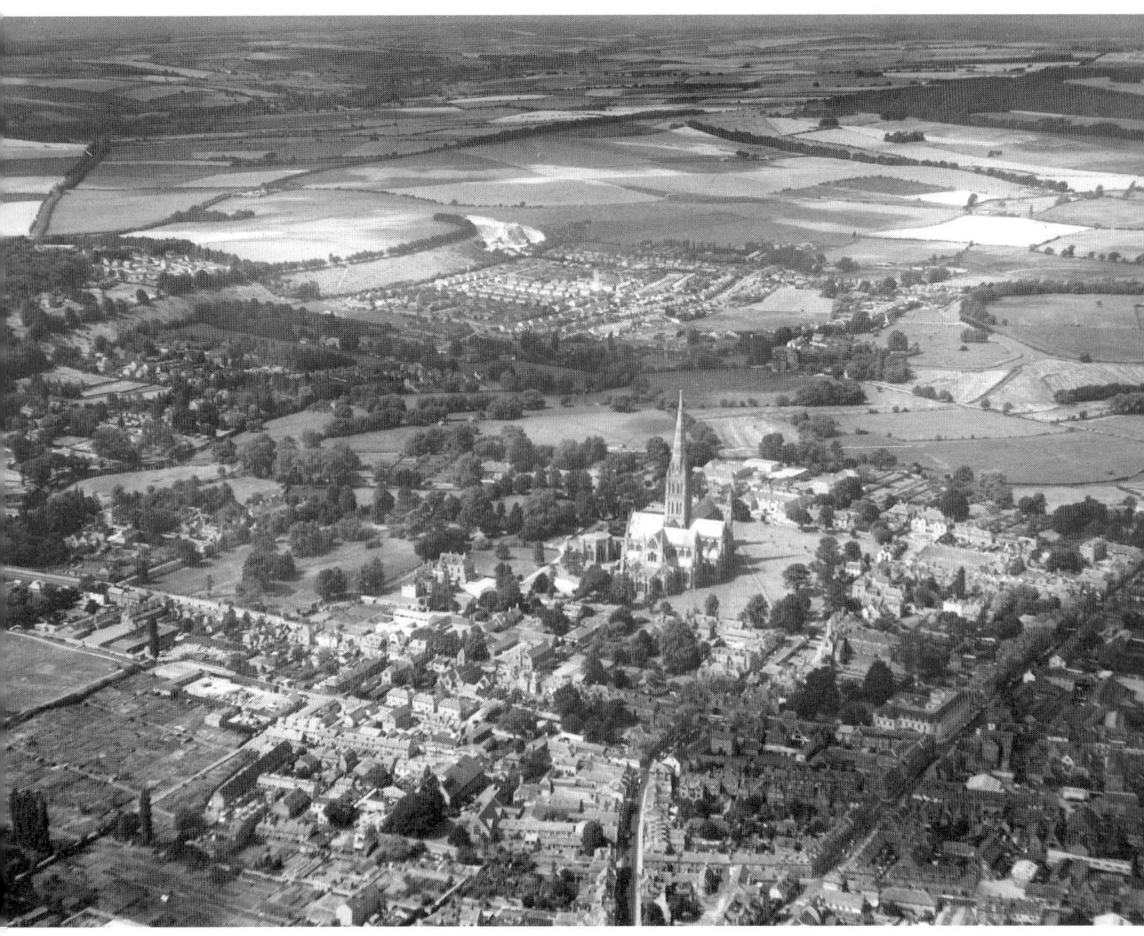

A View of Salisbury from the North East, 1950s

St Ann Street can easily be seen at the bottom of the photograph, to the left of which is an area then known as Bugmore, which was purchased by Salisbury City Council in 1874 as a suitable location for the construction of a sewage processing facility and garden allotments. The Friary Housing Estate now occupies the site. Coming into view in the distance, to the south-west of Salisbury Cathedral, is Harnham chalk pit, and also the post-war council housing estate at West Harnham.

British Telecom Depot, Lower Road, Salisbury, 1989

Opposite bottom: Formerly the Scout Motor Works built for Messrs Dean and Burden Brothers in 1906/7. Agricultural and marine engines were manufactured here, and also cars and commercial vehicles, until June 1921. In August 2000, soon after the old buildings had been demolished, a branch of Sydenhams Ltd, building material suppliers, opened on the site. The photograph was taken by Peter Daniels from the top of a 100-foot turntable ladder kindly provided by Wiltshire Fire Service. It is unlikely that such a favour would to be granted today due to health and safety issues.

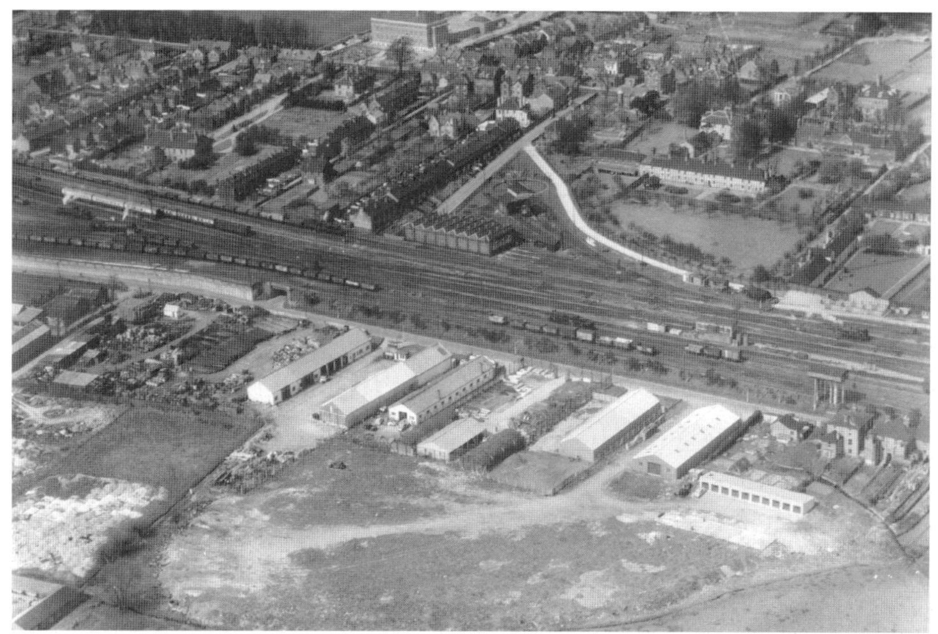

The West End, Wilton Road and Churchfields, Late 1950s

The photograph can be dated to around 1957 because the newly built headquarters of the Wiltshire County Constabulary in Wilton Road comes into view on the very top edge of the picture – it opened in 1956. On the east side of Ashfield Road, a railway turntable can be seen, and three steam locomotives and numerous goods wagons are clearly visible on the railway tracks. Development of the Churchfield's Road Industrial Estate had not yet begun, with just a few sheds by the side of the road, occupied at that time by SCATS, agricultural engineers; William Didden, builders; G. Bickham, sheet metal works; W. Gamblin, road transport contractors; V. W. Pointing, coach builders; W. G. Keen, scrap merchants; and Anglo American Asphalt.

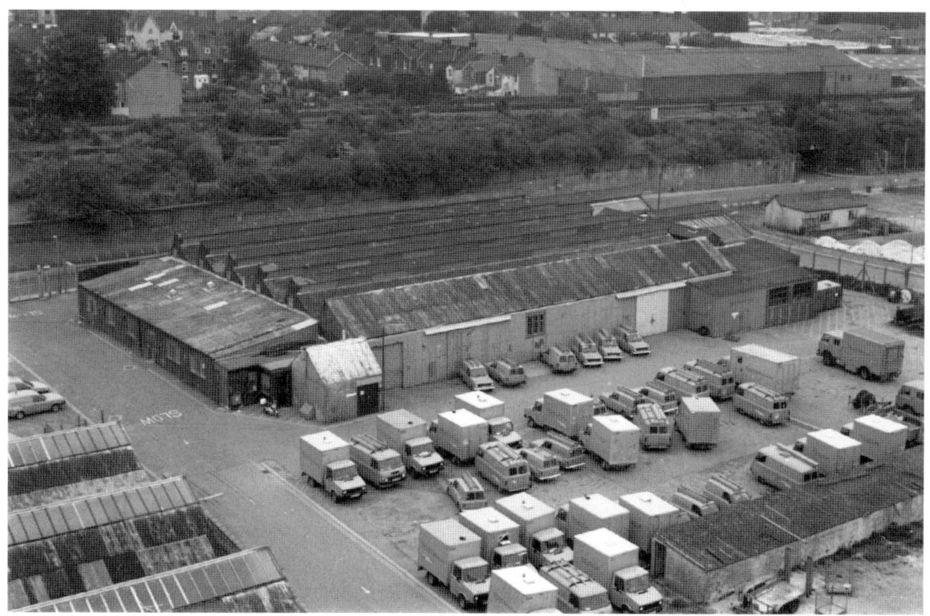

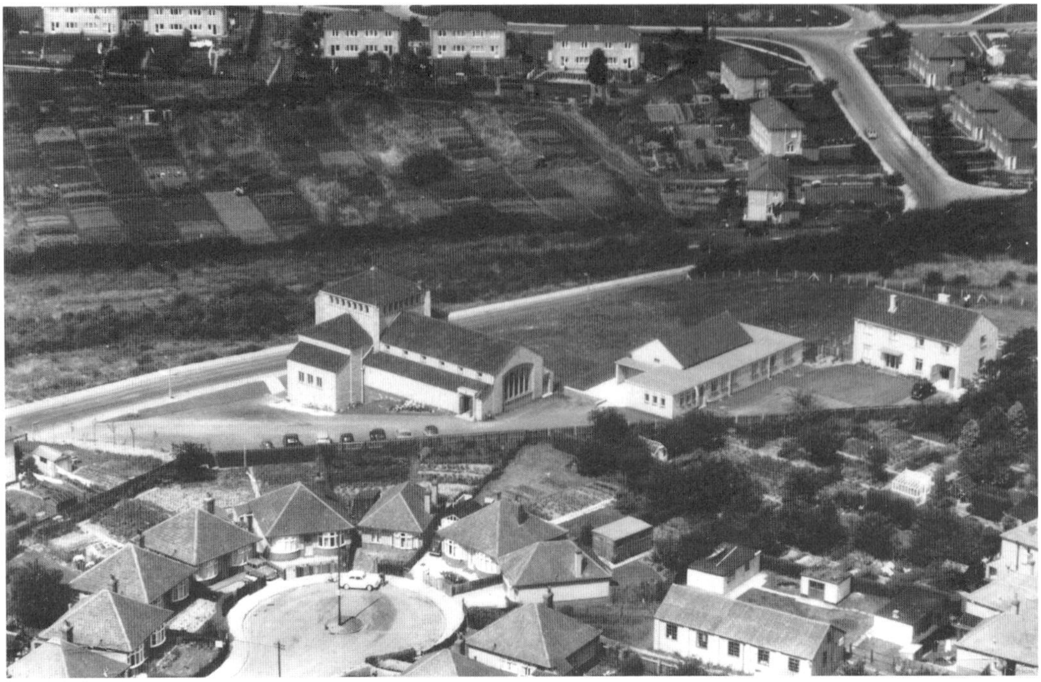

St Michael's Church and Surrounding Area, *c.* 1960
The foundation stone of St Michael and All Angels' church was laid by the Earl of Pembroke in April
1956. In the upper part of the picture we can see the newly built houses in St Michael's Road and
Woodside Road, and at the bottom, the distinctive layout of the bungalows at the end of Queen Mary
Road.

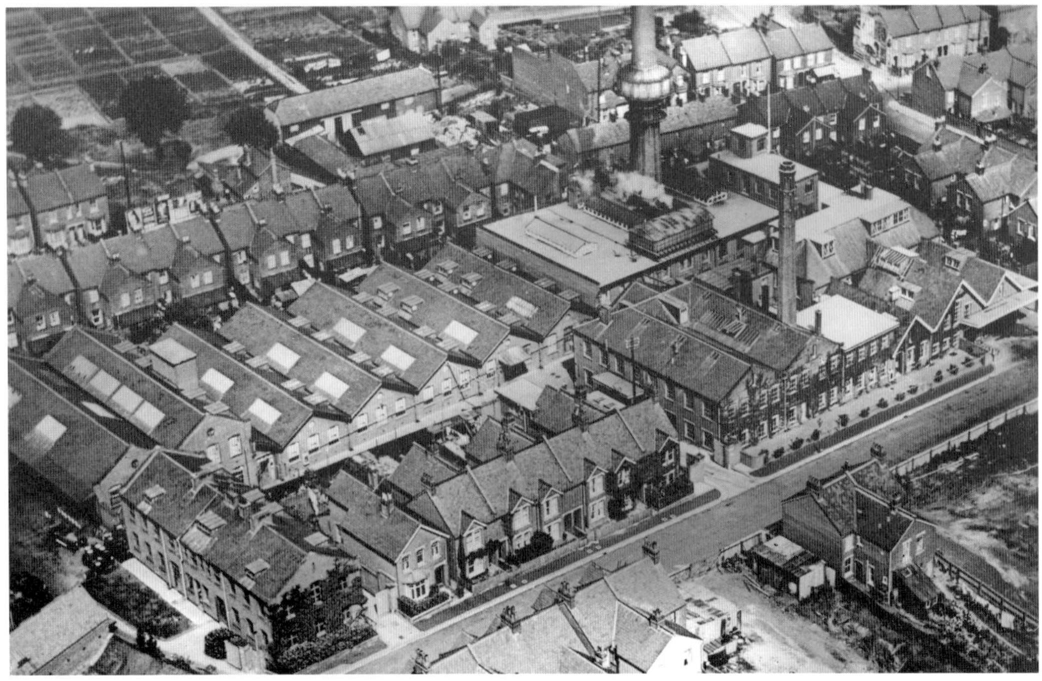

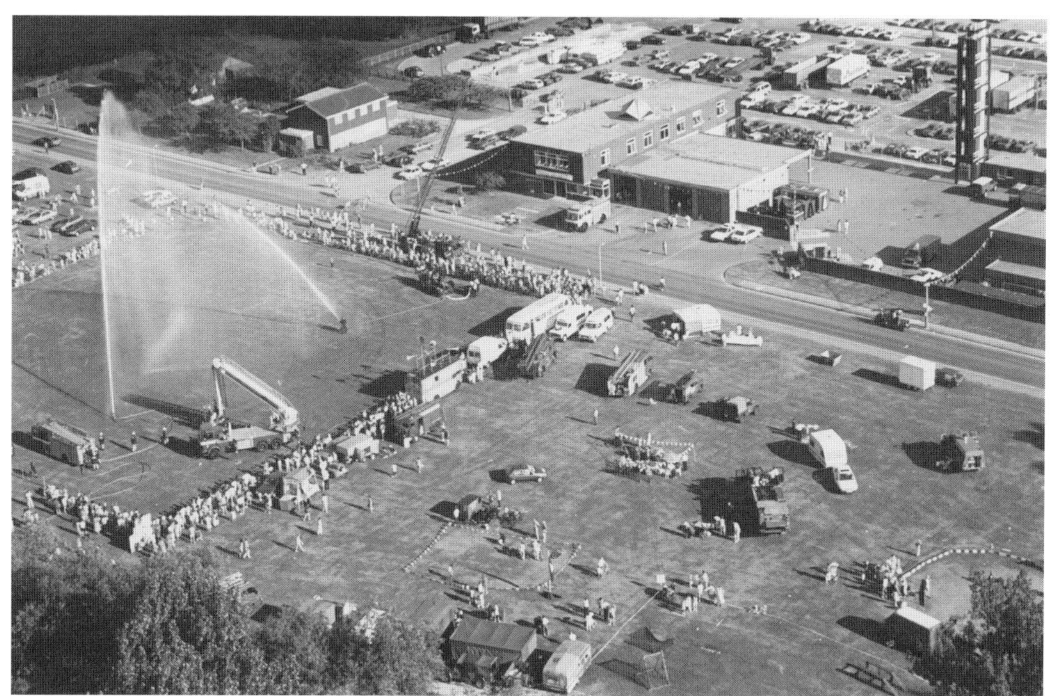

Salisbury Five Station and Ashfield Road, 1991

Much to the delight of everyone involved, 'Water Fun Day' took place in the fields opposite the fire station on Saturday 7 September 1991. The author Peter Daniels took this particular photograph from a helicopter when water pumping demonstrations were being performed below by Wiltshire Fire Service – we can clearly see water jets shooting high into the air. In the upper right corner of the picture, the fire station training tower comes into view, and also many cars parked on the former site of Salisbury Cattle Market on which a Waitrose supermarket later appeared.

Fussell's Condensed Milk Factory, 1924

Opposite bottom: Russell Road can be seen in the lower part of the photograph, with the factory's milk receiving bay coming into view to the right, with canopy above. The tall industrial chimney with water tank attached was a familiar site on the Salisbury skyline for very many years but it was not generally known that there were originally two chimneys in use at the factory. In 1927, or thereabouts, the Nestlé and Anglo-Swiss Condensed Milk Co. acquired the Fussell business along with the Russell Road factory.

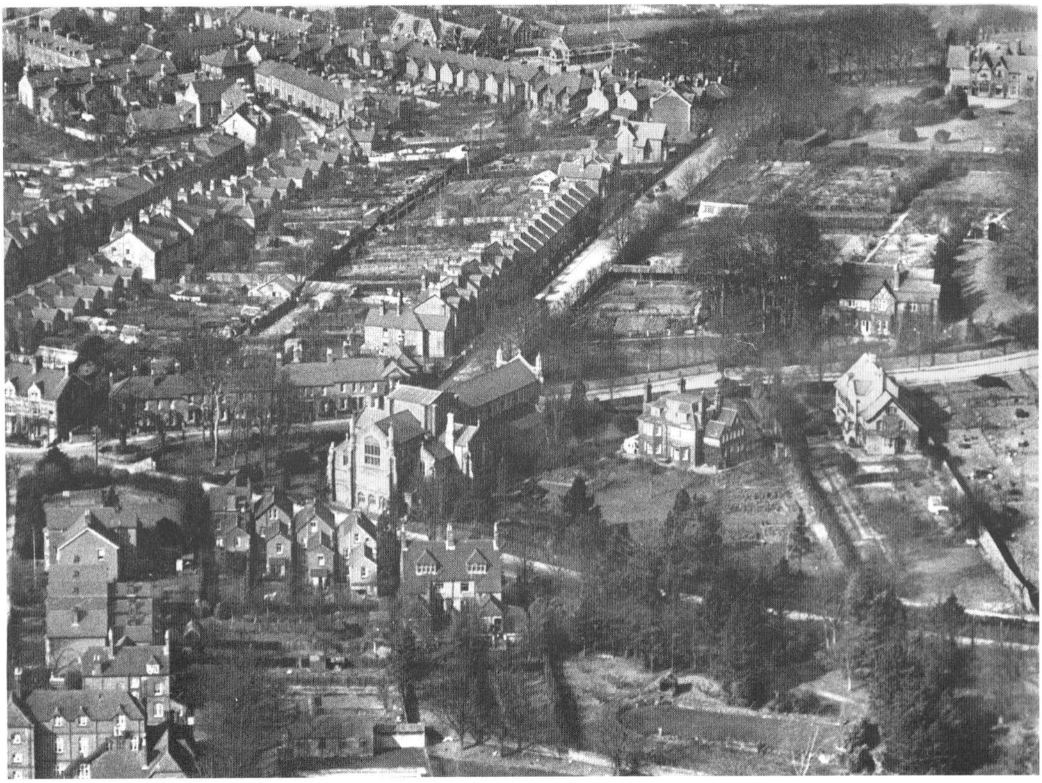

Saint Mark's Church and Weeping Cross, 1930s
Probably dating from the early 1930s, the photograph was taken by an RAF chaplain serving
at Old Sarum. His creation shows St Mark's church and vicarage in the centre; and to the left,
Weeping Cross (called Whipping Cross in earlier times) and the different layout of the roads at
that time. We can see that the Churchill Way relief road swallowed up quite a few of the gardens
behind the houses in St Mark's Road and Wyndham Road.

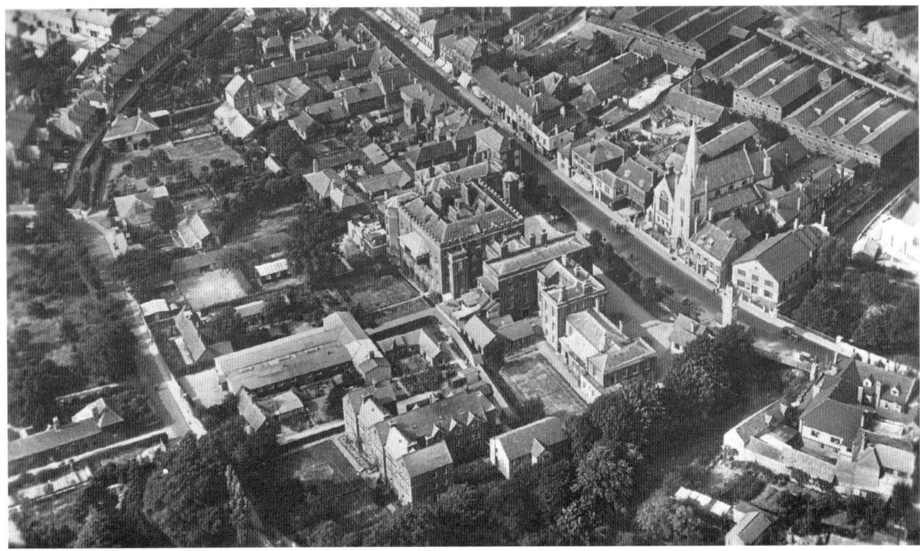

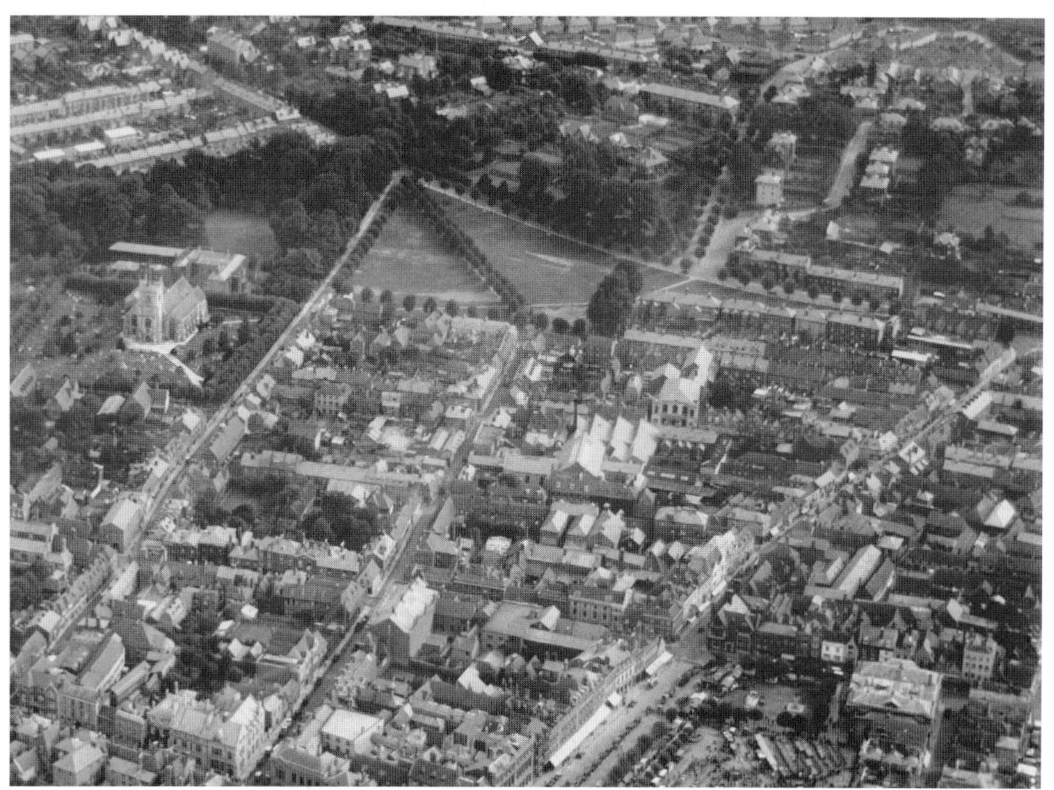

St Edmund's Church, Greencroft and Winchester Street, 1926
A fascinating image that clearly shows the mediaeval chequered layout of the city of Salisbury. Looking at Bedwin Street and Bourne Hill to left of the photograph leads us to St Edmund's church and the former St Edmund's College that became the Salisbury Council offices on 29 June 1927. Bourne Hill, Greencroft, London Road and Kelsey Road can be seen at the top of the picture. Winchester Street is on the right, which opens out into Market Place in the lower right corner.

Salisbury General Infirmary and Congregational Church, 1947
Opposite bottom: Coming into view in the top right corner of the picture is Maundrel Hall, Princess Christian Hostel, the Congregational church, and the former malthouses of Samuel Thompson & Sons Ltd, after which the Maltings Shopping Centre was named. In the centre of the photograph can be seen Salisbury General Infirmary and Victoria Nurses Home, which were vacated in January 1993 before the area was tastefully redeveloped for residential purposes. Crane Bridge Road is to the left.

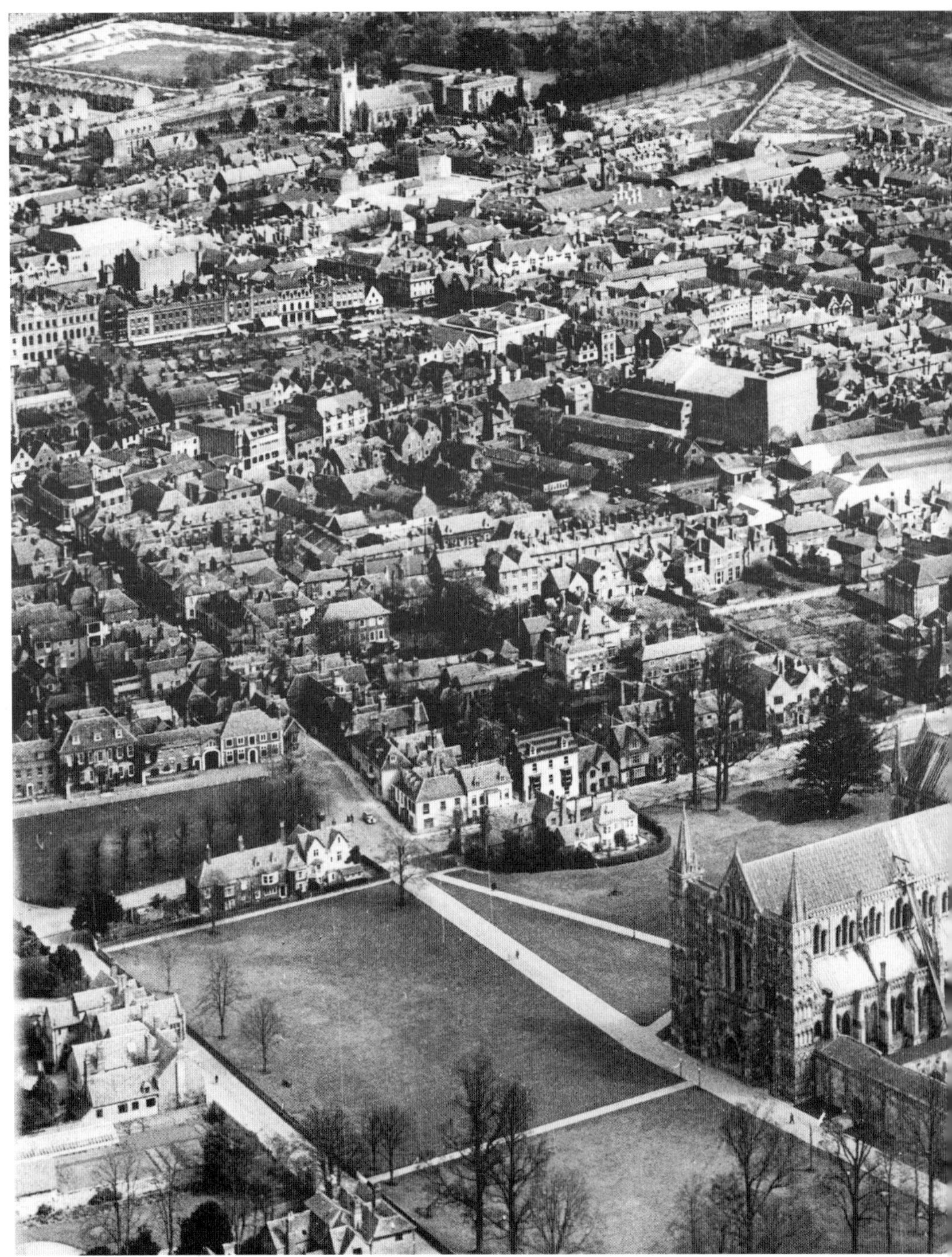

The Cathedral and Medieval City of Salisbury, 1937
The cathedral provides an ideal platform from which to take photographs of this historic city. A few examples have been reproduced on the next few pages.

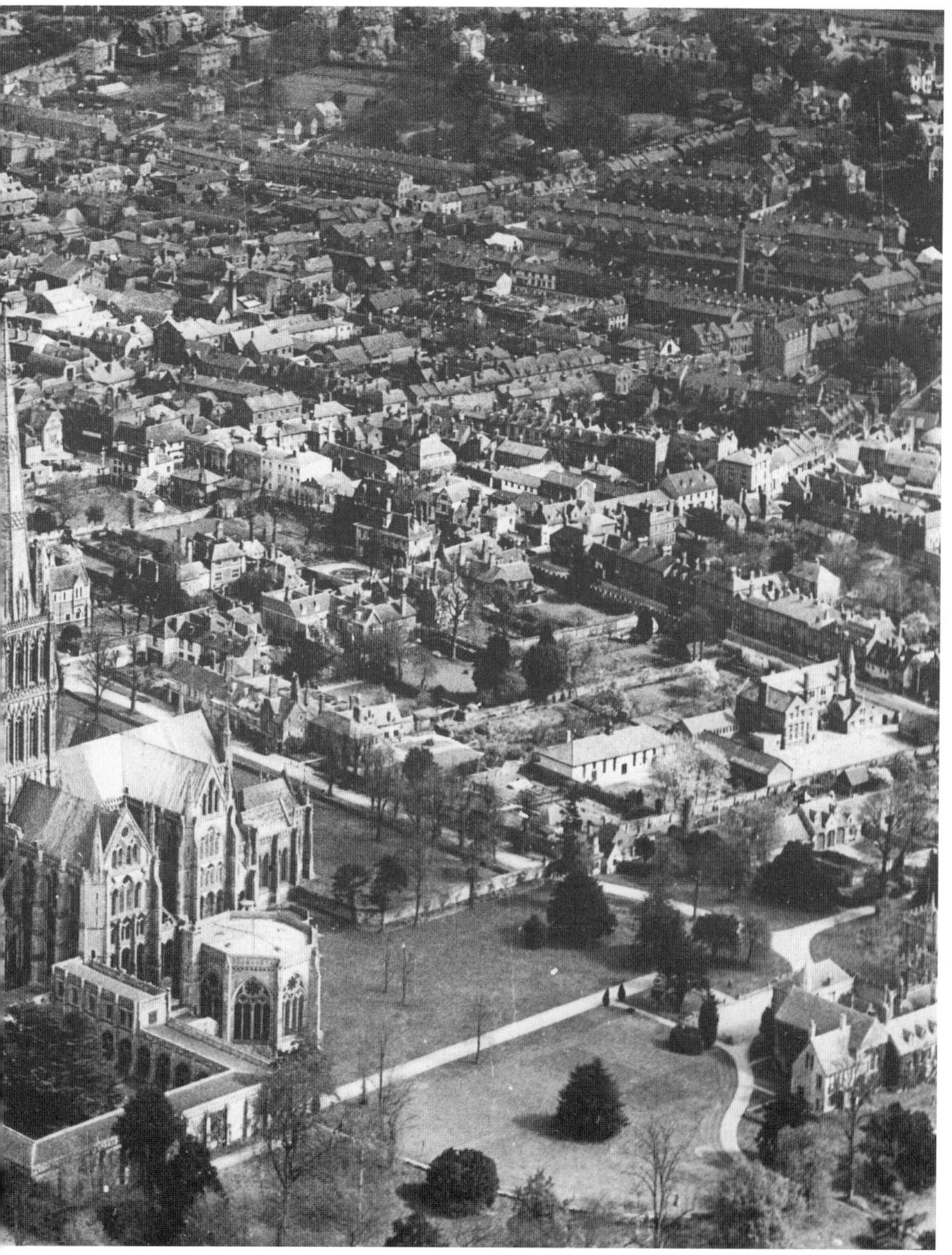

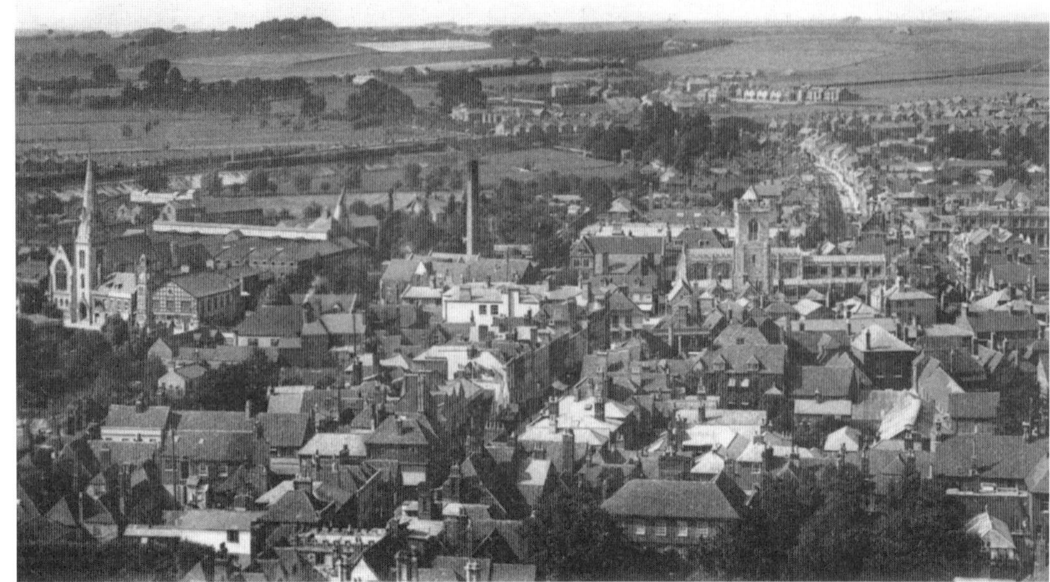

A General View of the City From the Cathedral Spire, 1903
The much smaller spire of the Congregational church in Fisherton Street can be seen on the left, and just to the right of centre, the church of St Thomas. On the right, Castle Street curves round and points in the direction of Old Sarum that stands on horizon.

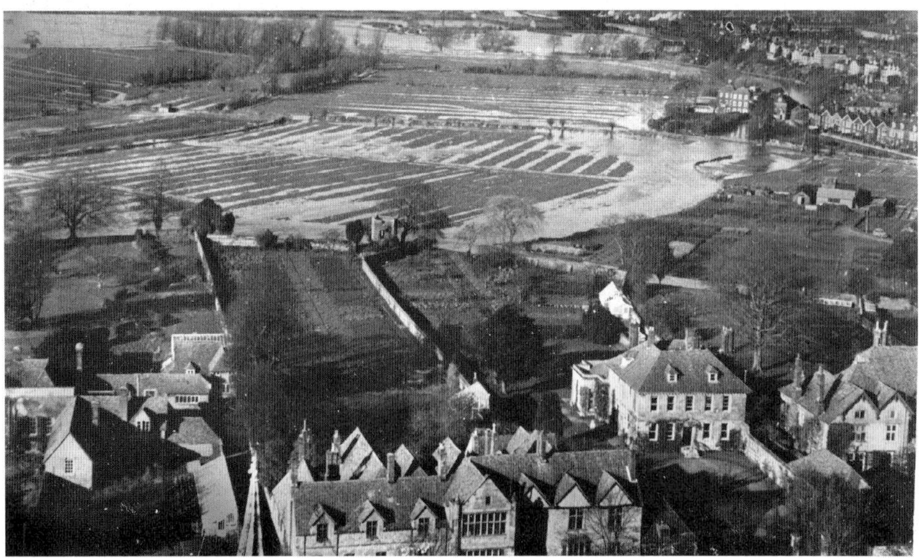

Looking West From the Base of the Cathedral Spire, 1943
The North Canonry appears at the bottom of the photograph, this building faces West Walk. The detached house to the right is Arundells, the residence of former Prime Minister Sir Edward Heath from 1985 until the time of his death on 17 July 2005. The flooded area behind the houses was developed in the mid-1950s to become Queen Elizabeth Gardens.

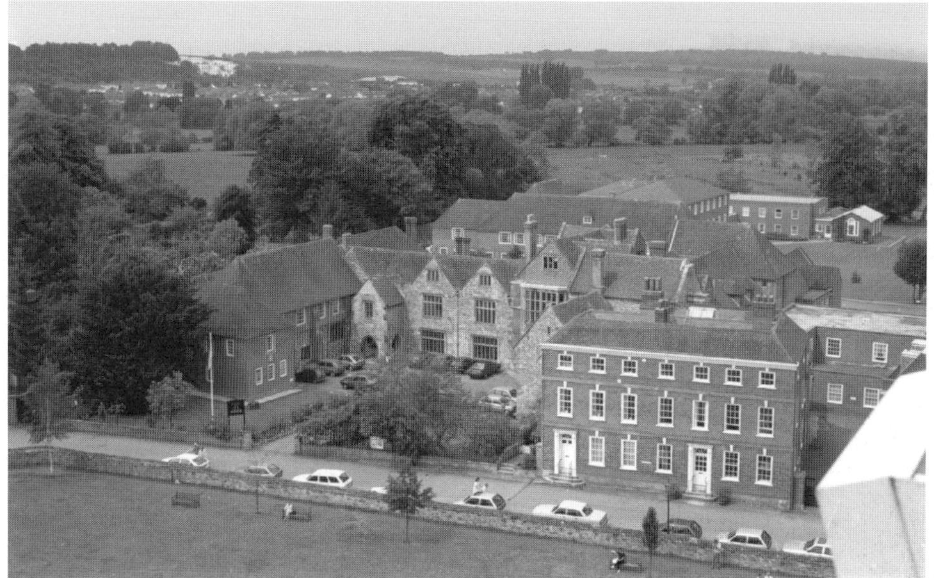

Salisbury Museum – Kings House, 65 the Close, 1987
For many years occupied by the College of Sarum St Michael (a teacher training college), this became the new home of Salisbury and South Wiltshire Museum in 1981. The photograph was taken by the author Peter Daniels from the cage of a 26-metre aerial appliance from Wiltshire Fire Service. Use of the hydraulic platform had been requested by the former Clerk of Works, Roy Spring, who wanted to inspect the statuary on the west front of Salisbury Cathedral.

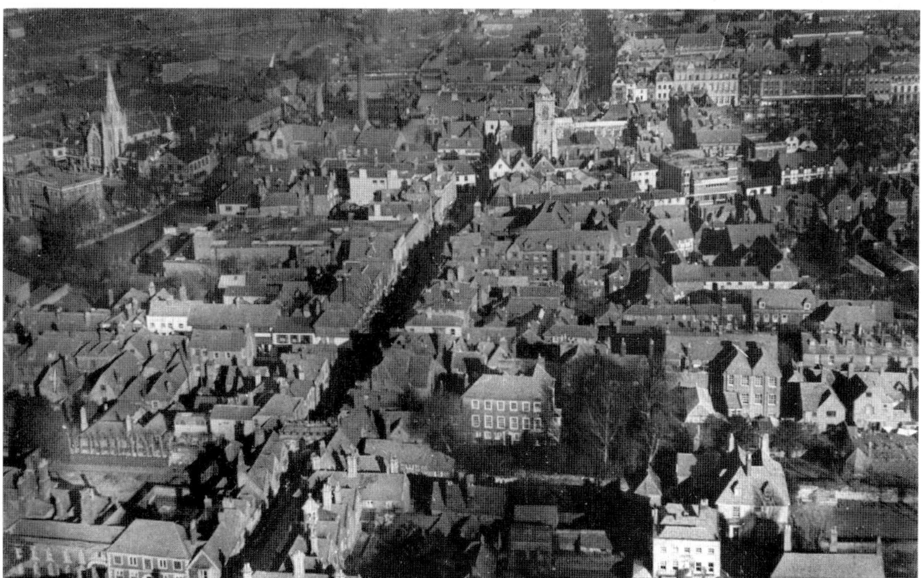

A City-Centre View from the Top of the Spire, 1943
Taken on the same day as the photograph on the opposite page, Thursday 4 February 1943. It is not a great image from a technical point of view, but a very interesting one because it shows the city at the time of the Second World War when photography was generally forbidden. Films, papers and chemicals used to develop prints were in short supply at that time.

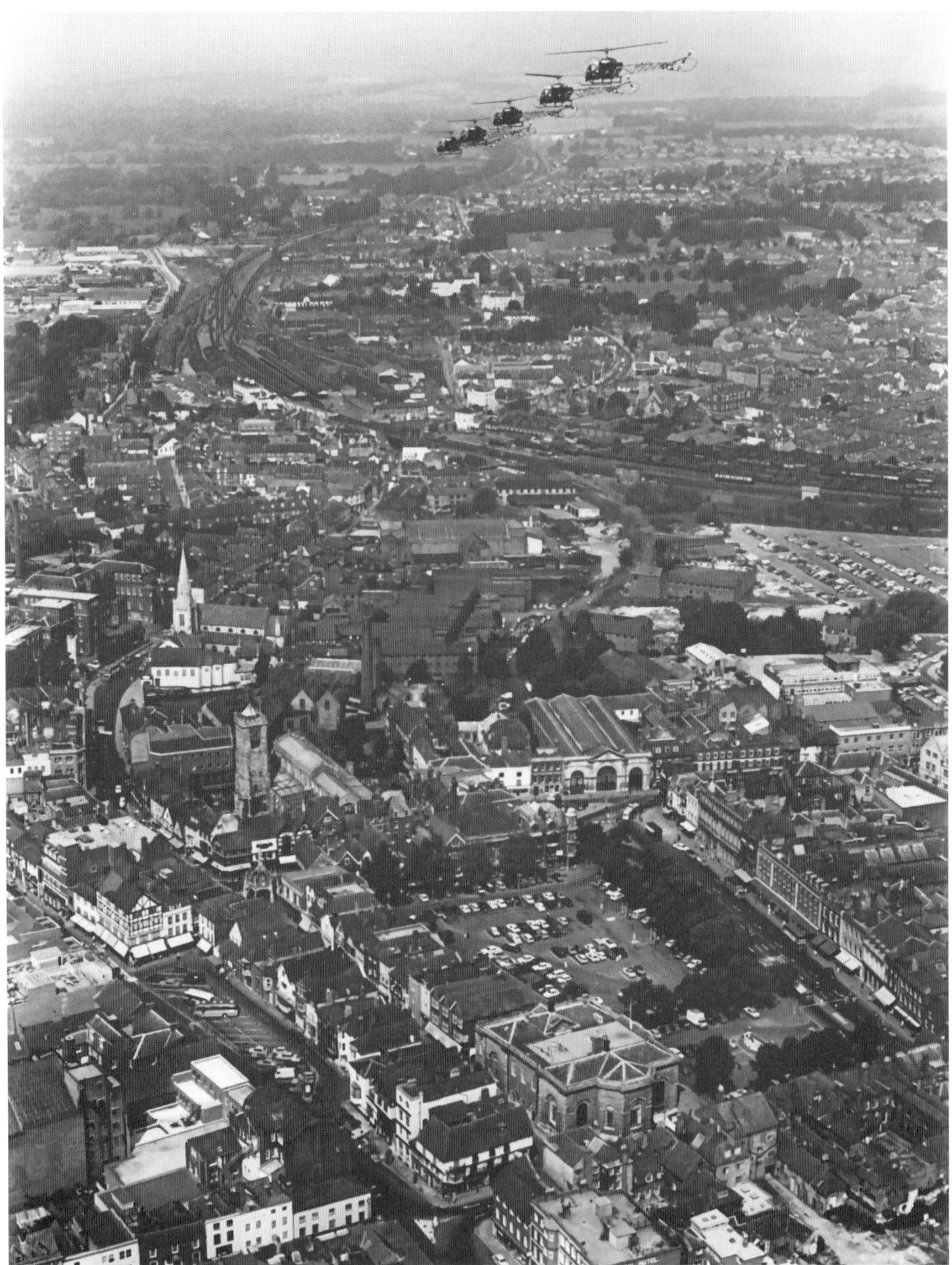

The Blue Eagles Fly Over Salisbury City Centre, 1969
Based at HQ Army Aviation, Middle Wallop, the Blue Eagles helicopter acrobatic team was formed in
the spring of 1968, and twelve months later was permanently established with five Bell-47G3B1 Sioux
helicopters. At the bottom of this remarkable photograph we can see the Guildhall and Market Place
with Fisherton Street leading us to the top of the picture where the five helicopters come into view.

Chapter 5
Wilts & Dorset
(First Fifty Years)

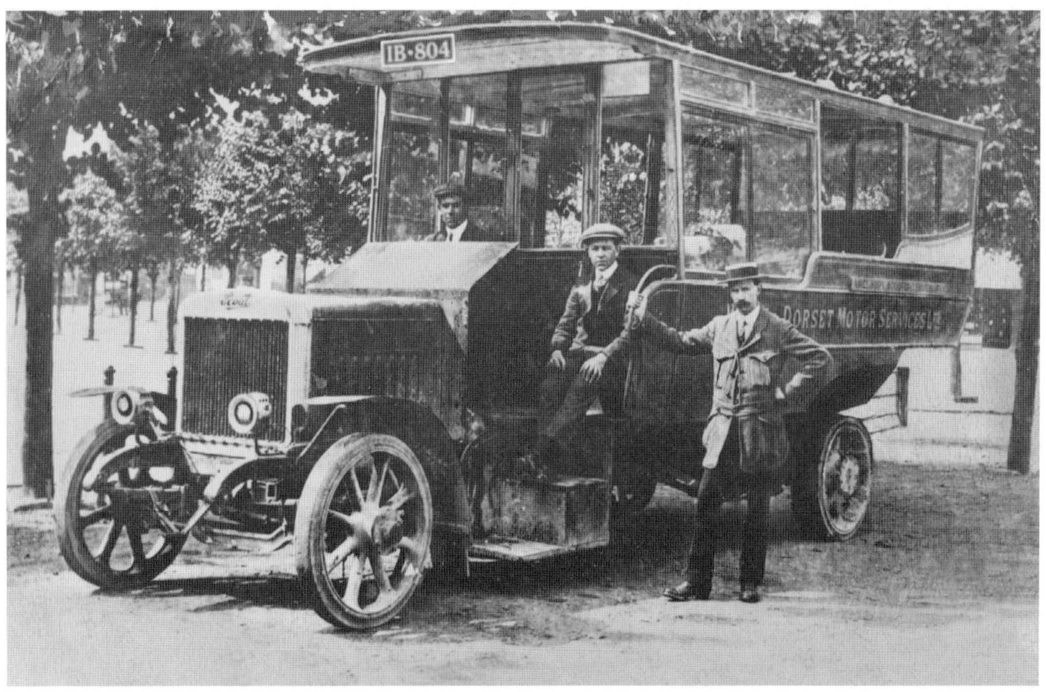

Scout Motor Bus in Market Place, 1915
The first four vehicles acquired by Wilts & Dorset Motor Services Ltd were manufactured locally
by Scout Motors Ltd at Bemerton. There were three saloon buses, registered IB-801, IB-802
and IB-804, and one charabanc, IB-803. Here we can see IB-804, nicknamed 'The Greenhouse',
waiting at the bus terminus in Market Place, Salisbury. Taking his place in the driver's seat is
William Leonard, with Inspector Bean standing beside the bus.

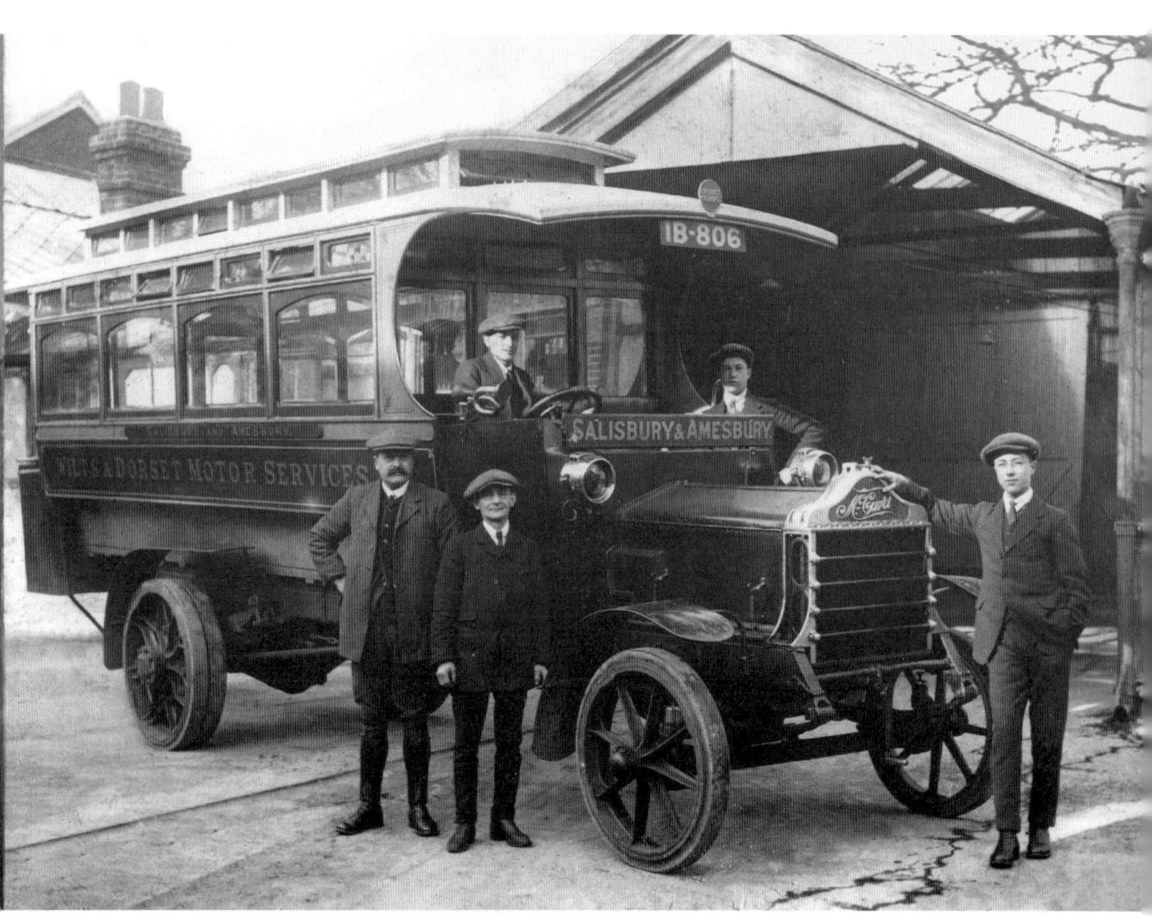

McCurd Saloon Bus with Clerestory Roof, 1916

Purchased in October 1916, this 40-hp machine was designed to carry twenty-six passengers seated around the perimeter of the body. Commercial vehicle chassis manufactured by the McCurd Lorry Manufacturing Co. Ltd, of Hayes, Middlesex, had a reputation for reliability, aptly demonstrated by the fact that Wilts & Dorset Motor Services kept IB-806 in the company fleet for ten years. We believe the bus is shown here at the Amesbury bus garage.

An AEC Bus Departing for Bournemouth, March 1921

Opposite bottom: Here we can see one of the two AEC single-deck buses acquired in 1920. Due to Wilts & Dorset's association with Southdown Motor Services, of Sussex, the company's vehicles at this time were registered in Brighton, and therefore allocated CD number plates. CD-3177 is pictured here at Sly's Corner in Blue Boar Row, Salisbury, on route to Bournemouth via Ringwood.

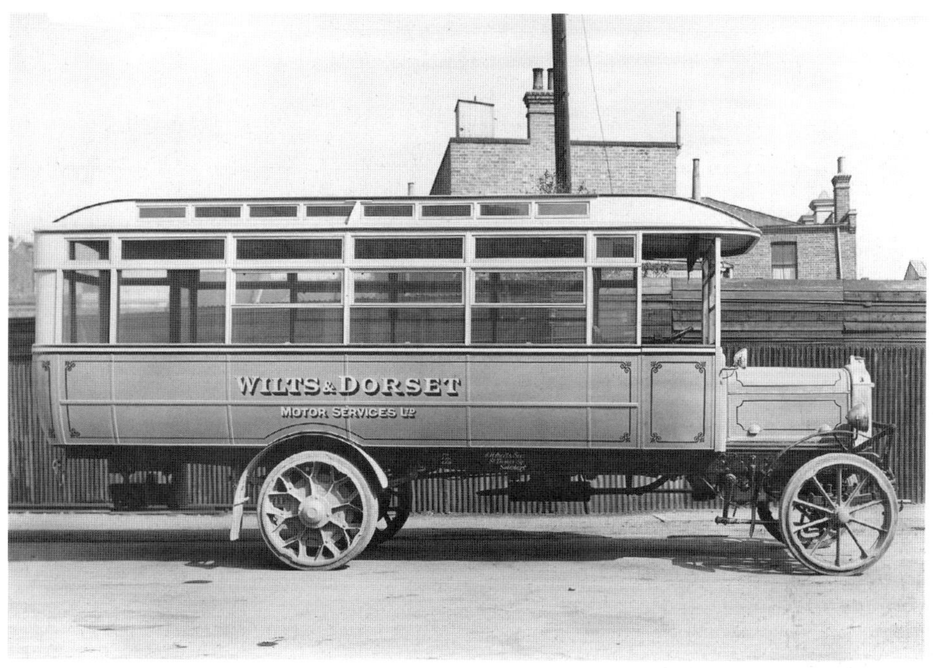

AEC Single-Deck Omnibus, 1919

Positive identification of this particular vehicle is difficult because no fleet number or registration mark is visible. The bus is definitely based on an AEC 3-ton YC type chassis, of which five were put into service by Wilts & Dorset in 1919 and 1920. Only two of the five chassis were originally fitted with single-deck bodywork. The lower half of this bus appears to be very light in colour which would indicate that it was originally painted yellow, as some new Wilts & Dorset buses were in the early days.

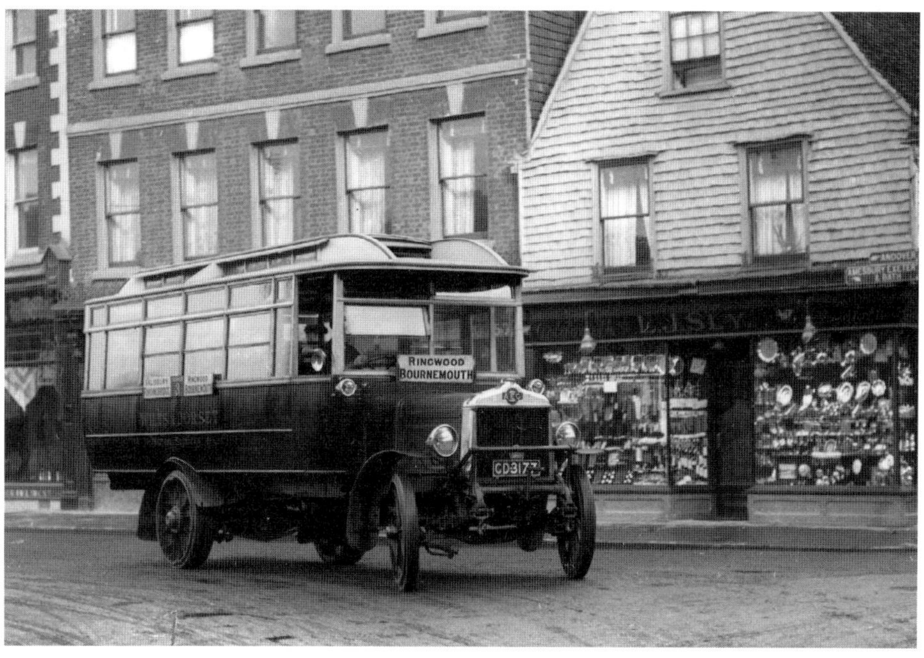

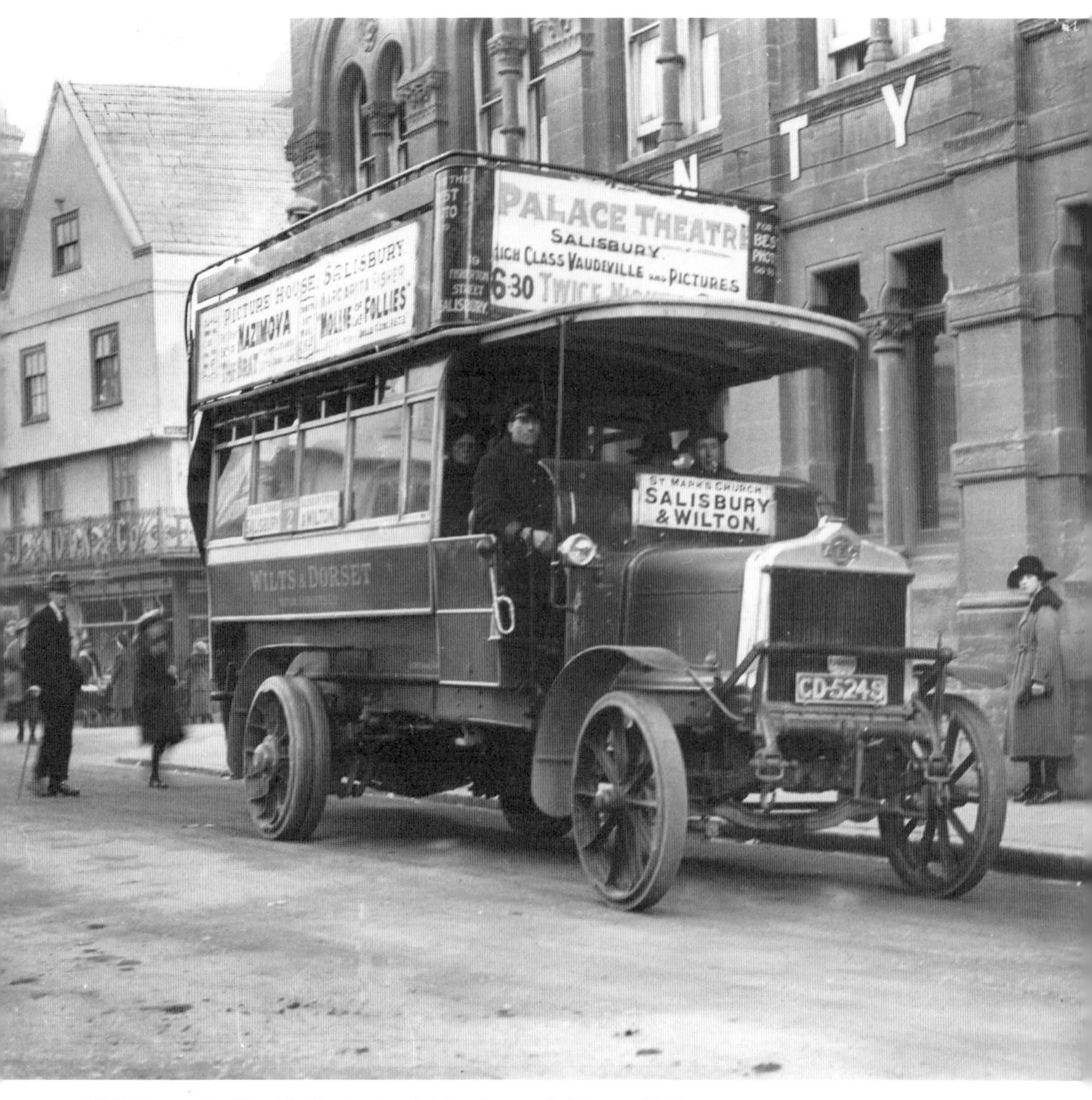

AEC Open-Top Double-Decker in Bridge Street, Salisbury, 1921

Having been acquired with the assistance of Southdown Motor Services, CD-5249 joined the Wilts & Dorset fleet (allocated fleet No. 13) in April/May 1920 along with three other public service vehicles: a Leyland S5 charabanc (CD-5247) and two AEC YC type single-deck rear-entrance buses (CD-3177 and CD-5248). No. 13 pulled up momentarily near the County Hotel in Bridge Street for this publicity photograph to be taken, it then continued on service No. 2 to Wilton.

A Four-Vehicle Line Up in Castle Street, Salisbury, 1921

Opposite bottom: An AEC thirty-five-seat bus (CD-3177) comes into view at the back of the line, in front of which appears a Leyland charabanc (CD-2556), the McCurd bus (IB-806), and the Maxwell sixteen-seat charabanc (HR 3186) that joined the Wilts &Dorset fleet in December 1920. This was the first W&D vehicle to display a Wiltshire registration mark.

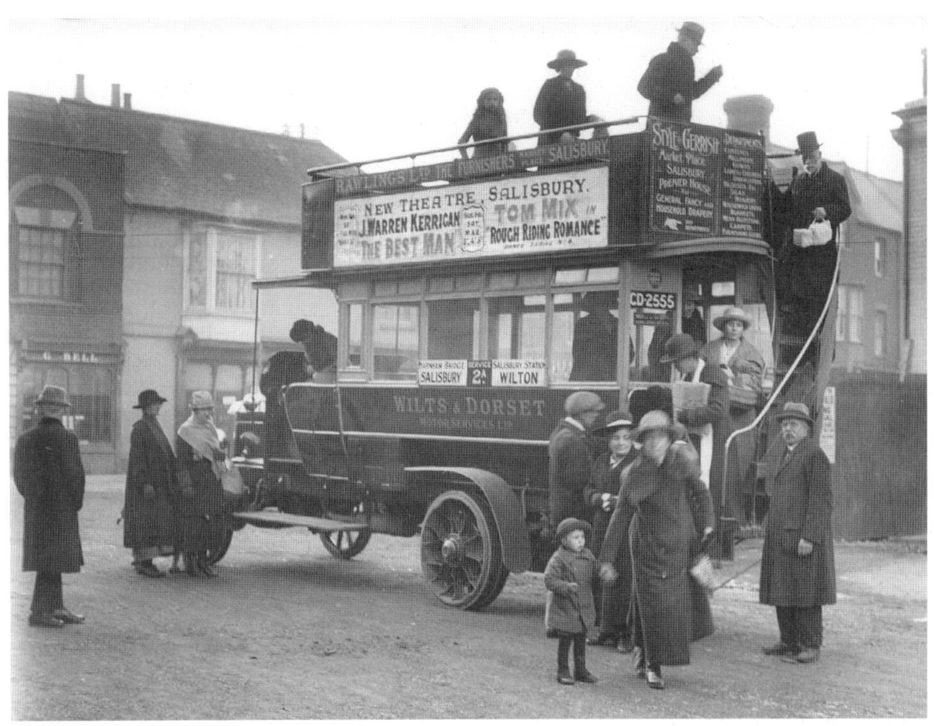

AEC Double-Decker Arrives at Wilton on Service 2A, March 1921
This fascinating photograph clearly shows the type of outside curved staircase that was a common feature on open-topped double-deck omnibuses at that time. The vehicle was given fleet No. 8 in July 1919 and it displayed the registration mark CD-2555.

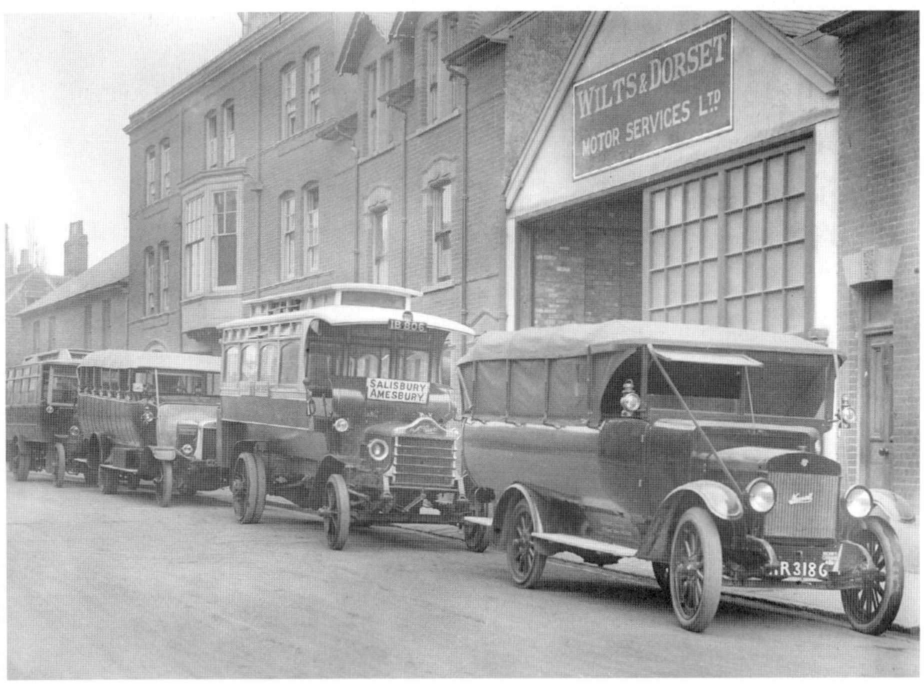

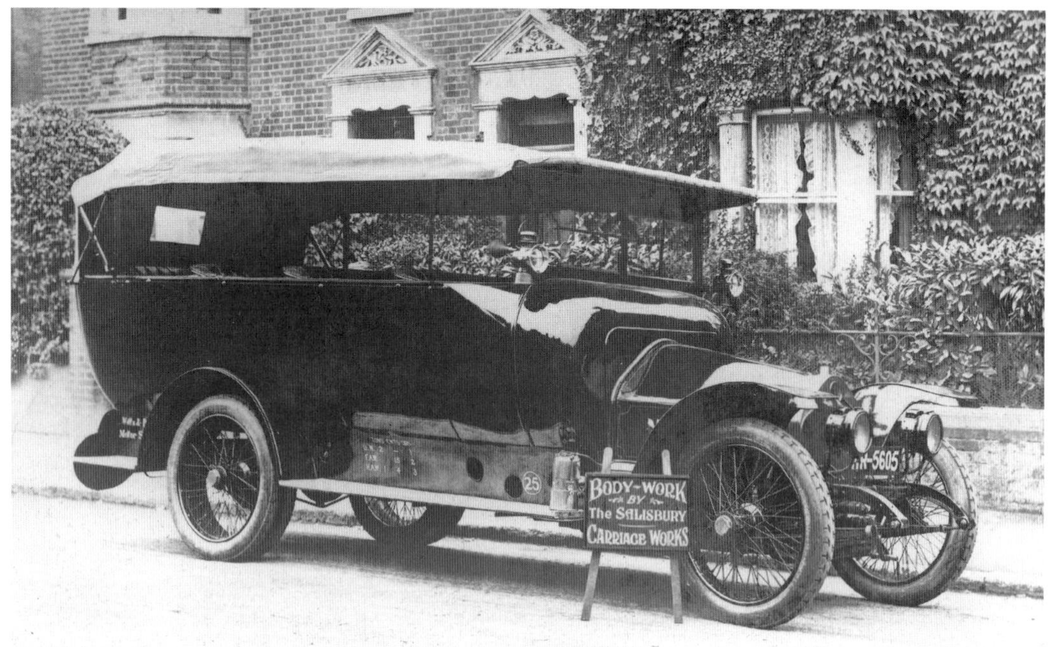

Crossley Charabanc with Salisbury Carriage Works Body, 1921
This is one of two Crossley charabancs operated by Salisbury & District Motor Services Ltd when the company was taken over by Wilts & Dorset in August 1921. At the time of the First World War, both vehicles were owned by the War Department and served as airfield tenders with the RAF. Having been allocated the Wiltshire registration mark HR-5605, this particular Crossley is pictured here in Wilts & Dorset colours.

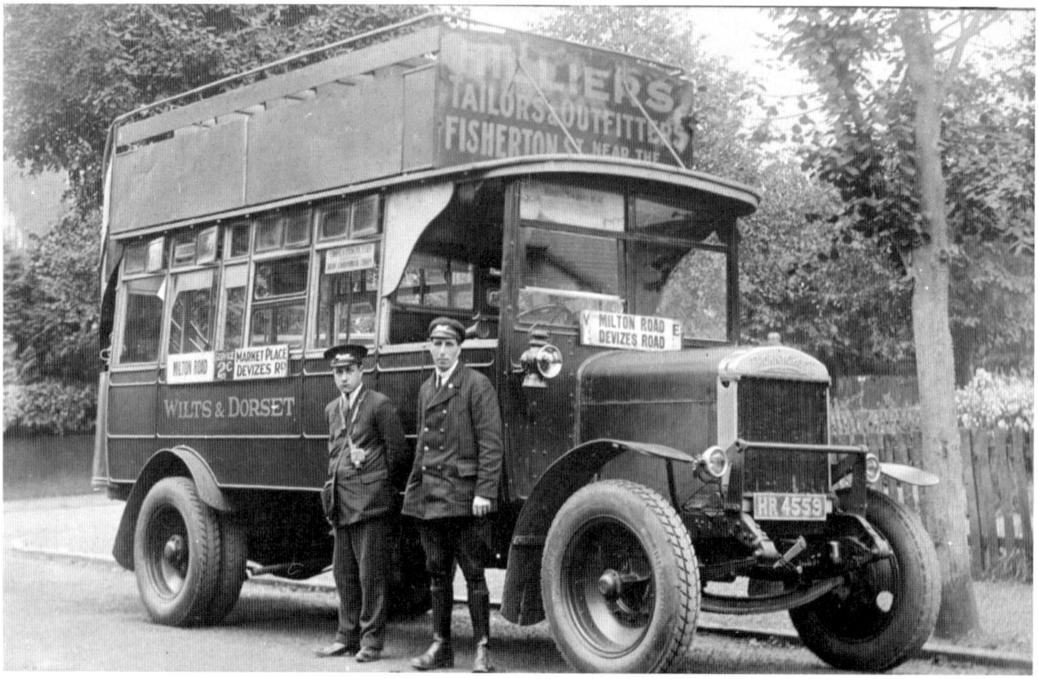

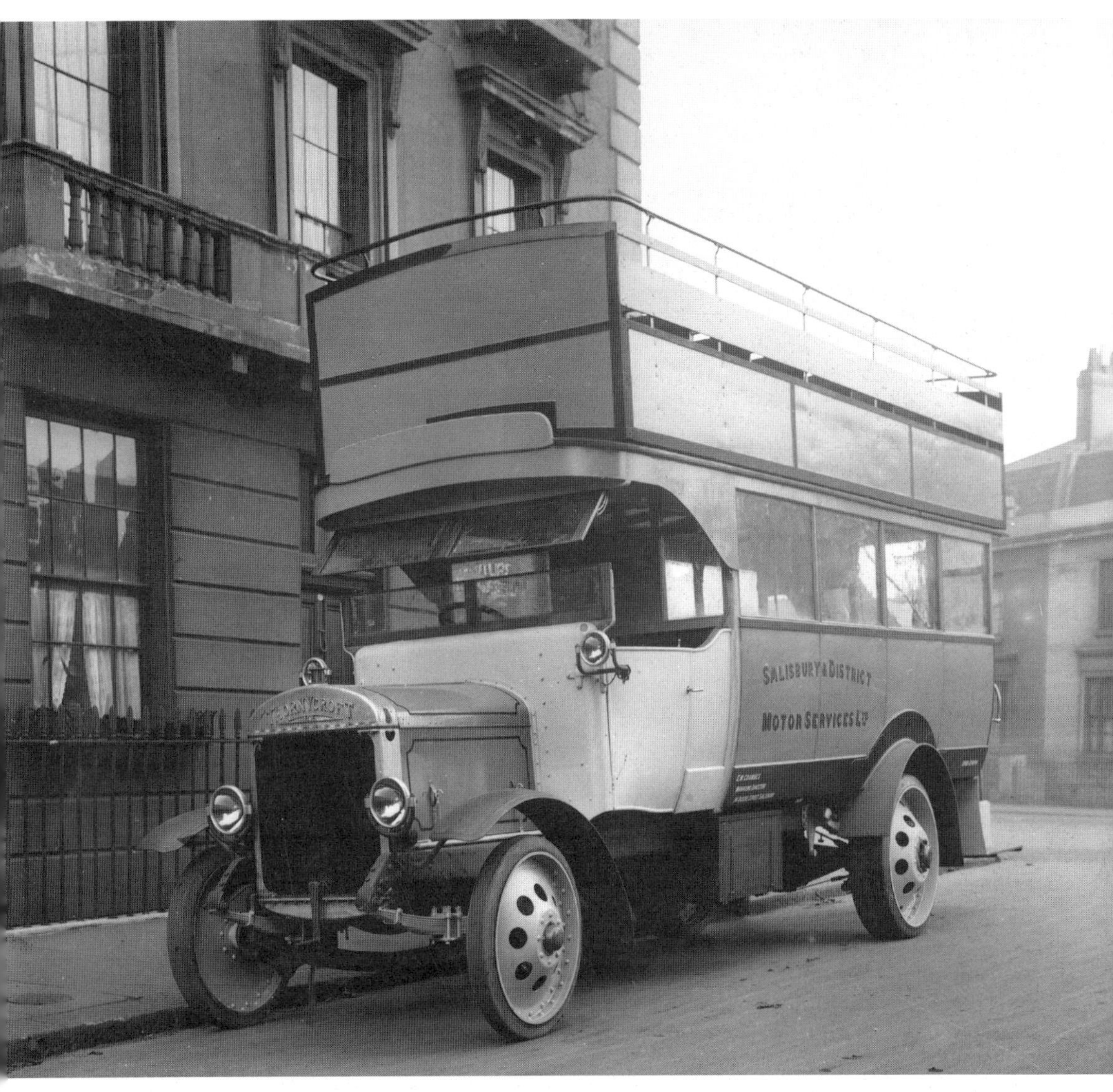

Thornycroft Omnibus in Salisbury & District Livery, 1921
Of the nine vehicles that joined the Wilts & Dorset fleet in August 1921, when the business of its main rival Salisbury & District Motor Services Ltd was acquired, seven were 40-hp Thornycrofts. Featured here in this official Thornycroft photograph, the bus is not yet displaying its Wiltshire registration mark, HR-3037. The double-deck bodywork was fabricated at Acton's motor and carriage works in Greencroft Street, Salisbury – it is finished in pale yellow. When in Wilts & Dorset ownership it was repainted and given fleet No. 23.

Former Salisbury & District Thornycroft on Service 2C, *c.* 1927
Opposite bottom: Originally a charabanc with Salisbury & District, this vehicle was re-built to operate as a saloon bus in the Wilts & Dorset fleet. The second body was removed two years later and a double-deck body was fitted, as shown here. The driver, pictured to the right with HR-4559, is Abel Gilbert, a native of Broad Chalke.

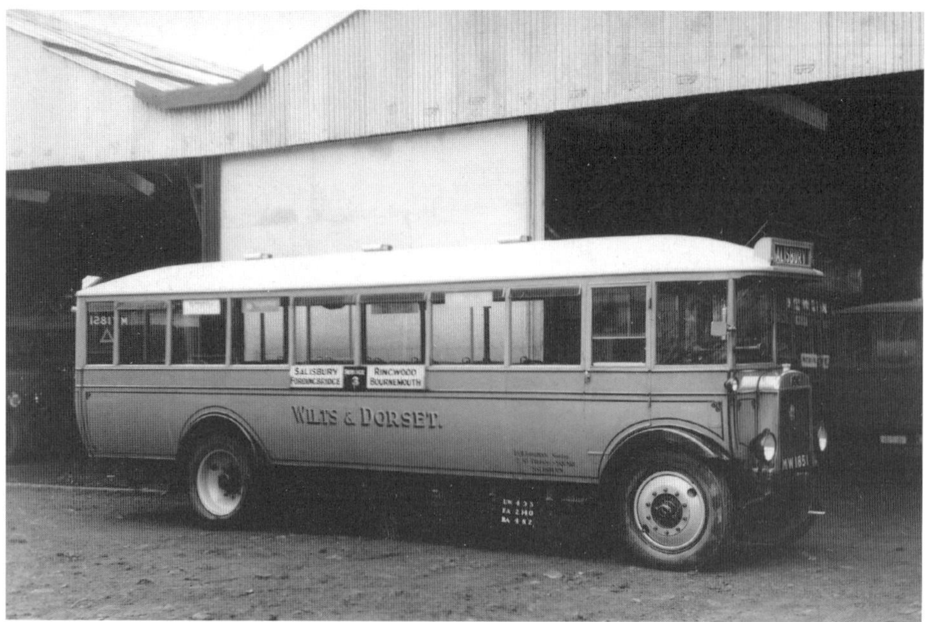

Leyland Lion Thirty-Six-Seater, 1928
This is one of a pair of Leyland single-deck buses purchased by Wilts & Dorset in May 1928 and allocated registration marks MW 1851 and MW 1852. The first of the pair is pictured here with 'Service 3' destination boards fitted, for the return journey to Bournemouth via Fordingbridge and Ringwood. A third machine, MW 1853, joined the fleet a month later in June 1928. Fleet Nos 55, 56 and 57.

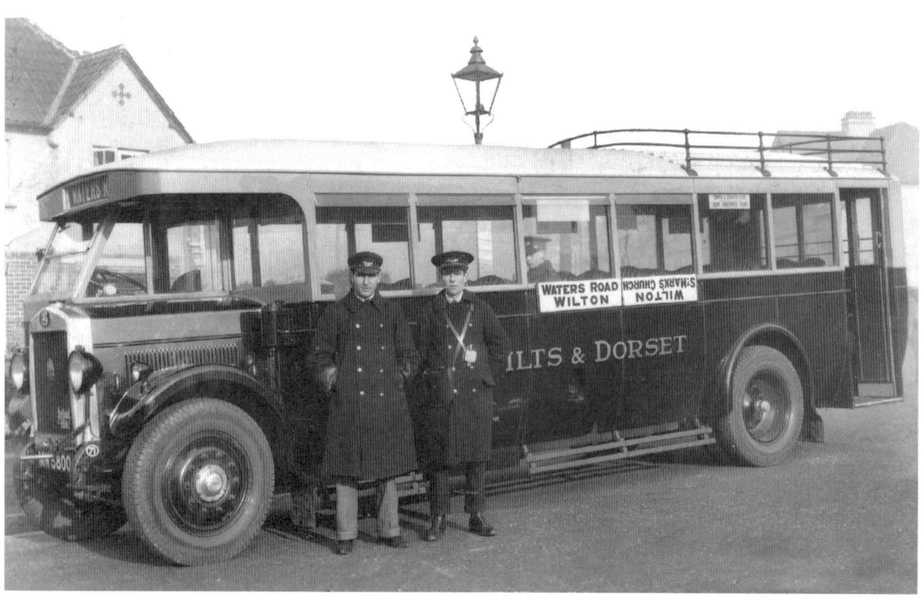

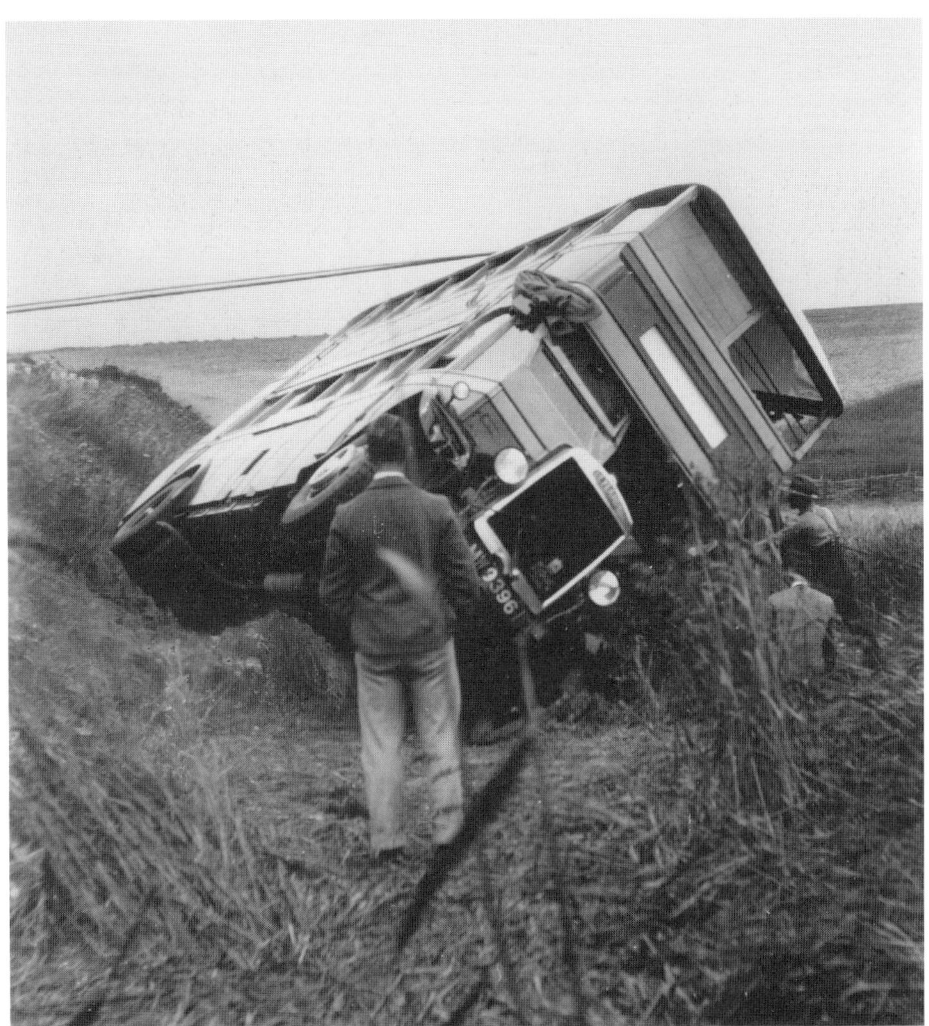

A Titan Takes a Tumble, 28 July 1931
The accident involved the Leyland Titan double-decker MW-9396 (fleet No. 102), which was running on the 'Workmen's Service' through Amesbury to Salisbury. As he approached Stockport Bottom (popularly known as White Railings) at about 8.30 a.m., driver Arthur Cleverley pulled over to allow another vehicle to pass on this narrow stretch of road. The front wheel sank into the ground, which had been undermined by rabbits, and his bus slowly toppled over and slid down the bank. There were mostly adults downstairs and around thirty children on the upper deck, including pupils of the South Wilts School for Girls and Bishop Wordsworth School for Boys. Although badly shaken, the children thankfully escaped without injury. The photo was taken shortly before the bus was recovered and taken to Heaver's Coachworks at Durrington. Bert Elliott was the conductor on this occasion.

Leyland Thirty-One-Seater on a Salisbury to Wilton Service, 1929
Opposite bottom: Three Leyland Lion LT1 buses were purchased in July 1929, registered MW 4595–MW 4597, with an additional three identical machines, MW 5799–MW 5802, joining the fleet in November 1929. The last three of this batch were converted for use as ambulances in 1939, at the start of the Second World War.

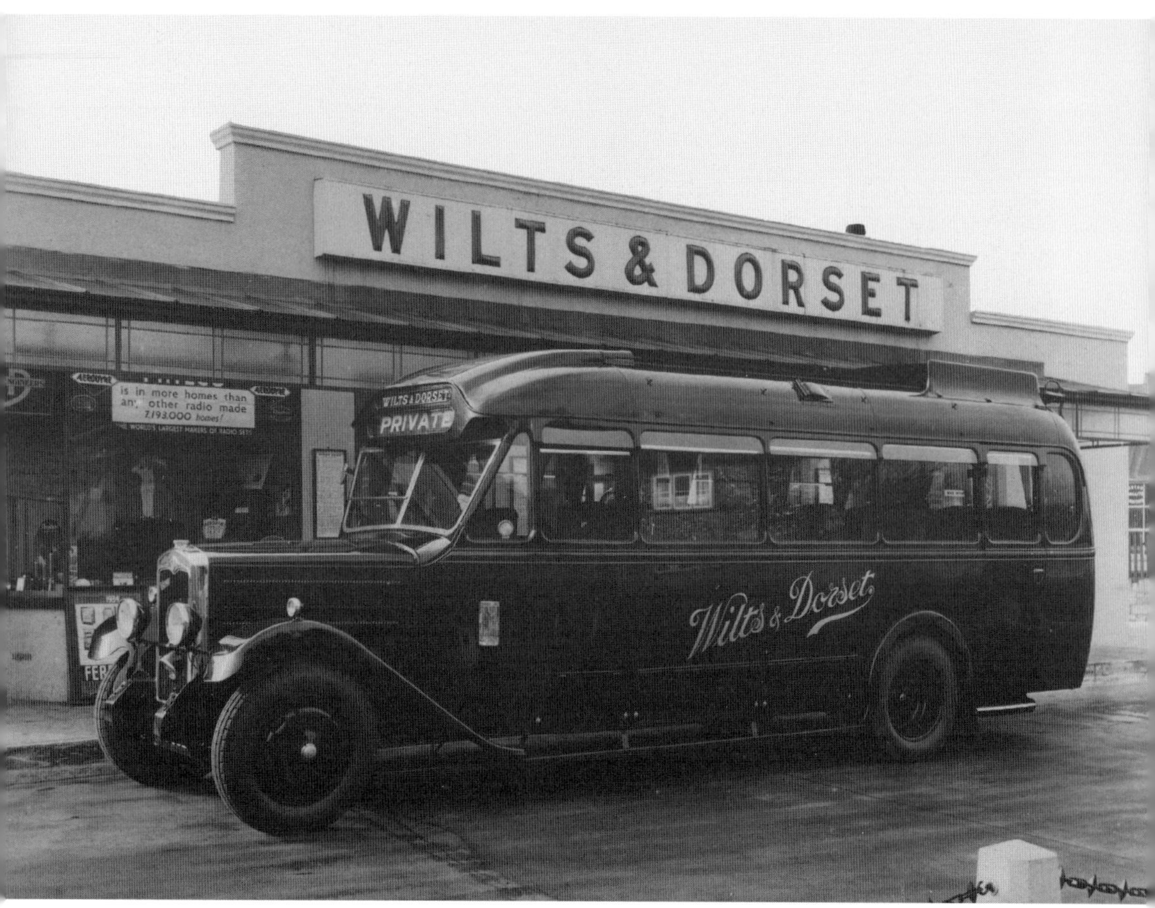

Morris Commercial Saloon Coach, 1932
Pictured here at Amesbury bus station is WV 652 (fleet No. 127), a smartly turned out Morris Commercial Viceroy coach built by Thomas Harrington Ltd, Motor Coach Builders and Automotive Engineers, at Sackville Works, Old Shoreham Road, Hove. This, and its twin, WV653, were designed to accommodate twenty passengers. They remained in service until the early 1940s.

Leyland TS6 Coach with Thirty-Two-Seat Harrington Body, 1934
Opposite bottom: Photographed on New Bridge Road by F. Futcher & Son, WV 5526 was one of a pair of identical coaches purchased by Wilts & Dorset in July 1934. This one was allocated fleet No. 117, and WV 5527 was given No. 118. Both vehicles were powered by a Leyland six-cylinder petrol engine. A secure luggage area was installed on the roof at the rear of the coaches.

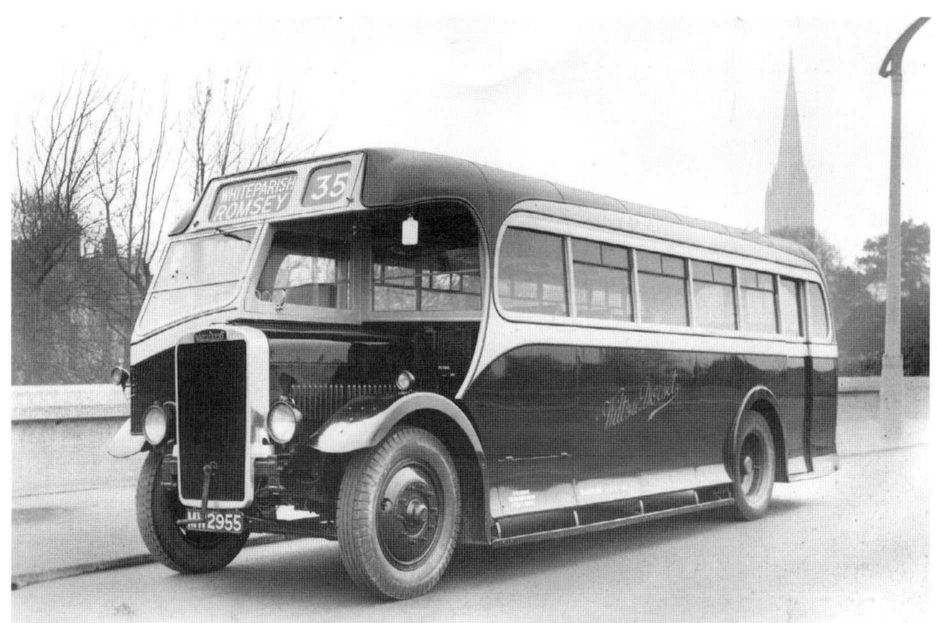

Leyland Thirty-Six-Seat Bus with Leyland Rear Entry Bodywork, 1934
This is a former Sparrow & Vincent vehicle that was added to the Wilts & Dorset fleet in December 1933 following the company's takeover. Displaying the Wiltshire registration mark MW 2955, and fleet No. 133, the bus is pictured here in the aptly named New Bridge Road, which had opened just a few months earlier. The Leyland badge on top of the radiator has been replaced with that of Wilts & Dorset.

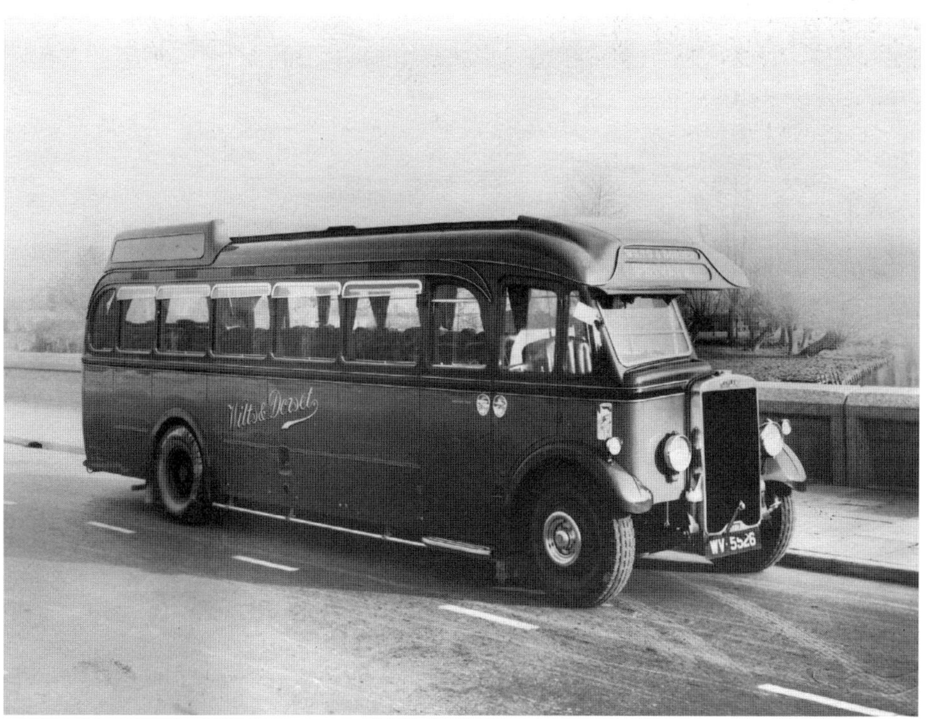

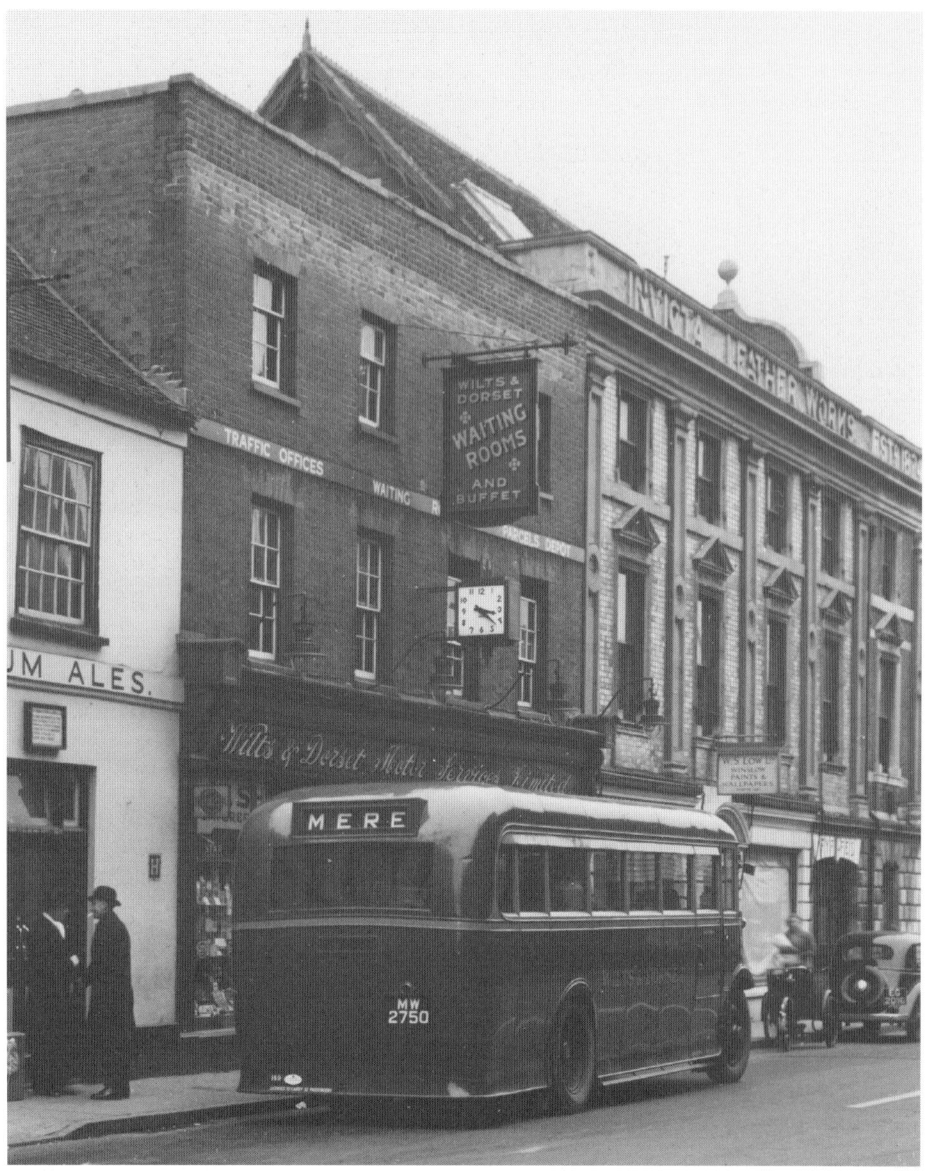

'Coronation Coach' in Endless Street, 1937

A Leyland Lion bus (MW 2750) with London Lorries bodywork stands outside the Wilts & Dorset Motor Services Parcels Office, Travel Office, Waiting Rooms and Buffet at 6 Endless Street, Salisbury. The vehicle was formerly owned by Sparrow & Vincent, motor coach proprietors, of 79a Fisherton Street, but became part of the Wilts & Dorset fleet when the firm was taken over in 1933.

A Leyland Titan Takes to the Water, *c.* 1939

Opposite bottom: Purchased by Wilts & Dorset in the summer of 1931, along with three other identical double-deckers, MW 7049 (fleet No. 88) can be seen here motoring along Fisherton Street on a very wet day in the late 1930s. Depicted here in the very attractive red and grey livery of that era, the bus continued to provide good service until withdrawn from the fleet in the April 1952.

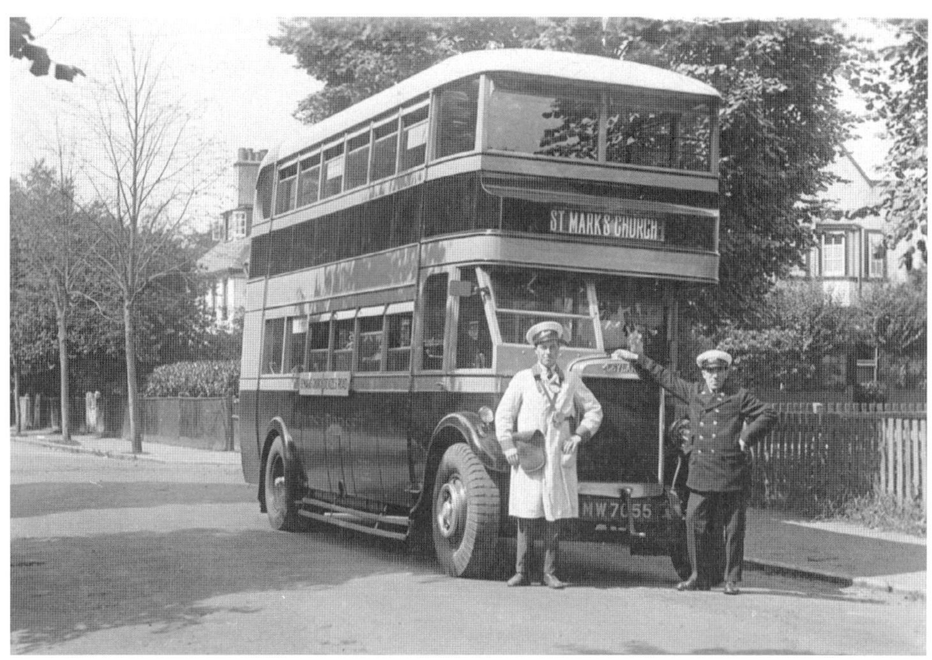

Leyland Double-Decker on Return Service to St Mark's Church, *c.* 1937
Driver Charles James Lucas and conductor Frederick Dredge stand for a photo opportunity with a Leyland Titan double-decker (MW 7055), at the terminus near the junction of Roman Road and Coronation Road on the Pembroke Park residential estate.

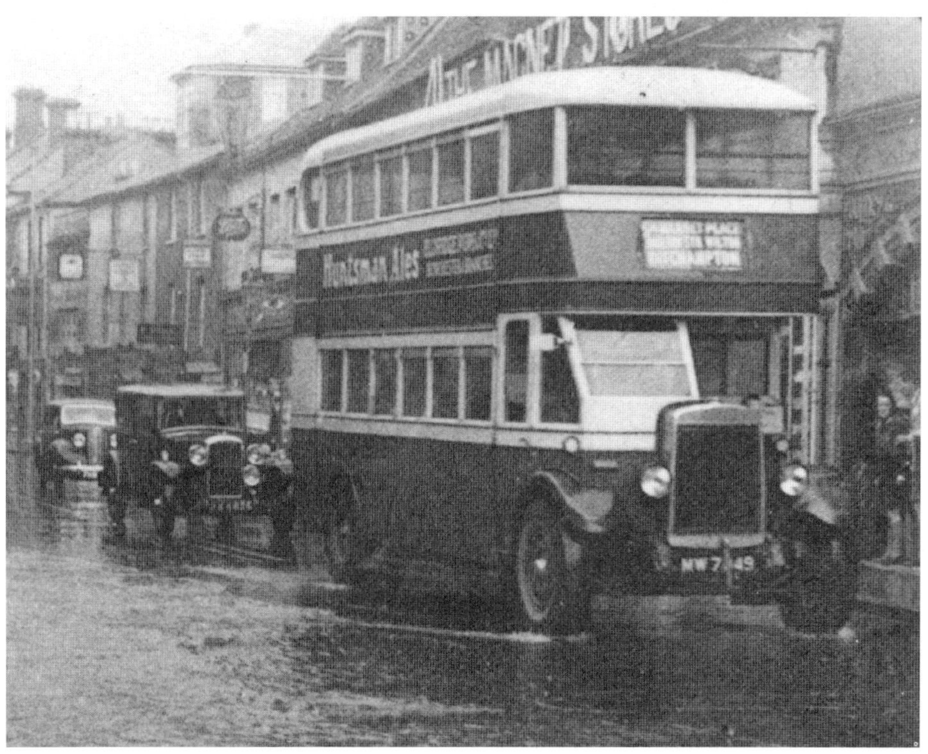

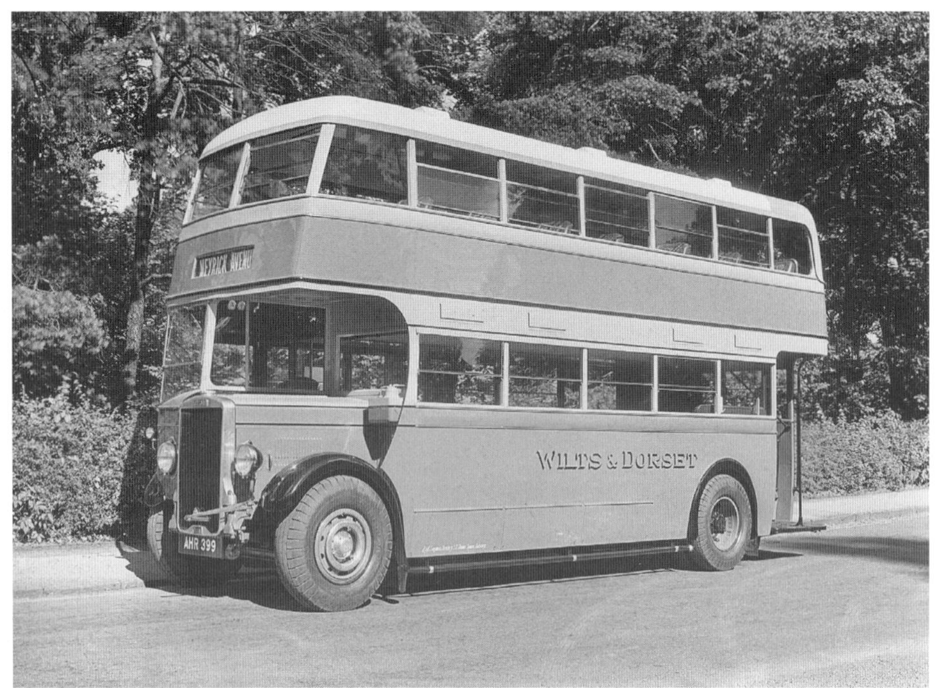

Two Additional Leyland Titans Added to the Fleet, 1936
A new series of three-letter registration marks was introduced by Wiltshire County Council in February 1936 to replace the former two letter series, AM, HR, MR, MW and WV, that had all been allocated. The first Wilts & Dorset vehicles to receive the new look registration plates was AHR 399 (pictured above and below) and AHR 400. Both Leyland Titan TD4 buses, they were to display fleet Nos 144 and 145.

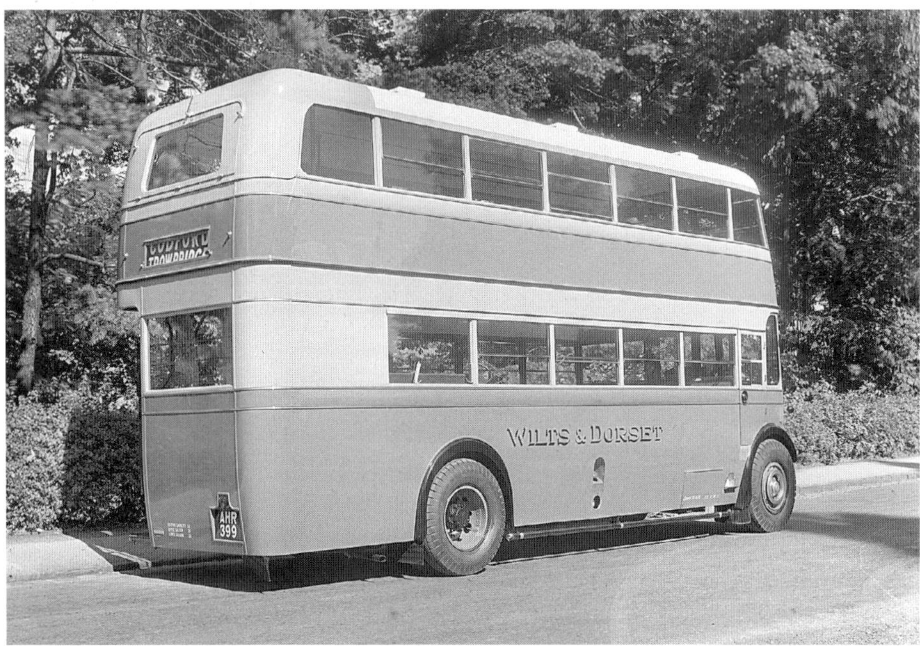

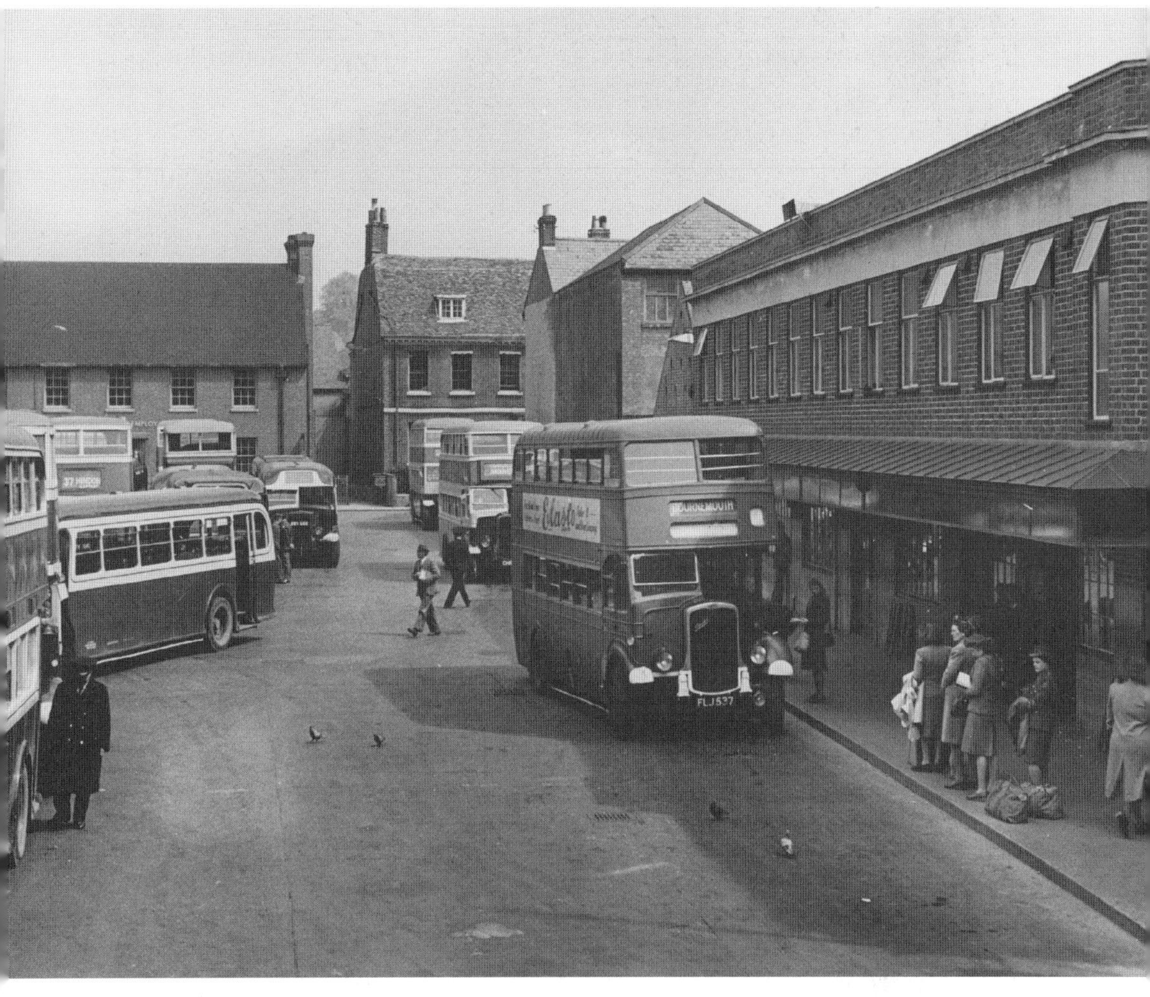

Salisbury Bus Station Opens in Endless Street, August 1939
This new facility opened just one month before the start of the Second World War, and although no-one would have realised it at the time, it was the commencement of seventy-five years of service to regional bus travellers. We can clearly see that all but one of the vehicles parked in the bus station on this particular day appears in the red and cream livery of the Wilts & Dorset fleet at that time. The odd one out is the Bristol double-decker, FLJ 537, which is painted green for the Hants & Dorset bus company. We can tell from the destination blind that the bus was soon to depart on a return service to Bournemouth. Salisbury bus station closed for the very last time on Saturday 4 January 2014.

Rear View of the All-New Leyland Titan TD4 Double-Deckers, 1936
Opposite bottom: AHR 399 and AHR 400 were the first of Leyland Motors newly designed, metal-framed double-deck bodies to enter service with Wilts & Dorset. Very elegant buses they were, cutting quite a dash in the attractive 1930s Wilts & Dorset red and grey colour scheme.

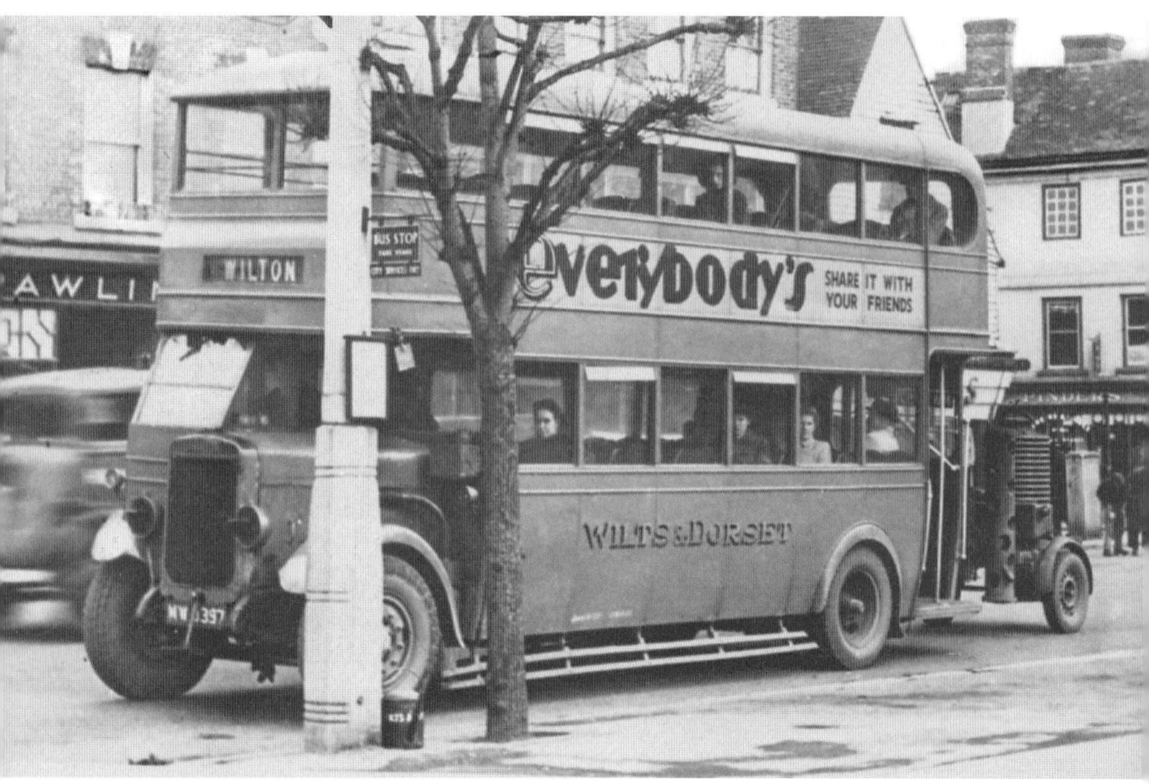

Alternative Fuel Source During the Second World War, 1939–45

To overcome the problem of severe fuel shortages, Wilts & Dorset converted nine Leyland buses to run on 'producer-gas', a by-product of burning fossil fuels. MW 9397 towing a gas-producer trailer can be seen pulled up at a bus stop in Blue Boar Row, Salisbury. A sign attached to the lamp post informs us that this is a 'fare stage stop for city services only'. A Wilts & Dorset watering can stands at the base of the lamp post, no doubt kept there for topping up bus radiators. It is interesting to see that the headlights of the bus are fitted with blackout covers. Official known as 'slit masks', these devices were designed to deflect the beam downwards, permitting a dim light to be seen at street level only but not from above. In the pitch blackness collisions were commonplace so matt white bands were painted on lamp posts, postboxes, and also on the mudguards of many vehicles as can be seen here on the front of this particular bus.

The First Post-War Buses Delivered, 1946

Opposite bottom: Two Bristol K5G double-deckers joined the Wilts & Dorset fleet in April 1946, they were fitted with Eastern Coachworks low bridge, rear entrance bodies to accommodate fifty-five passengers (twenty-seven lower deck/twenty-eight upper deck). Registered DMR 836 and DMR 837, they were allocated fleet Nos 264 and 265. DMR 836 is pictured here at Salisbury bus station.

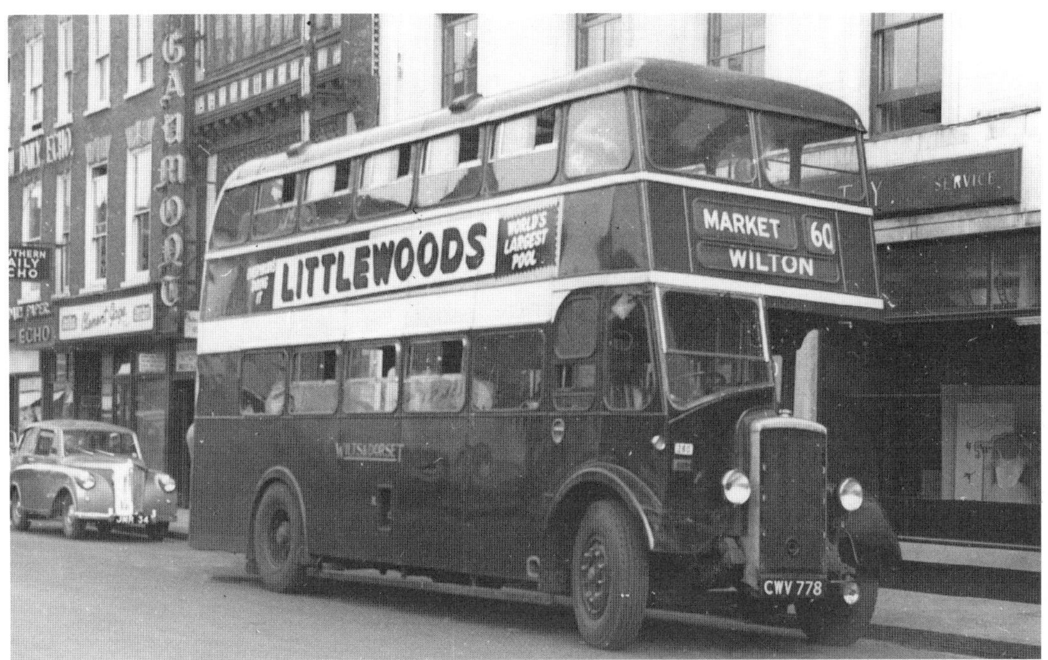

Government-Approved Austere Bus Delivery for Salisbury, 1943
There were strict restrictions placed on the purchase of new vehicles at the time of the Second World War, but in 1943 the Ministry of War Transport allocated four Daimler double-deckers to Wilts & Dorset. Registered CWV 778–CWV 781, the buses were fitted with Utility-type bodies manufactured by Brush Coachworks Ltd. Here we can see CWV 778 pulled up near the Gaumont cinema (now Odeon) in New Canal in 1953, having already given ten years of service. The Daimlers were eventually withdrawn in 1957 and 1958.

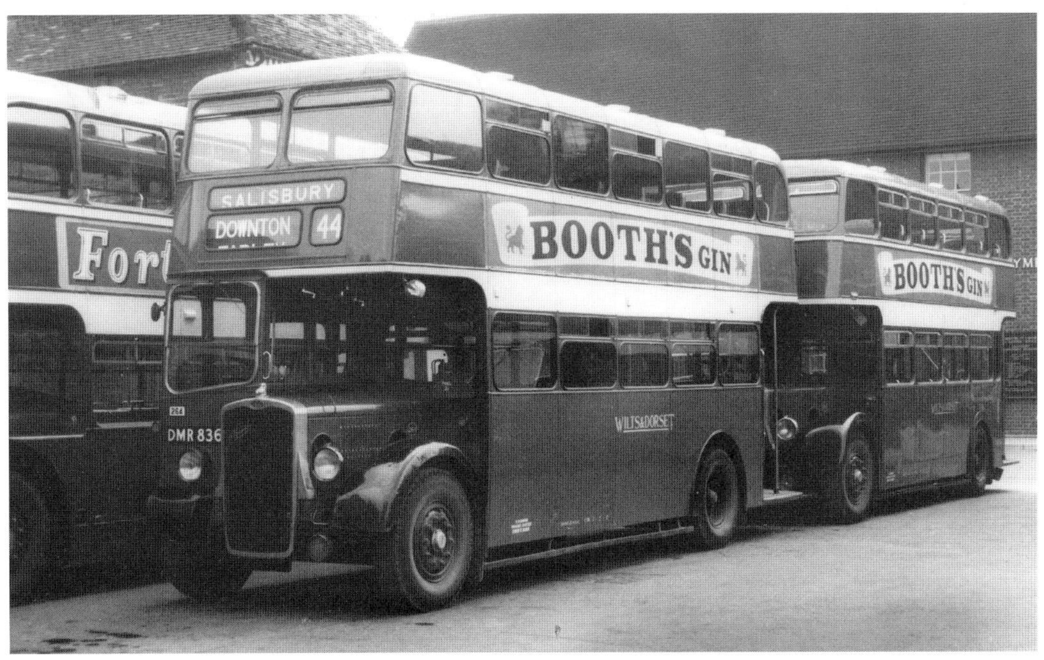

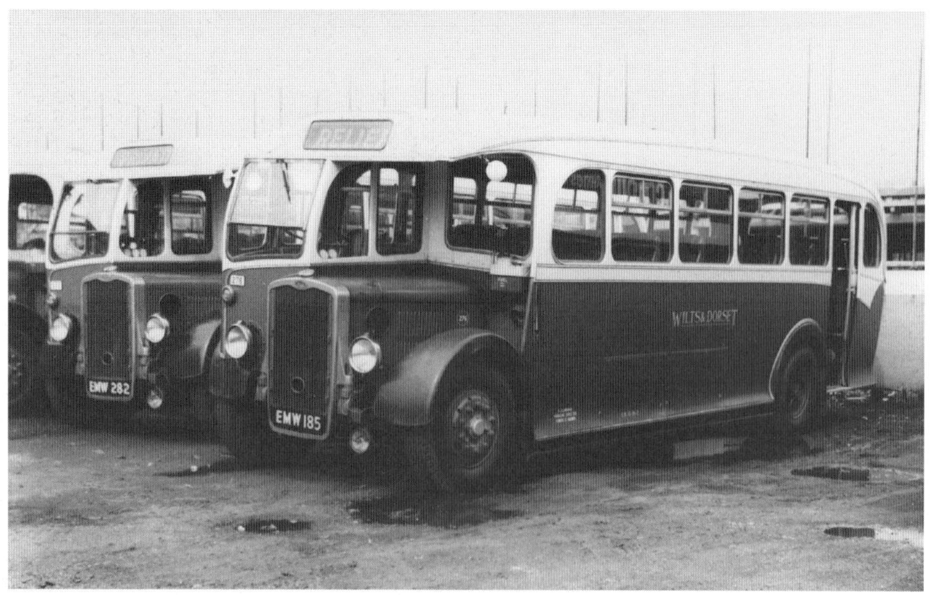

The First New Post-War Coaches Arrived, 1948

A batch of six Bristol L6B coaches with twenty-three-seat rear entry bodies by John C. Beadle Ltd, of Dartford, was taken into service by Wilts & Dorset between December 1948 and March 1949. The vehicles were issued with the Wiltshire registration marks EMW 183–185 and EMW 282–284 (fleet Nos 274–279). In this archive photograph we can see EMW 185 (nearest to the camera) and EMW 282.

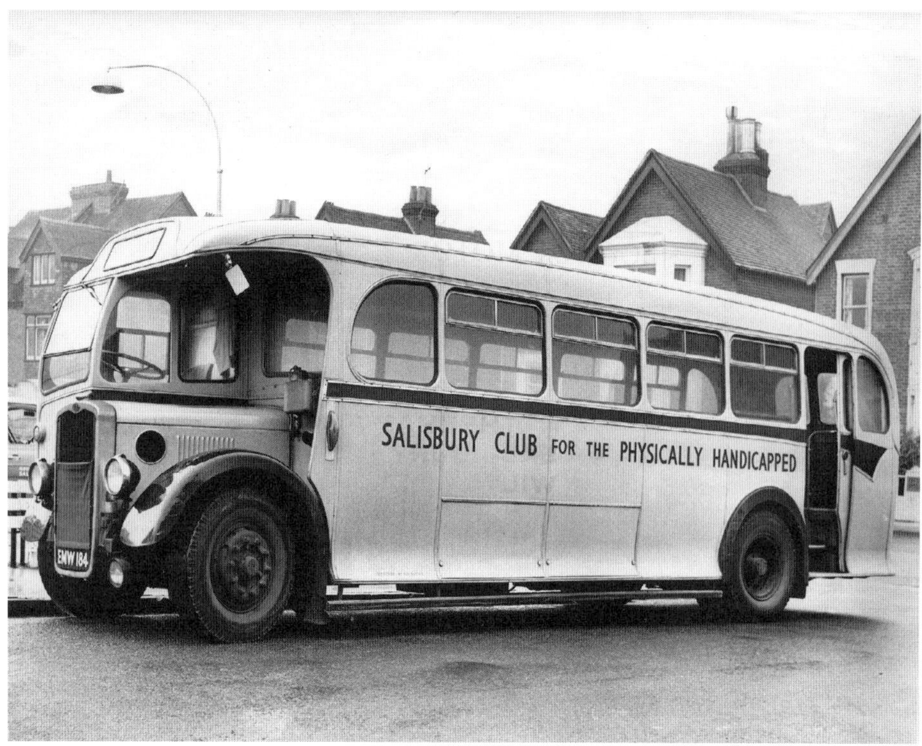

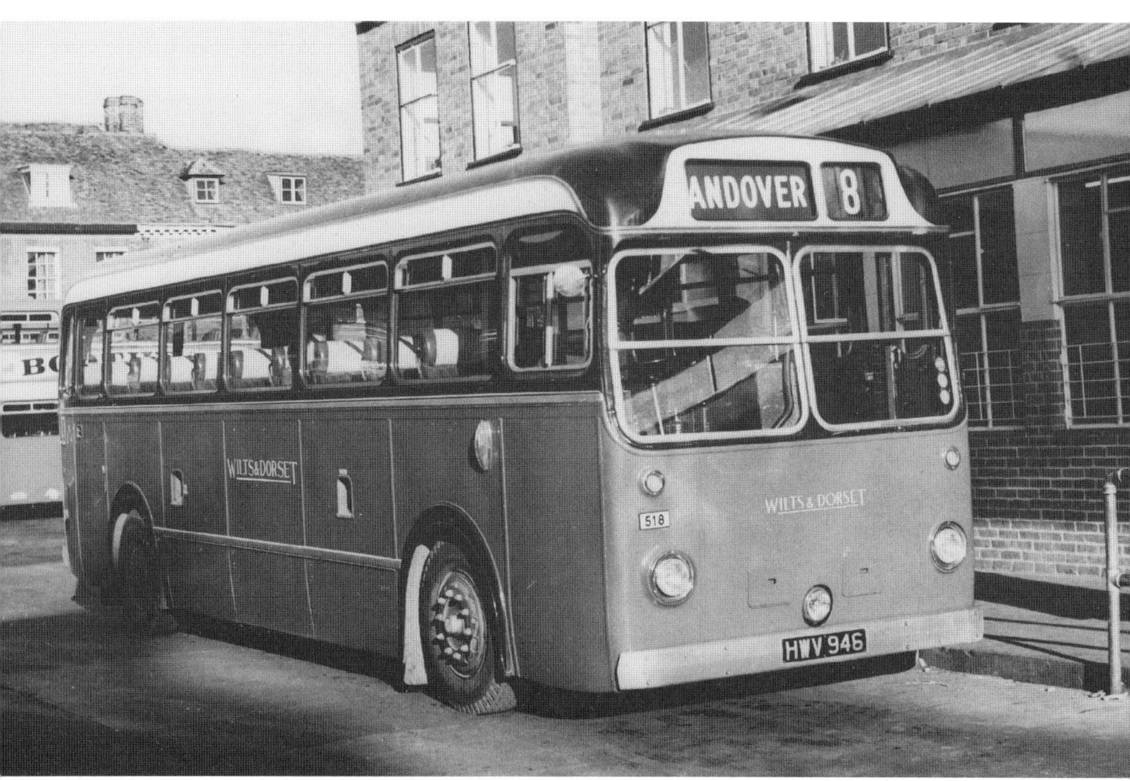

The First Underfloor Engined, Dual-Purpose Buses Ordered, 1952
Twenty-eight Bristol LS6Gs were delivered between November 1952 and April 1953. They all featured Eastern Coachworks dual-entrance, dual-purpose, thirty-nine-seat bodies. Having been issued with fleet Nos 516–534, they displayed a selection of Wiltshire registration marks from the HWV, JAM and JHR series. HWV 946 (fleet No. 518) can be seen here at Salisbury bus station prior to departing on Service 8 to Andover.

Former Wilts & Dorset Bristol Coach Given a New Purpose, 1961
Opposite bottom: Having provided twelve years of reliable service to Wilts & Dorset, Bristol coach EAM 184 was sold to the Salisbury Club for the physically handicapped in May 1961. The vehicle was converted for its new use by Hayden & Sons, coachbuilders, of Netherhampton. A ramp and doors were fitted at the rear of the body. Painted in two shades of blue, the ambulance can be seen here parked up in Australian Avenue, with Wilton Road in the background.

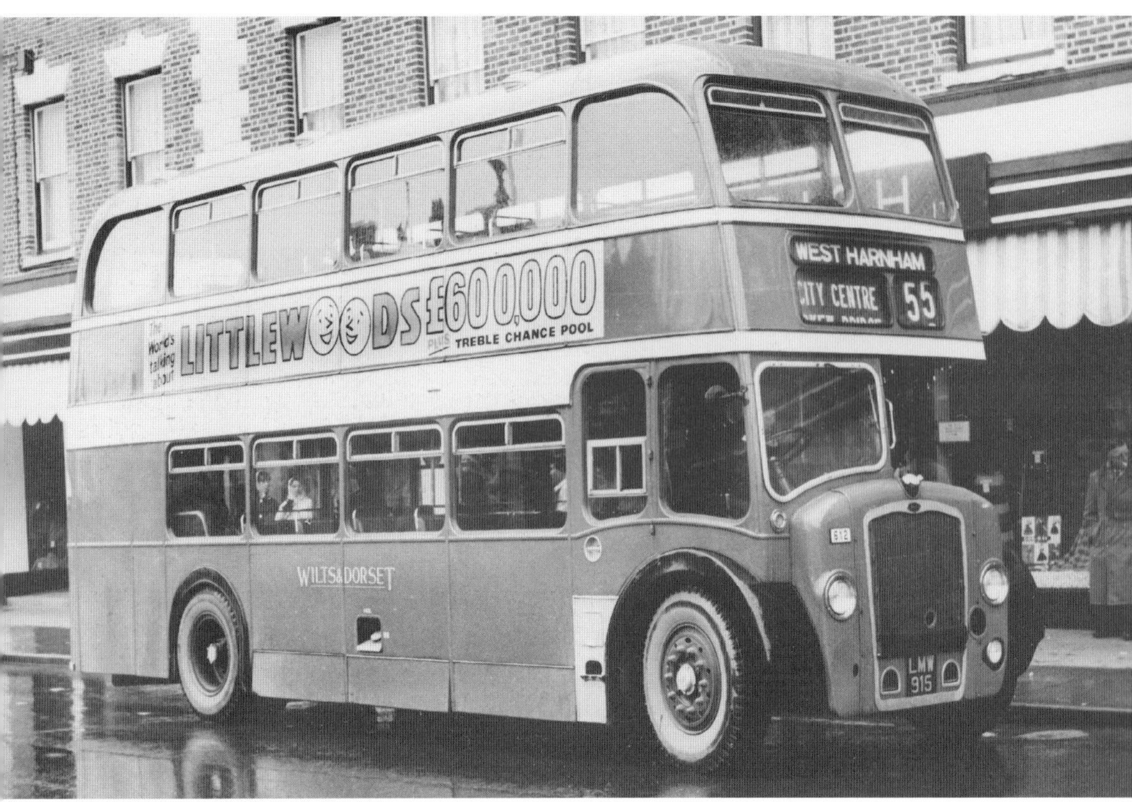

New Bristol Lodekkas for Salisbury City Services, 1955

Pictured here in the familiar location of the Style & Gerrish (later Debenhams) department store in Blue Boar Row, Salisbury, is LMW 915 (fleet No. 612), a Bristol LD6B with Lodekka double-deck body by Bristol and Eastern Counties Coach Works. The first seventeen of these revolutionary new fifty-eight-seat buses were delivered between March 1954 and October 1955, to replace the ageing pre-war Leyland Titan double-deckers. More were to follow.

Coaches for Long-Distance Excursions and Private Hire, 1962

Opposite bottom: Three of these Bristol MW6G coaches with Eastern Counties coachwork were purchased in May 1962, featuring a new livery of cream with a red waistband. Allocated the registration marks 673 AAM, 674 AAM and 675 AAM, they were the first Wilts & Dorset vehicles to have been issued with the new look registration marks issued by Wiltshire County Council from October 1961. There were no more combinations of the former series of three letter marks followed by one, two or three numbers so the new series was simply displayed in a reverse format.

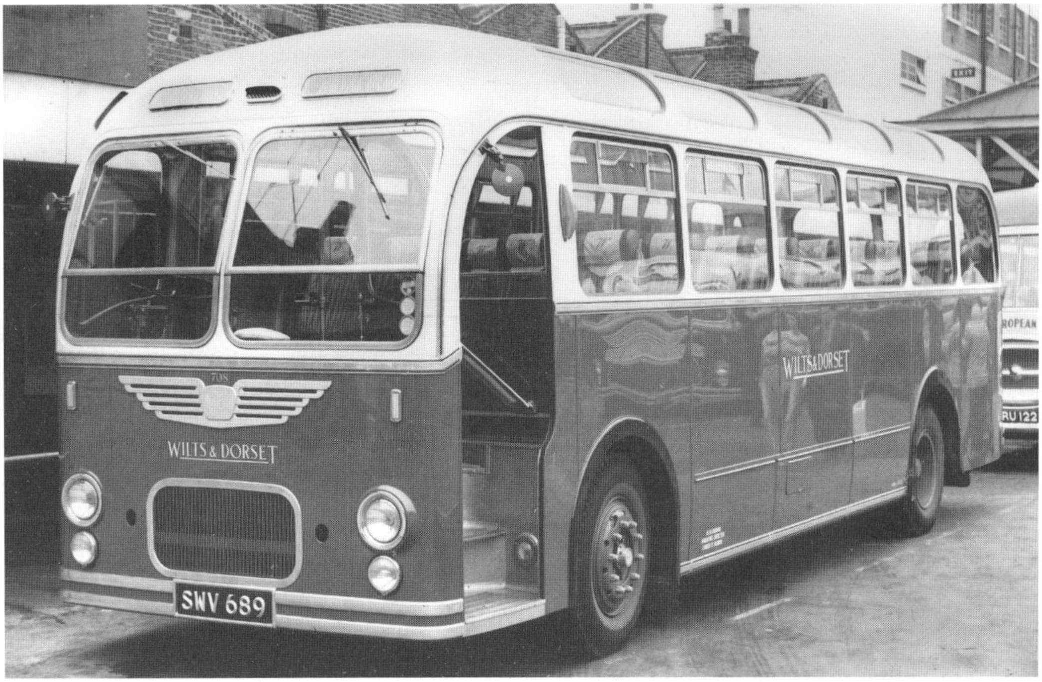

Luxury Coaches with a Cream-Over-Red Livery, 1959
Two of these elegant coaches were received just in time for the 1959 tourist season. Based on the Bristol MW6G chassis with Eastern Counties thirty-nine-seat front entry bodies, SWV 688 and SWV 689 (fleet Nos 707 and 708) joined six other coaches of the same type that were taken into the Wilts & Dorset fleet in June and July 1958.

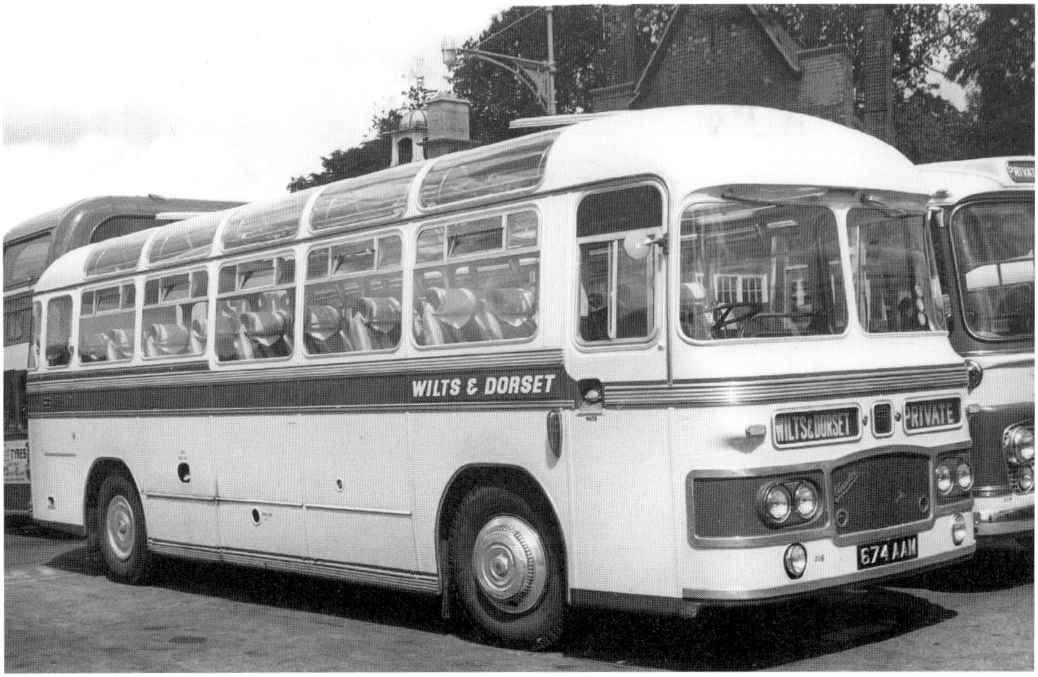

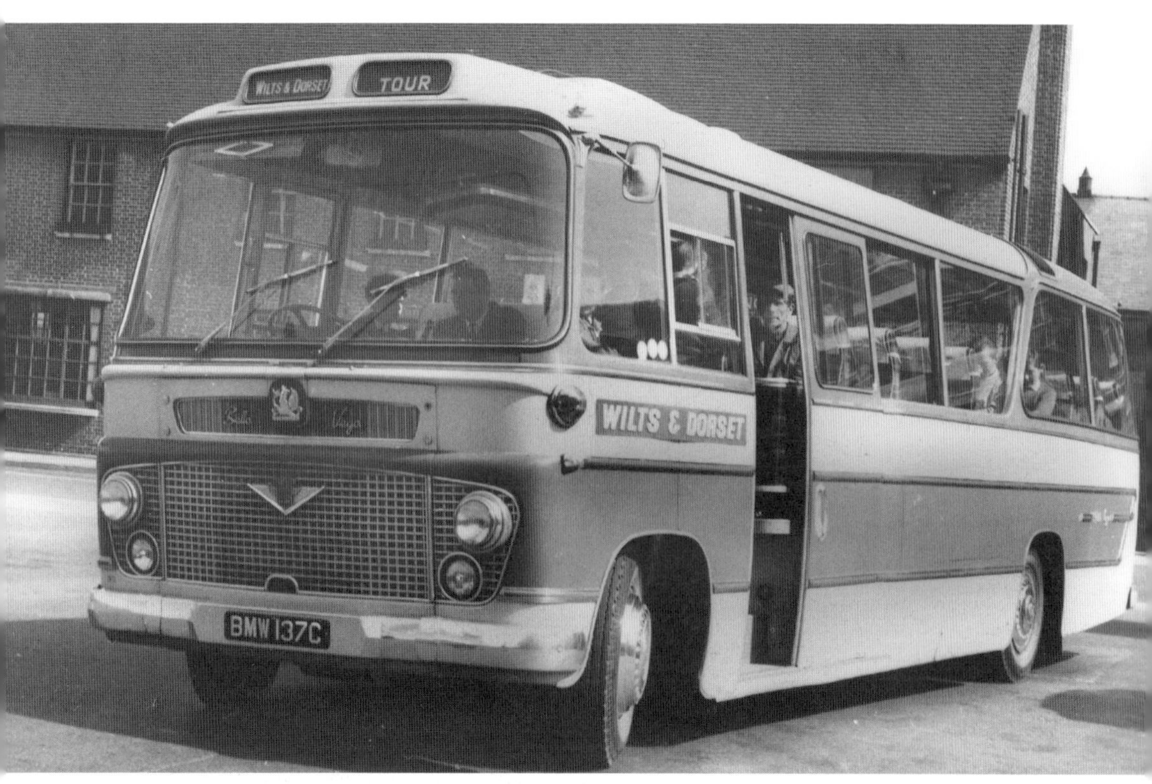

Bedford with Duple Coachwork, 1965

Five Bedford SB13s with forty-one-seat Duple Bela Vega bodies were purchased by Wilts & Dorset in 1965, the only vehicles to have be acquired by the company in that particular year. Issued with registration marks BMW 135C – BMW 139C, they were allocated fleet Nos 910–914. BMW 137C is shown here at Salisbury bus station. Our tour around the first fifty years of Wilts & Dorset buses ends here, but we will continue by taking a look at a few of the people associated with the company.

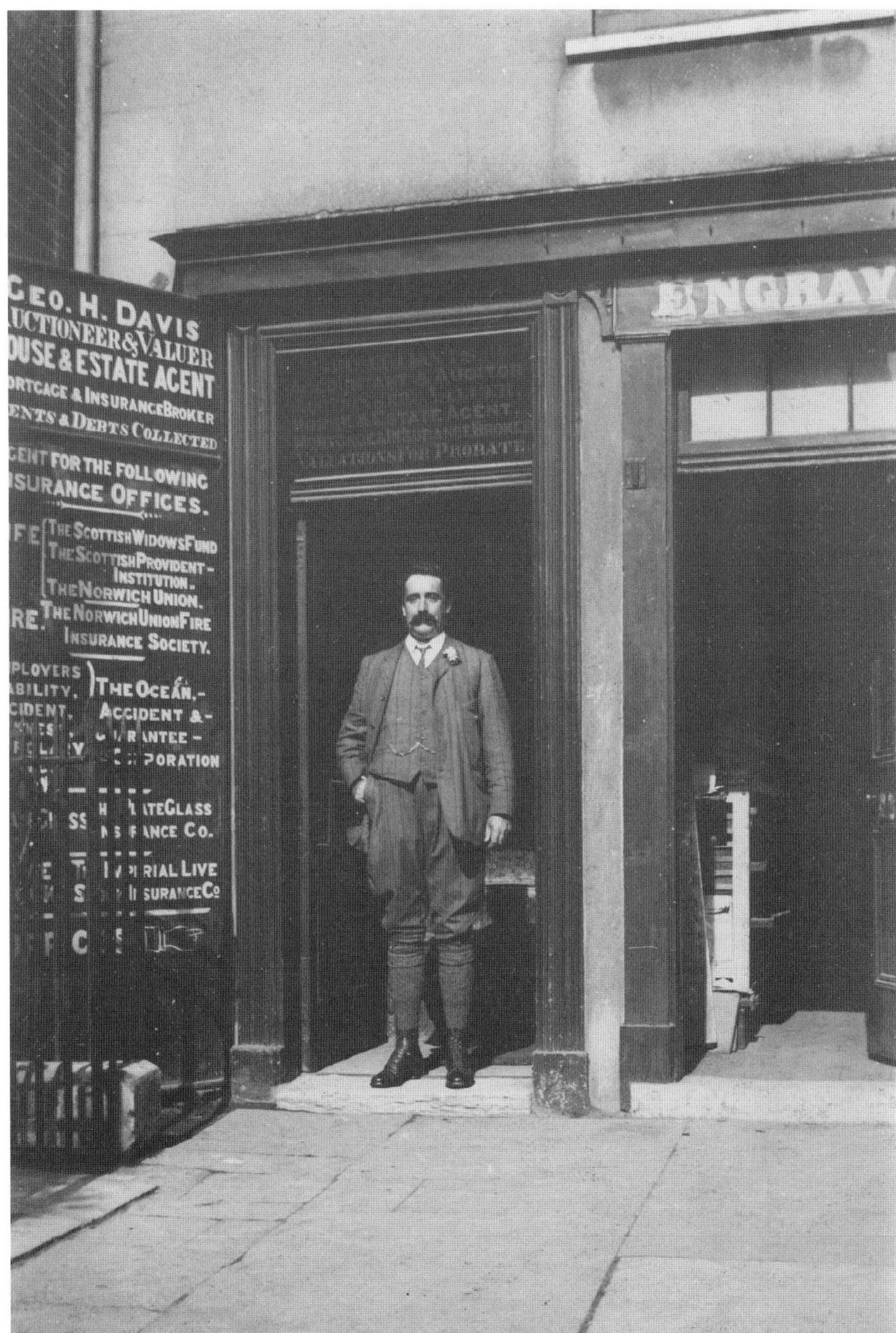

George H. Davis

A director of Wilts & Dorset Motor Services Ltd from 1915–1924, Mr Davis is pictured here at the front door of the company's registered office at 2 St Thomas' Square, Salisbury. It is quite apparent from the sign-writing on the display board that he had a lot of other business interests in addition to his involvement with Wilts & Dorset.

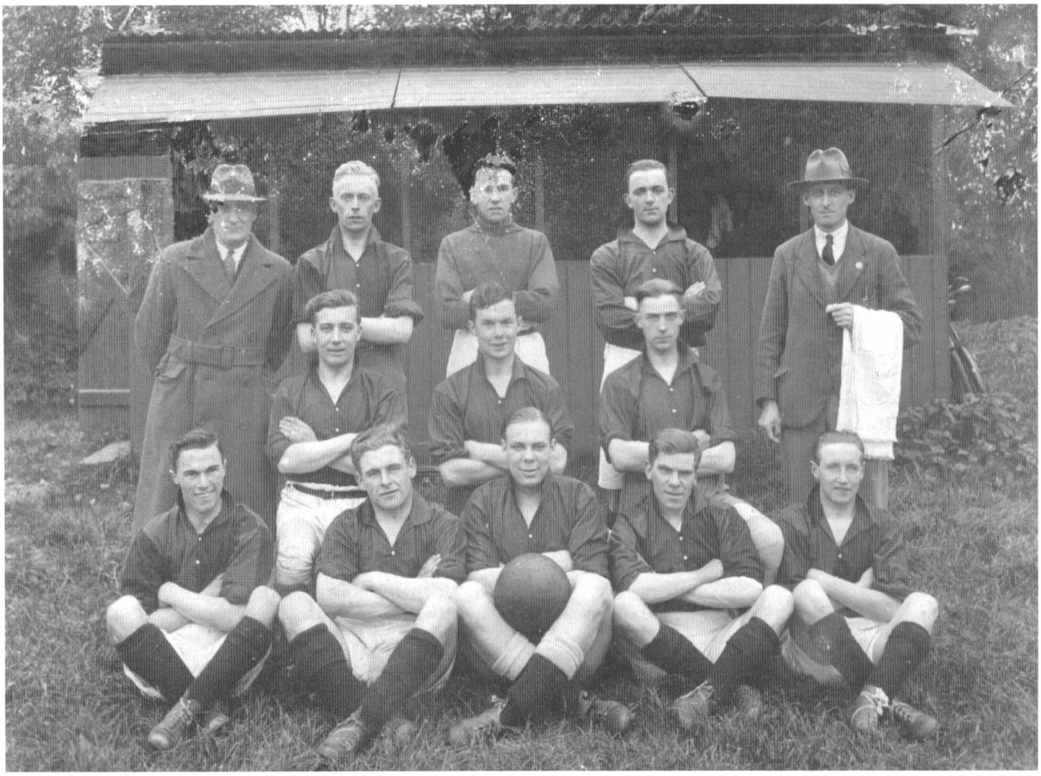

Wilts & Dorset Motor Services Football Team, 1930s
Sadly the names of the team players have been lost with the passage of time. If you can put a name to face then do please get in touch with Peter Daniels. The original photograph was taken by F. Futcher & Son of Fisherton Street, Salisbury.

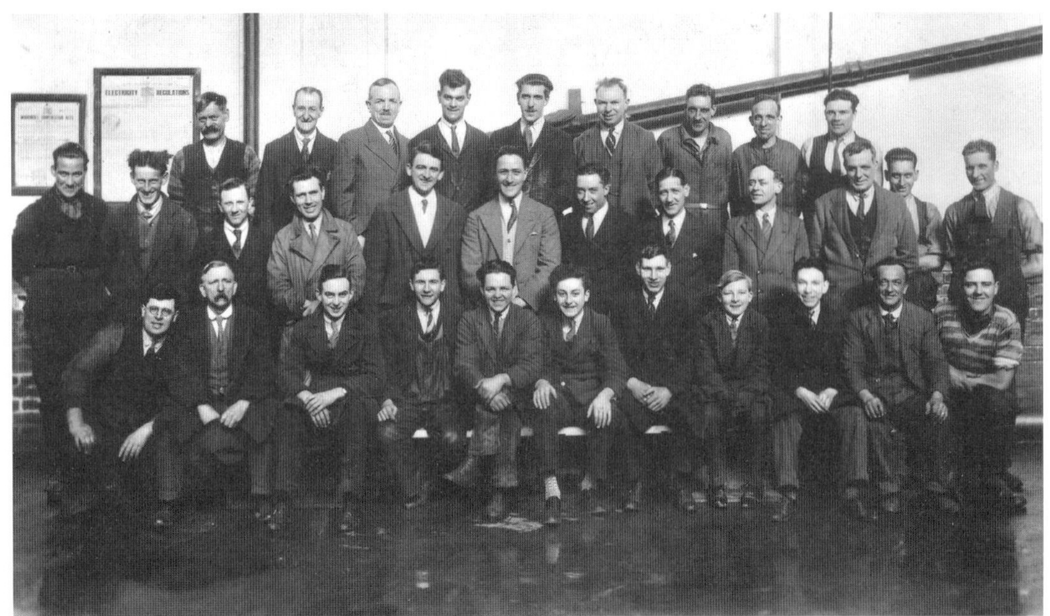

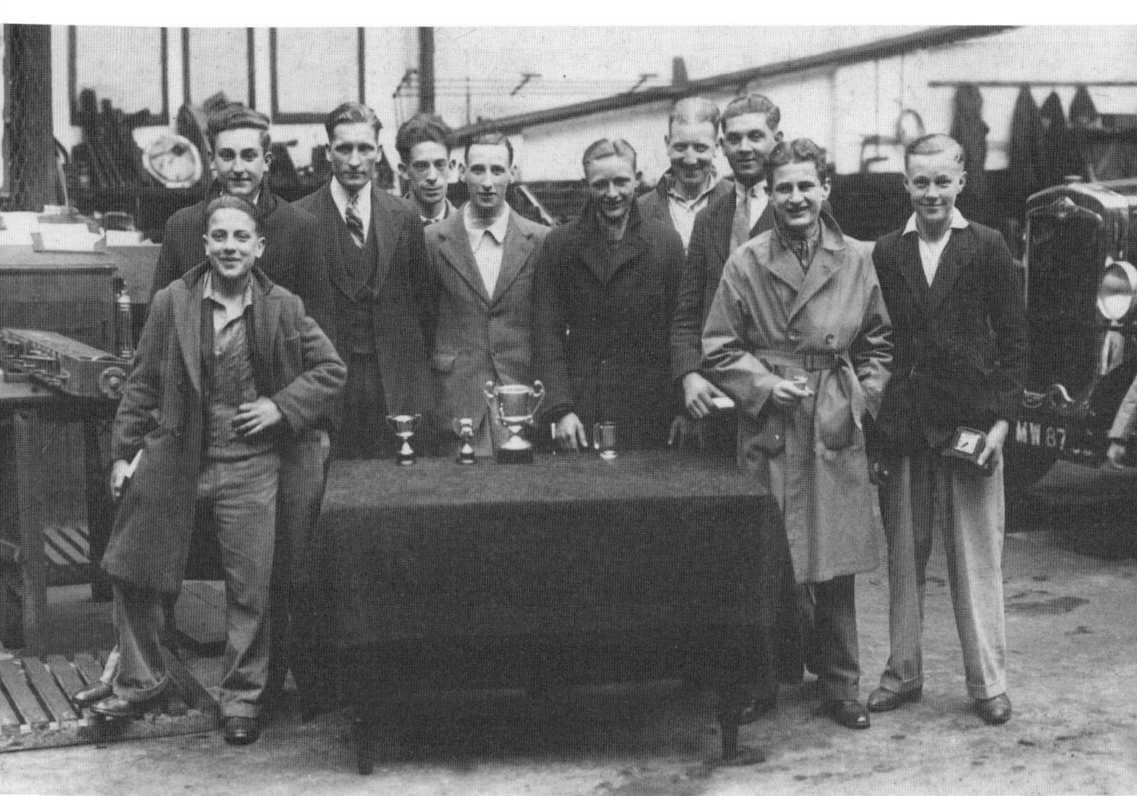

Busmen's Road Race Prize Winners, 1933
Pictured here at the Castle Street garage are the winners of the 8-mile championship walk from Amesbury to Salisbury that took place on Sunday 9 April 1933. Pictured left to right: Cecil Longhurst, Harry Hailstone, Charles Francis, Charles Warren, George Ross, Neuve Lock, Reg Wilton, Spencer Gwinnell, an unknown competitor and Arthur Beeston.

Maintenance Staff at Castle Street Garage, Mid-1930s
Opposite bottom: Standing in the back row, from the left: Harry Steele, 'Uncle' Holbourn, Jack Wheble (sign writer), Richard 'Dick' Scammell (gear boxes); Leonard 'Len' Newman (foreman); 'Rummy' Rumbold (driver), and Billy Waters. In the second row: 'Burt' (?) Kelly, Fred Treadgold, Robert 'Bob' Edsor (electrician), Albert E. Tutt (coachwork), George Wallis (general manager), Albert 'Burt' Crabb (charge-hand), J. E. 'Ernie' Engelbretsen (body shop), Harry Serpell (chargehand-turner), Charlie and Ron Francis (cleaners). In the front row: Reginald William 'Reg' Newman, A. E. Tutt (senior), Don Serpell, Reginald 'Smiler' Mortimer, 'Smudger' Smith, Dennis Whatley, Harry Hailstone, Arthur 'Tarzan' Laney, Harold Smeeth, Harry Fulford and Alfie Duffin (welder).

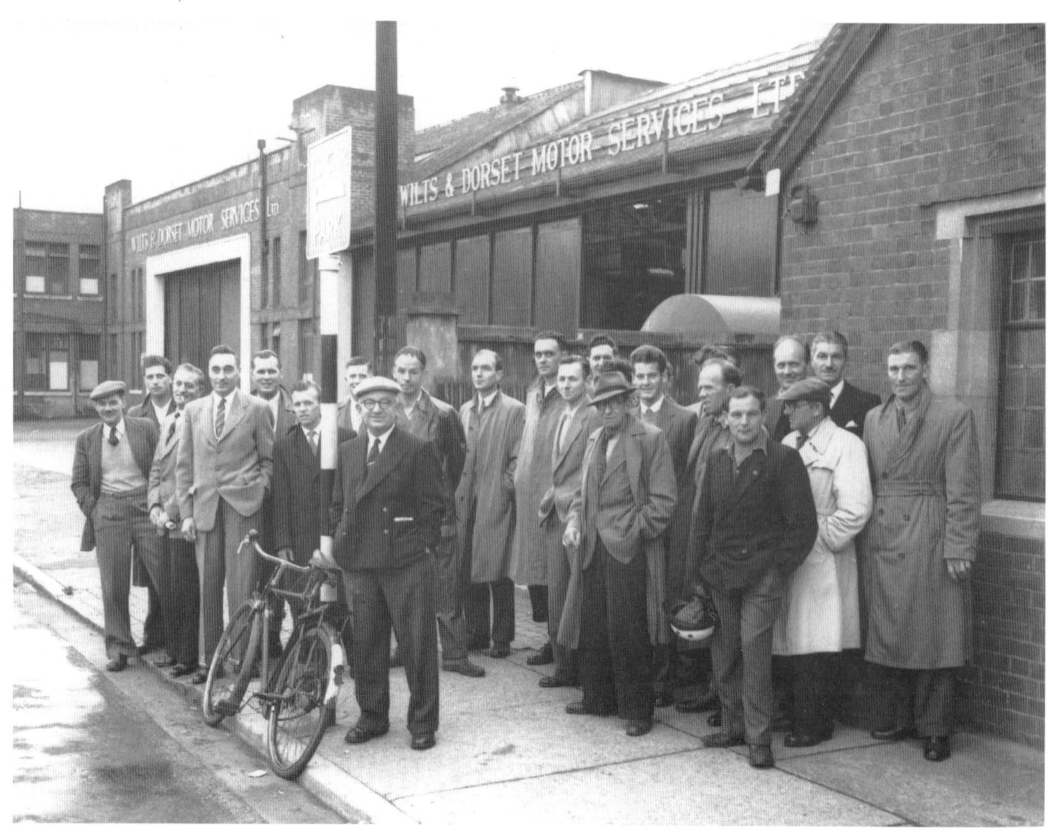

Salisbury Busmen on Strike, 1957

The photograph was taken by Austin Underwood in July 1957 when the men were striking for higher pay. Among those to be seen in the picture is Don Bealing, Albert Blackmore, Bill Boniface, Arthur Butt, Maurice Denham, Bill Douthwiate, Alfie Duffin, Jim Foord, Edward 'Knocker' Goddard, Ron Morris, George Moxham, Trevor Palmer, Ernest 'Ernie' Parks, Douglas 'Danny' Pearce, Jim Read, Leslie Smith, Stan Thick, Jim Walsh and Bert 'Woodbine' Williams'.